GED

PREPARATION FOR THE
HIGH SCHOOL EQUIVALENCY EXAMINATION

SOCIAL STUDIES

NEW GED TEST 2

KAREN SCOTT DIGILIO

Project Editor
Mark Boone

CONTEMPORARY
BOOKS, INC.
CHICAGO ▪ NEW YORK

Library of Congress Cataloging-in-Publication Data

Digilio, Karen Scott.
    The new GED social studies test.

    1. Social studies—Examinations, questions, etc.
2. General educational development tests—Study guides.
I. Title.
H62.D54   1987   300'.72   86-29284
ISBN 0-8092-5037-3

Published by Contemporary Books, Inc.
180 North Michigan Avenue, Chicago, Illinois 60601
Manufactured in the United States of America
International Standard Book Number: 0-8092-5037-3

Published simultaneously in Canada by
Fitzhenry & Whiteside
91 Granton Drive
Richmond Hill, Ontario L4B 2N5
Canada

Editorial Director
Caren Van Slyke

Editorial
Sarah Schmidt
Christine M. Benton
Patricia Reid

Production Editor
J. D. Fairbanks

Art Director and Cover Design
Georgene G. Sainati

Illustrator
Rosemary Morrissey-Herzberg

Art & Production
Jan Geist
Princess Louise El
Arvid Carlson
Lois Koehler

Typography
Lisa A. Waitrovich

Cover photo © Imtek Imagineering, Masterfile

ACKNOWLEDGMENTS

Pretest

Graph on page 12 adapted from *Encyclopedia of World Geography*—Elsevier International Projects Limited, © 1974.

Cartoon on page 13 by Don Hesse, © 1978. Reprinted courtesy of the *St. Louis Globe/Democrat*.

Cartoon on page 14 reprinted with permission from the *Minneapolis Star and Tribune*.

Excerpt on page 16 reprinted by permission of OISE Press, The Ontario Institute for Studies in Education, Toronto.

Illustrations on page 17 adapted from *World Geography* by John Hodgdon Bradley, © copyright 1945 by Silver, Burdett & Ginn Inc. Used with permission.

Graph on page 19 adapted from *Economics* by Paul A. Samuelson. © 1980 by McGraw-Hill Book Company. Reprinted by permission of the publisher.

Text

Cartoon on page 48 by Steve Kelley, © 1985. Reprinted by permission of Copley News Service.

Cartoon on page 49 by Tom Flannery, from *Best Editorial Cartoons of the Year*, © 1978, edited by Charles Brooks. Reprinted by permission of Tom Flannery.

Cartoon on page 55 reprinted with permission from the *Minneapolis Star and Tribune*.

Cartoon on page 56 by Lou Erickson, from *Best Editorial Cartoons of the Year*, © 1978, edited by Charles Brooks. Reprinted by permission of Lou Erickson.

Cartoon on page 66 by Karl Hubenthal, from *Best Editorial Cartoons of the Year*, © 1978, edited by Charles Brooks. Reprinted by permission of Karl Hubenthal.

Cartoon on page 67 reprinted with permission from the *Minneapolis Star and Tribune*.

Cartoon on page 74 by Ken Alexander, from *Best Editorial Cartoons of the Year*, © 1978, edited by Charles Brooks. Reprinted by permission of Ken Alexander.

Cartoon on page 75 by John Knudsen, © 1978 by *The Tidings*, Los Angeles. Reprinted by permission of John Knudsen.

Cartoon on page 79 by Le Pelley in The *Christian Science Monitor* © 1977 TCSPS.

Cartoon on page 81 by Sandy Campbell, from *Best Editorial Cartoons of the Year*, © 1978, edited by Charles Brooks. Reprinted by permission of Sandy Campbell.

Chart on page 85 adapted from *The Woman's Guide to the Stock Market* by Barbara Lee, © 1982 by Barbara Lee. Reprinted by permission of Harmony Books, a division of Crown Publishers, Inc.

Cartoon on page 89 by Dick Locher. Reprinted by permission: Tribune Media Services.

Map on page 120 adapted from *The National Experience*, 6th ed., by John M. Blum et al., copyright © 1985 by Harcourt Brace Jovanovich, Inc. Reproduced by permission of the publisher.

Posttest

GED
PREPARATION FOR THE
HIGH SCHOOL EQUIVALENCY EXAMINATION

SOCIAL STUDIES
NEW GED TEST 2

CONTENTS

TO THE STUDENT
Introducing the Social Studies Test

Part of preparing for a test is working through the doubts and questions that you have. Perhaps it has been a long time since you took an important test. Maybe you are not sure what is required to pass the GED Social Studies Test, or you are nervous about the test-taking situation.

This book has been designed so that you can succeed on the test. It will provide you with instruction in the skills you need to pass the test, background information on key social studies concepts, and plenty of GED-type practice. If you work carefully through this book, you should do well. The material on pages 8 and 9 will give you advice on how to use this book.

What Kind of Test Is This?

The GED Social Studies Test consists of multiple-choice questions. These questions require you to know some of the basic social studies concepts that will be covered in this book. However, the test emphasizes your ability to think about these concepts. You will not have to recall an isolated fact or date as on some tests. Rather, you will read a passage or look at an illustration and answer questions based on it. To answer successfully, you will need to:

- have an understanding of basic social studies concepts

- be able to interpret illustrations and reading passages

- be able to show that you can:
  - understand what you read
  - apply information to a new situation
  - analyze relationships between ideas
  - make judgments about the material presented

Actually, you already do all of these different kinds of thinking in daily life. In this book, we will help you apply these skills to social studies materials.

What Does the Test Look Like?

There are 64 multiple-choice questions, and you will be given 85 minutes to complete the test. About 2/3 of the questions will be based on reading passages of up to 250 words each, and 1/3 will be based on maps, charts, graphs, or political cartoons. To get an idea of what the test is like, look at the practice test at the end of this book. This practice test was based on the real GED test.

What's on the Test?

The GED Social Studies Test can be broken down into the content areas it covers and the skills it tests.

These subjects make up the content of the test.

History	25%
Economics	20%
Political Science	20%
Behavioral Science	20%
Geography	15%

These essential social studies concepts are covered in chapters 5–9 of this book. However, keep in mind that a given question may draw from a number of these subjects. It's hard to discuss society or people without touching on a number of topics. For example, a question on the *U.S. Constitution* may draw from material covered in both political science and history.

Also, remember that you are being tested on your ability to think about certain ideas and concepts. You will be asked to do more than just find an answer that was given in a passage.

Thinking skills that you will be tested on include:

Understanding Ideas	20%
Applying Ideas	30%
Analyzing Ideas	30%
Evaluating Ideas	20%

Chapters 1–4 of this book focus on these thinking skills and all of the activities and questions in this book will help you practice answering these types of questions. However, when you answer a question, you shouldn't be concerned about which thinking skill is being tested. The chart above is intended simply to show you how the GED Social Studies Test may differ from other tests you have taken.

The Five GED Tests

The following section answers some of the questions asked most frequently about the GED tests.

Q: WHAT DOES *GED* STAND FOR?

A: *GED* stands for the Tests of General Educational Development. The GED is a national examination developed by the GED Testing Service of the American Council on Education. The credential received for passing the test is widely recognized by colleges, training schools, and employers as equivalent to a high school diploma.

While the GED measures skills and knowledge normally acquired in four years of high school, much that you have learned informally or through other types of training can help you pass the test.

The GED test is available in English, French, and Spanish, on audiocassette, in Braille, and in large print.

Q. WHAT SHOULD I KNOW TO PASS THE TEST?

A. The test consists of five examinations in the areas of writing skills, social studies, science, literature and the arts, and mathematics. The chart below outlines the main content areas, the breakdown of questions, and the time allowed per test.

The GED Tests

Test	Minutes	Questions	Percentage
Writing Skills Part I	75	55	Sentence Structure 35% Usage 35% Mechanics 30%
Part II	45	1 topic	
Social Studies	85	64	History 25% Economics 20% Political Science 20% Geography 15%* Behavioral Science 20%
Science	95	66	Biology 50% Physical Sciences 50%
Literature and the Arts	65	45	Popular Literature 50% Classical Literature 25% Commentary 25%
Mathematics	90	56	Arithmetic 50% Algebra 30% Geometry 20%

In Canada, 20% of the test is based on geography and 15% on behavioral sciences.

On all five tests, you are expected to demonstrate the ability to think about many issues. You are also tested on knowledge and skills you have acquired from life experiences, television, radio, books and newspapers, consumer products, and advertising. In addition to the above information, keep these facts in mind:

1. Three of the five tests—literature, science, and social studies—require that you answer questions based on reading passages or inter-

preting cartoons, diagrams, maps, charts, and graphs in these content areas. Developing strong reading and thinking skills is the key to succeeding on these tests.

2. The writing skills test requires you to be able to detect and correct errors in sentence structure, grammar, punctuation, and spelling. You will also have to write a composition of approximately 200 words on a topic familiar to most adults.

3. The math test consists mainly of word problems to be solved. Therefore, you must be able to combine your ability to perform computations with problem-solving skills.

Someone once said that an education is what remains after you've forgotten everything else. In many ways, this is what the GED measures.

Q: CAN I TAKE THE TESTS?

A: Each year, more than 700,000 people take the GED Test. In the United States, Canada, and many territories, people who have not graduated from high school and who meet specific eligibility requirements (age, residency, etc.) may take the test. Since eligibility requirements vary, it would be useful to contact your local GED testing center or the director of adult education in your state, province, or territory for specific information.

Q: WHAT IS A PASSING SCORE ON THE GED?

A: Again, this varies from area to area. To find out what you need to pass the test, contact your local GED testing center. However, you must keep two scores in mind. One score represents the minimum score you must get on each test. For example, if your state requires minimum scores of 40, you must get at least 40 points on every test. Additionally, you must meet the requirements of a minimum average score on all five tests. For example, if your state requires a minimum average score of 45, you must get a total of 225 points to pass. The two scores together, the minimum score and the minimum average score, determine whether you pass or fail the GED.

To understand this better, look at the scores of three people who took the test in a state that requires a minimum score of 40 and a minimum average score of 45 (225 total). Ann and Sarah did not pass, but Ramon did. See if you can tell why.

	Ann	Sarah	Ramon
Test 1	44	42	43
Test 2	43	43	48
Test 3	38	42	47
Test 4	50	40	52
Test 5	50	40	49
	225	207	239

Ann made the total of 225 points but fell below the minimum score on Test 3. Sarah passed each test but failed to get the 225 points needed; just passing the individual tests was not enough. Ramon passed all the tests and exceeded the minimum average score. Generally, to receive a GED credential, you must correctly answer half or a little more than half of the questions on each test.

Q: WHAT HAPPENS IF I DON'T PASS THE TEST?

A: You are allowed to retake some or all of the tests. Again, the regulations governing the number of times that you may retake the tests and the time you must wait before retaking them are set by your state, province, or territory. Some states require you to take a review class or to study on your own for a certain amount of time before taking the test again.

Q: HOW CAN I BEST PREPARE FOR THE TEST?

A: Many libraries, community colleges, adult education centers, churches, and other institutions offer GED preparation classes. Some television stations broadcast classes to prepare people for the test. If you cannot find a GED preparation class locally, contact the director of adult education in your state, province, or territory.

Q: I NEED TO STUDY FOR THE OTHER TESTS. ARE THERE OTHER MATERIALS AVAILABLE?

A: Contemporary Books publishes a wide range of materials to help you prepare for the tests. These books are designed for home study or class use. Contemporary's GED preparation books are available through schools and bookstores and directly from the publisher, at Contemporary Books, 180 N. Michigan Ave., Chicago, IL 60601.

Now let's focus on some useful test-taking tips. As you read this section, you should feel more confident about your ability to succeed on the social studies test.

Test-Taking Tips

1. **Prepare physically.** Get plenty of rest and eat a well-balanced meal before the test so that you will have energy and will be able to think clearly. Last-minute cramming will probably not help as much as a relaxed and rested mind.

2. **Arrive early.** Be at the testing center at least fifteen to twenty minutes before the starting time. Make sure you have time to find the room and to get situated. Keep in mind that many testing centers refuse to admit latecomers.

3. **Think positively.** Tell yourself you will do well. If you have studied and prepared for the test, you should succeed.

4. **Relax during the test.** Take half a minute several times during the test to stretch and breathe deeply, especially if you are feeling anxious or confused.

5. **Read the test directions carefully.** Be sure you understand how to answer the questions. If you have any questions about the test or about filling in the answer form, ask before the test begins.

6. **Know the time limit for each test.** The social studies test has a time limit of 85 minutes.

    Some testing centers allow extra time, while others do not. You may be able to find out the policy of your testing center before you take the test, but always work according to the official time limit. If you have extra time, go back and check your answers.

    For this 64-question test, you should allow a maximum of one-and-a-half minutes per question. However, this is not a hard and fast rule. Use it only as a guide to keep yourself within the time limit.

7. **Have a strategy for answering questions.** You should read through the reading passages or look over the pictorial materials once and then answer the questions that follow. Read each question two or three times to make sure you understand it. It is best to refer back to the passage or illustration in order to confirm your answer choice. Don't try to depend on your memory of what you have just read or seen. Some people like to guide their reading by skimming the questions before reading a passage. Use the method that works best for you.

8. **Don't spend a lot of time on difficult questions.** If you're not sure of an answer, go on to the next question. Answer easier questions first and then go back to the harder questions. However, when you skip a question, be sure that you have skipped the same number on your answer sheet. Although skipping difficult questions is a good strategy for making the most of your time, it is very easy to get confused and throw off your whole answer key.

    Lightly mark the margin of your answer sheet next to the numbers of the questions you did not answer so that you know what to go back to. To prevent confusion when your test is graded, be sure to erase these marks completely after you answer the questions.

9. **Answer every question on the test.** If you're not sure of an answer, take an educated guess. When you leave a question unanswered, you will *always* lose points, but you can possibly gain points if you make a correct guess.

    If you must guess, try to eliminate one or more answers that you are sure are not correct. Then choose from the remaining answers. Remember, you greatly increase your chances if you can eliminate one or two answers before guessing. Of course, guessing should be used only when all else has failed.

10. **Clearly fill in the circle for each answer choice.** If you erase something, erase it completely. Be sure that you give only one answer per question; otherwise no answer will count.

11. **Practice test-taking.** Use the exercises, reviews, and especially the posttest in this book to better understand your test-taking habits and weaknesses. Use them to practice different strategies such as skimming questions first or skipping hard questions until the end. Knowing your own personal test-taking style is important to success on the GED.

HOW TO USE THIS BOOK

If you are a student about to prepare for the GED tests, you are to be admired. You have decided to resume an education that had been cut short. It is never easy to get back on track after you have been derailed. While it may not be easy, it will not be impossible. It will require determination and a lot of hard work.

This book will guide you through the types of questions you can expect to find on the social studies test. To answer some questions successfully, you will need to recall facts that you may have heard or read about previously. You may be surprised at what you already know about issues and events in social studies. If you read newspapers, magazines, historical novels, or travel guides, you are already on the road to success. If you do not read very much, now is the time to start. Not only will you improve your social studies skills, you will also set a pattern for lifelong learning.

1. Before beginning this book, you should take the pretest. This will give you a preview of what the social studies test includes, but more importantly, it will help you identify which areas you need to concentrate on most. Use the chart at the end of the pretest to pinpoint the types of questions you answered incorrectly and to determine what skills you need special work in. You may decide to concentrate on specific areas or to work through the entire book. We strongly suggest that you do work through the whole book to prepare yourself best for the actual test.

2. This book has a number of features designed to help make the task of test preparation easier, as well as effective and enjoyable. These features include:

   - a preliminary "warm-up" section of four chapters that isolates the four thinking skills—*comprehension, analysis, application,* and *evaluation*—and provides you with plenty of practice in applying these skills; this section includes a broad sampling of passages, graphics, and cartoons from all five subject areas covered on the social studies test; these sections are indicated by the symbol

   - skill builders (in the reading chapters only) that are concise hints for reinforcing social studies skills and concepts; these are indicated by the symbol

- content chapters that cover the essential social studies concepts that you need to know; these chapters are indicated by the symbol

- questions from the four levels of thinking skills in a similar format to the GED test
- high-interest reading passages that deal with current issues
- a variety of exercise types to maintain reader interest—matching, fill-in-the-blank, true/false, multiple-choice, and short essay questions
- writing activities based on thought-provoking issues that provide an opportunity to practice critical thinking and writing skills for the essay portion of the GED Writing Skills Test; these are indicated by the symbol

- over 300 practice questions for strengthening social studies reading and thinking skills
- an answer key (coded by skill level) for each section that explains the correct answers for the exercises; if you make a mistake, you can learn from it by reading the explanation that follows the answer and then reviewing the question to analyze the error

3. After you have worked through the five subject areas—U.S. History, Political Science, the Behavioral Sciences, Geography, and Economics—you should take the posttest. The posttest is a simulated GED test that presents questions in the format, level of difficulty, and percentages found on the actual test. The posttest will help you determine whether you are ready for the test and, if not, what areas of the book need to be reviewed. The posttest evaluation chart is especially helpful in making this decision.

SOCIAL STUDIES PRETEST

Directions: Before beginning to work with this book, take this pretest. The purpose of this test is to help you determine which skills you need to develop in order to pass the Social Studies Test.

The Social Studies Pretest consists of 30 multiple-choice questions. Some of the questions are based on maps, charts, graphs, cartoons, and reading passages.

Answer each question as carefully as possible, choosing the best of five answer choices and blackening in the grid. If you find a question too difficult, do not waste time on it. Work ahead and come back to it later when you can think it through carefully.

When you have completed the test, check your work with the answers and explanations at the end of the section.

Use the Evaluation Charts on page 20 to determine which areas you need to review most. For the best possible preparation for the Social Studies Test, however, we advise you to work through this entire book.

Pretest Answer Grid

1 ① ② ③ ④ ⑤	11 ① ② ③ ④ ⑤	21 ① ② ③ ④ ⑤
2 ① ② ③ ④ ⑤	12 ① ② ③ ④ ⑤	22 ① ② ③ ④ ⑤
3 ① ② ③ ④ ⑤	13 ① ② ③ ④ ⑤	23 ① ② ③ ④ ⑤
4 ① ② ③ ④ ⑤	14 ① ② ③ ④ ⑤	24 ① ② ③ ④ ⑤
5 ① ② ③ ④ ⑤	15 ① ② ③ ④ ⑤	25 ① ② ③ ④ ⑤
6 ① ② ③ ④ ⑤	16 ① ② ③ ④ ⑤	26 ① ② ③ ④ ⑤
7 ① ② ③ ④ ⑤	17 ① ② ③ ④ ⑤	27 ① ② ③ ④ ⑤
8 ① ② ③ ④ ⑤	18 ① ② ③ ④ ⑤	28 ① ② ③ ④ ⑤
9 ① ② ③ ④ ⑤	19 ① ② ③ ④ ⑤	29 ① ② ③ ④ ⑤
10 ① ② ③ ④ ⑤	20 ① ② ③ ④ ⑤	30 ① ② ③ ④ ⑤

Questions 1 and 2 refer to the following passage.

Psychologists at Rutgers University found that men whose wives worked had lower degrees of self-esteem than men whose wives did not. One explanation that the researchers offered was that the higher living standards made possible by the dual income raised the family's expectations. In the men's minds, the second income became a necessity. As a result, the men believed themselves to be incapable of solely supporting their families in the manner to which they had become accustomed.

1. The psychologists at Rutgers University attribute the cause of low self-esteem in men whose wives work to

   (1) the family's high living standards and high expectations.
   (2) the fact that their wives' income is higher than their own.
   (3) their inability to fulfill the traditional male role of breadwinner.
   (4) society's attitude toward men whose wives work.
   (5) their wives' inattentiveness and unwillingness to do housework.

2. The same Rutgers study found that women who worked outside the home generally showed sounder mental health than women who did not.

   This fact implies that

   (1) maintaining a career has a positive effect on women.
   (2) maintaining a career is stressful for women.
   (3) housewives do not get enough respect.
   (4) women benefit by competing with men in the workplace.
   (5) working women do not get sick as much as housewives.

Questions 3 and 4 are based on the explanation below.

To a sociologist, your family is not your family; it is your primary group. The purpose of primary groups is to share human intimacies and teach society's ways and norms. You have other primary groups—close friends and confidants—around whom you can "be yourself."

The main purpose of secondary groups is to enable individuals to perform tasks efficiently. Secondary groups are more formal and less relaxed than primary groups. Most work settings involve secondary groups as do most political and community organizations.

3. Which of the following would a sociologist probably call a primary group?

   (1) a supervisor and the employees in her charge
   (2) a parent-teacher organization dedicated to improving its neighborhood school
   (3) next-door neighbors who get together regularly to share gossip
   (4) members of the Young Republicans
   (5) volunteers who work together during a United Way campaign

4. Which of the following would a sociologist probably call a secondary group?

   (1) poker-playing buddies
   (2) members of one's immediate family
   (3) officers of a school's student council
   (4) neighbors who participate in a car pool
   (5) members in a therapy group who meet regularly with their psychotherapist

Questions 5 and 6 are based on the following graph.

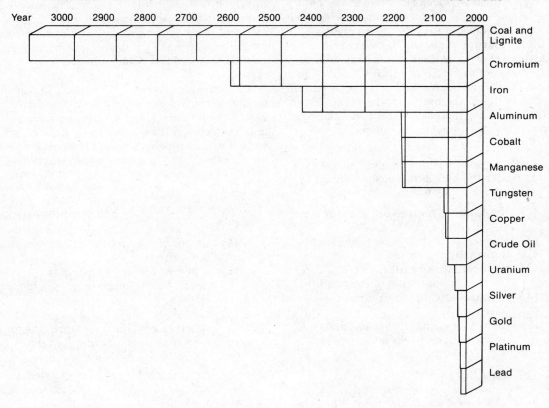

ESTIMATED DATES FOR DEPLETION OF WORLD'S MAJOR MINERAL RESOURCES

5. The information in the graph supports which of the following statements?

    (1) The supply of coal in the U.S. will be in danger by the year 2000.
    (2) There will be a glut in the world's crude oil supply by the year 2000.
    (3) Gold and silver are more scarce than oil and, therefore, are more important resources to be conserved.
    (4) By the year 3000, virtually all the major mineral resources of the world will be gone.
    (5) Manufacturing with iron and aluminum will be possible through the year 3000.

6. In the graph, the artist did not consider that

    (1) there is no limit to the world's resources.
    (2) man-made substitutes might extend the supply of scarce mineral resources.
    (3) gold is the most scarce of all mineral resources.
    (4) all of the world's mineral resources will be exhausted by the end of this century.
    (5) coal is the most important of all mineral resources.

Question 7 is based on the following cartoon.

'I'M TRYING TO KEEP HIM ON HIS FEET'

7. In the cartoon, the artist is saying that

(1) the U.S. economy is dead on its feet.
(2) Congress is killing the U.S. economy by its own excessive spending.
(3) deficit spending is killing the U.S. economy, and Congress is trying to control it.
(4) inflation is running away with the national economy.
(5) deficit spending can't be controlled by Congress or anyone else.

———

Questions 8–10 are based on the information in the following passage.

In 1986, according to the U.S. Bureau of Labor Statistics, some 50 million American women were employed outside of the home. Also, more than 50 percent of women with children under 18 years of age were in the labor market. Married mothers spent up to 85 hours per week working at two jobs: career and family.

Statistics from another report sponsored by a pharmaceutical company reveal that mothers who work outside the home are more likely to report headaches, stomach pains, premenstrual pain, and dental pain than homemakers. Further, the survey indicates that women report pain more often than men.

8. The results of both of these reports tend to suggest that

(1) working women report pain in order to gain sympathy for their cause.
(2) no link exists between stress and physical pain.
(3) physical pain contributes to stress and overwork.
(4) women, as a rule, are able to withstand more pain than men.
(5) stress and overwork contribute to physical pain.

9. The survey states that women report pain more often than men and that, although women may experience more physical pain, men have more heart attacks and ulcers due to stress than women. Which of the following hypotheses best explains why men suffer more heart attacks than women?

(1) Men's and women's biological makeup is different, which causes men to experience more stress than women.
(2) Men are traditionally the breadwinners, which causes them to experience more stress than women.
(3) Men perform more heavy labor than women, which results in greater stress on the heart and abdominal muscles.
(4) In America, men are discouraged from admitting that they are under stress; internalizing stress can lead to heart attacks and ulcers.
(5) Men are more competitive than women are; the drive to compete leads to stress, which results in heart attacks and ulcers.

10. Which of the following suggestions might be most effective in reducing the stress and pain that working mothers with young children experience?

(1) setting aside private time to meditate and relax
(2) exercising three times a week
(3) taking more vitamin supplements
(4) dividing household responsibilities more evenly with their mates
(5) postponing childbearing

Questions 11 and 12 refer to the following quote.

"Justice of this kind is obviously no less shocking than the crime itself and the new 'official' murder, far from offering redress for the offense committed against society, adds instead a second defilement to the first."

U.S. Supreme Court Justice Brennan, in a 1975 dissenting opinion on a controversial issue

11. In the quote above, the "official murder" refers to

   (1) suicide.
   (2) mercy killing.
   (3) assassination.
   (4) the death penalty.
   (5) manslaughter.

12. Based on the quote, we can infer that Justice Brennan

   (1) supports pardoning those on death row.
   (2) is in favor of life imprisonment for murder.
   (3) is against capital punishment.
   (4) believes it is the state's responsibility to sentence convicted killers.
   (5) supports capital punishment.

---

13. In 1890, the Sherman Anti-Trust Act was passed by the U.S. Congress to prevent monopolies from forming or price-fixing from occurring among producers of similar products. In general, such monopolies are seen as being harmful to the economy. However, the Sherman Anti-Trust Act does not apply directly to certain business activity that is perceived as beneficial to society as a whole. An example of this would be

   (1) service companies such as gas and electric companies because such competition would lead to waste of natural resources and inefficiency.
   (2) such companies as McDonald's and Burger King that get together to set prices for their similar products.
   (3) a company such as Kodak that manufactures related products such as cameras, film, projectors, etc.
   (4) a corporation such as IBM that has holdings throughout the world.
   (5) a communications corporation such as AT&T that provides a vital service in the communications industry.

Questions 14 and 15 are based on the cartoon below.

MODERN ECONOMICS

Reprinted with permission from the *Minneapolis Star and Tribune*

14. The main idea that the cartoonist is expressing is that

   (1) modern economics is too involved with Buddhism.
   (2) modern economics is like a game that only certain people can play.
   (3) modern economics is unfair to consumers.
   (4) modern economics is complicated and confusing.
   (5) modern economics is simple and straightforward.

15. With which of the following opinions would the cartoonist most likely agree?

   (1) A separation of church and state should extend to economic policies.
   (2) The direction that the economy will take is difficult to predict these days.
   (3) People are spending money at a much greater rate than they are saving it today.
   (4) The ability to stretch one's income to meet new economic demands is necessary today.
   (5) The economic policies of the government should be centralized and controlled.

Questions 16–18 are based on the following graph.

JURY AWARDS
Average judgments in Cook County civil cases

In millions of dollars

$1,508.7

$422.5

$145.2

$143.5

$99.2

$40.5

1974   '80*   '81   '82   '83   '84

*Includes $600 million ATT-MCI verdict; figures for years ending Sept. 1

16. According to the information in the graph, the average judgment in Cook County civil cases since 1974 has

   (1) decreased in dollar amount.
   (2) remained virtually the same in dollar amount.
   (3) increased in dollar amount.
   (4) leveled off in dollar amount.
   (5) exceeded the defendants' ability to pay.

17. The professional occupation most negatively affected by the increase in jury awards would be

   (1) corporate executives.
   (2) lawyers.
   (3) college professors.
   (4) physicians.
   (5) accountants.

18. Which of the following would be a direct result of the increase in the amounts that juries have awarded to plaintiffs in civil suits?

   (1) The taxpayers are forced to foot the bill.
   (2) Insurance costs for those most often sued have risen dramatically.
   (3) Jurors are in greater demand than ever before.
   (4) All lawyers representing plaintiffs in civil suits are getting rich.
   (5) Courts are more backlogged than ever before.

Questions 19 and 20 are based on the following passage.

Crime Stoppers is a private, citizen-run program formed in Lake County, Illinois, in 1981 to encourage residents to get involved in crime prevention. The organization rewards informers with cash, though only 30 to 40 percent of all callers accept the money.

Anonymous callers can call a special phone number to report any information they have about any crime. Though the program has been responsible for over 1,200 felony cases being solved, more than 900 felony arrests being made, and almost $2 million in stolen property and illicit narcotics being recovered, the program may be in jeopardy. A judge of the circuit court dismissed a case against a motorcycle thief because the chief prosecution witness was an anonymous tipster and police had made no attempt to find or identify him.

The Lake County State's Attorney's Office has now appealed the case. The Crime Stoppers hopes the ruling of the circuit court judge will be reversed and has stated that not doing so will victimize society.

19. Which of the statements below is an opinion based on the passage?

   (1) Only 30 to 40 percent of the callers to Crime Stoppers accept cash rewards for their information about a crime.
   (2) Callers to the special Crime Stoppers hotline may remain anonymous.
   (3) A judge of the circuit court dismissed a case against a thief because the main witness remained anonymous.
   (4) The ruling of the circuit court judge should be reversed because not doing so will harm society.
   (5) Anonymous callers are retaliating against their enemies by accusing them of committing crimes.

20. Crime Stoppers would be likely to support all of the following *except*

   (1) a whistlestop program in which citizens in distress use whistles to alert neighbors.
   (2) an armed neighborhood vigilante group that takes the law into its own hands.
   (3) a "neighborhood watch" program in which neighbors report any suspicious activity to local police.
   (4) a citizens patrol organization in which private citizens patrol the streets looking to report criminal activity.
   (5) a local chapter of the Guardian Angels, a volunteer group that supports the police in fighting crime.

Question 21 is based on the paragraph below.

"Adults need individualized help particularly in self-planned learning. Indeed, by definition, the self-planner has decided to build his or her own sequence of learning activities, rather than follow a sequence of learning activities determined by a group, by programmed instruction, or by a series of recordings or televised programs."
Allen Tough, *The Adult's Learning Projects*

21. Based on the information in the paragraph above, which of the tests listed below would be *most* helpful in designing an instructional program for an adult learner?

   (1) Wechsler Adult Intelligence Scale—A test that determines individual intelligence for adults
   (2) Rorschach Inkblot Test—a personality test in which the adult reveals personality characteristics by describing an inkblot
   (3) Vocational Aptitude Test—a test that measures the ability to perform specialized skills required in different jobs
   (4) Kuder Interest Survey—a test that shows a person's values, preferences and strengths in various areas
   (5) Minnesota Multiphasic Personality Test—a widely used personality questionnaire

Question 22 is based on the illustrations below.

Mountains

Hills

Plateaus

Plains

Valleys

22. The Grand Canyon, a magnificent example of a steep, walled valley, is surrounded by elevations of land that are broad and flat. These land features around the Grand Canyon are called

   (1) mountains.
   (2) hills.
   (3) plains.
   (4) plateaus.
   (5) valleys.

Questions 23 and 24 are based on the following passage.

The immigrants that came to America at the turn of the century were different from their predecessors. They were Italians, Austrians, Hungarians, Poles, Serbs, and Russians and were either Catholic or Jewish. Their traditions and ways of life seemed strange to more established Americans, and, because they were so different from the northern Europeans, ethnic prejudice became a problem. Years later, for much the same reason, Chinese immigrants to California were hated and feared by the very people who were victims of discrimination at the turn of the century.

23. The problems the new immigrants faced at the turn of the century were similar to the problems encountered by

   (1) British brides of American soldiers during World War II.
   (2) American draft dodgers who moved to Canada during the Vietnam War.
   (3) Russian artists who defected to the U.S. for political asylum.
   (4) U.S. servicemen living on American bases in Europe.
   (5) Cuban refugees fleeing to the U.S.

24. The writer of the passage above seems to believe that

   (1) the eastern European immigrants are not true Americans.
   (2) considering their treatment at the turn of the century, the eastern European immigrants might have been more tolerant.
   (3) the eastern European immigrants deserved the treatment given them by established Americans.
   (4) the Chinese deserved the treatment given them when they settled in California.
   (5) America is big enough for all people who want to come here.

Questions 25 and 26 are based on the information provided below.

In North America, people consume about 3 pounds of meat per person each week. Europeans eat about 2 pounds, South Americans 1-1/2 pounds, and Asians and Africans just 1/3 pound. If all meat were distributed equally throughout the world's population, each person would get about 1 pound per week.

25. Based on the information in the passage, we can conclude that

    (1) Americans eat more than their share of meat.
    (2) Europeans do not eat enough meat.
    (3) people cannot live on less than one pound of meat per week.
    (4) Americans, Canadians, and Mexicans eat more meat than people in other parts of the world.
    (5) the world's population could survive without meat in its diet.

26. Based on the facts presented in the passage above, we can infer that

    (1) Asians and Africans suffer from malnutrition.
    (2) Asians and Africans live only on fish and poultry.
    (3) most Asians and Africans subsist on grains and vegetables.
    (4) Asians and Africans do not raise cattle for food.
    (5) the cattle that normally would supply beef in Asia and Africa are used to plow fields.

Questions 27 and 28 are based on the passage below.

As the new immigrants increased their numbers in the U.S., the growth of the cities began displaying its full effects in this country. Tenement houses, lacking safety and health precautions, housed half of New York City's population in 1890. Open drainage gutters polluted water supplies with human and industrial sewage. Working conditions worsened as owners put more money into modern machinery and invested less in comfort and safety measures for employees. The new immigrants and the freedmen of the South took any work they could get without complaint. As a result, the anger of the more established American workers grew.

27. According to the passage, it was most likely that the established Americans were angry at the new immigrants and blacks because

    (1) they lowered the quality of the products companies sold.
    (2) they hadn't earned their jobs.
    (3) they were endangering the lives of other workers because of their unfamiliarity with modern machinery.
    (4) they protested too much about their living and working conditions.
    (5) they were unintentionally hurting working conditions for others by accepting lower pay and poorer working environments.

28. The passage illustrates the historic basis for prejudice against minority and foreign-born workers. For largely the same reasons, which of the following immigrant groups is resented by unskilled American workers?

    (1) Filipinos
    (2) Mexicans
    (3) Russians
    (4) Canadians
    (5) Japanese-Americans

Questions 29 and 30 are based on the following graph.

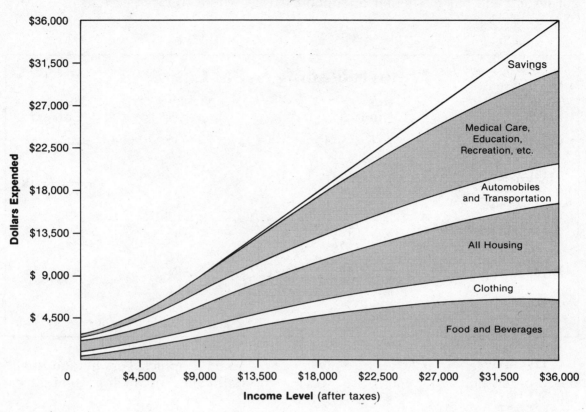

EXPENDITURES FOR CONSUMPTION AT DIFFERENT INCOME LEVELS, 1980

29. According to the graph, which of the following correctly summarizes the relationship between income and savings?

  (1) As incomes go up, savings go down.
  (2) As incomes go up, savings go up.
  (3) As incomes go down, savings go up.
  (4) Even when incomes go down, savings stay the same.
  (5) Even when incomes go up, savings stay the same.

30. According to this graph, the income level at which people can start saving money instead of spending it all is approximately

  (1) $4,500
  (2) $9,000
  (3) $13,500
  (4) $18,000
  (5) $20,000

Use the chart below to determine the reading skills areas in which you need to do the most work. These reading skills, covered on pages 23–98, are absolutely essential for success on the GED Social Studies Test. Circle any items that you got wrong and pay particular attention to areas where you missed half or more of the questions.

Pretest Reading Skills Chart

Skill Area	Item Number	Review pages	Number Correct
Comprehension	2, **7**, 11, **14**, **16**, **29**, **30**	23–36	_____/7
Analysis	1, 6, 8, 9, 12, **18**, 19, 25, 26, 27	37–67	_____/10
Application	3, 4, 13, **17**, 21, **22**, 23, 28	68–81	_____/8
Evaluation	**5**, 10, **15**, 20, 24	82–98	_____/5

Your score _____ out of 30 correct.

The numbers in boldface are questions based on graphics. For the questions based on graphics that you missed, review the skill pages in which graphics are found.

Now circle the same numbers for the items that you circled in the chart above. This will give you additional information about the social studies content areas in which you need the most work.

Pretest Content Areas Chart

Skill Area	Item Number	Review Pages	Number Correct
History	13, 23, 24, 27, 28	99–146	_____/5
Political Science	7, 11, 12, 16, 17, 18, 19, 20	147–175	_____/8
Behavioral Science	1, 2, 3, 4, 8, 9, 10, 21	176–209	_____/8
Geography	22, 25, 26	210–240	_____/3
Economics	5, 6, 14, 15, 29, 30	241–263	_____/6

Pretest Answer Key

1. **(3)** The passage states, "As a result, the men believed themselves to be incapable of solely supporting their families in the manner to which they had become accustomed." This means that men felt unable to fulfill the traditional male role of family breadwinner.

2. **(1)** The fact that working women showed sounder mental health than women who did not work suggests that working women get some benefit from maintaining careers.

3. **(3)** A primary group is described as "close friends and confidants around whom you can 'be yourself';" next door neighbors are examples of this relationship. The other choices describe secondary groups.

4. **(3)** Secondary groups are formed to carry out tasks efficiently, a characteristic of work groups. Officers of a school's student council represent a type of work group.

5. **(4)** Of the 14 minerals listed, only the line for coal and lignite is shown to extend to the year 3000.

6. **(2)** Choices (1), (3), and and (4) are untrue. Choice (5) is an opinion that cannot be supported by the graph.

7. **(2)** Congress is shown as strangling the economy with deficit spending.

8. **(5)** The first paragraph describes the overwhelming responsibilities of working mothers with young children. The second reports that working mothers are more likely to report pain than nonworking mothers. Together they imply a relationship between stress combined with overwork and physical pain.

9. **(4)** Only choice (4) is a reasonable hypothesis. It is a fact that not admitting to stress and pain can lead to more serious physical ailments. The other choices are either unrelated to the passage or generalizations that cannot be supported.

10. **(4)** If, as the passage suggests, the chief cause of pain that working mothers experience is overwork, then the only solution for reducing stress and pain would be an even distribution of household responsibilities between husband and wife.

11. **(4)** Of all the choices given, only the death penalty, or capital punishment, means the same as "official murder."

12. **(3)** Justice Brennan says the " 'official' murder . . . adds instead a second defilement to the first." This shows his opposition to capital punishment.

13. **(1)** Gas and electric companies are excluded from anti-trust legislation because competition between them would lead to waste of natural resources. Choice (2) is an example of price fixing and choices (3), (4), and (5) do not involve monopolies and price-fixing.

14. **(4)** The six arms pointing in different directions indicate complication and confusion.

15. **(2)** The cartoonist depicts economics as confusing. The only answer choice that supports this opinion is the statement that the direction that the economy will take is difficult to predict.

16. **(3)** Even though the amounts rose and fell, the graph shows an increase in the dollar amounts that juries awarded since 1974.

17. **(4)** Malpractice insurance costs for physicians have increased dramatically in recent years; therefore, as a professional group they have been most negatively affected. The other occupations have not been sued as often as doctors.

18. **(2)** Since the awards paid in civil judgments have increased, the insurance companies that cover those firms or individuals being sued have raised the cost of insurance.

19. **(4)** The clue word that indicates that an opinion is being expressed is *should*. Choices (1), (2), and (3) are facts stated in the passage, not opinions. Choice (5) is not an opinion.

20. **(2)** The only choice that does not suggest cooperation with the local law enforcement authorities is an armed neighborhood vigilante group.

21. **(4)** The Kuder Interest Survey is the only test instrument shown that includes some element of self-analysis similar to that which is described in the paragraph.

22. **(4)** From the illustration, you can see that plateaus are elevated, broad, and flat.

23. **(5)** Of the choices given, Cuban refugees are the only group that experienced the ethnic discrimination that the eastern European immigrants did.

24. **(2)** The passage states, ". . .Chinese immigrants to California were hated and feared by the very people who were victims of discrimination at the turn of the century." This ironic statement suggests that the eastern European immigrants, having had experiences similar to those of the Chinese, might have been more understanding.

25. **(4)** The passage compares the amount of meat eaten in different parts of the world. North Americans (Canadians, Mexicans, and Americans) do eat proportionally more meat than people in other parts of the world.

26. **(3)** If Asians and Africans consume the least of the world's meat, we can infer that they depend more on vegetables than the rest of the world. Choices (1), (2), (4), and (5) cannot be supported by the passage.

27. **(5)** The passage says that the established American workers were angry at the new immigrants and freedmen of the South because both groups took any work they could get without complaint. This statement suggests that, in their desperation to find work, the new immigrants and blacks contributed unintentionally to worsened working conditions and pay for established American workers.

28. **(2)** Mexicans are forced to accept unskilled, low-level jobs at the bottom of the pay scale and are perceived as threats by unskilled American workers.

29. **(2)** According to the graph, as income rises, the section that represents savings gets wider. This widening represents an increase in savings.

30. **(3)** According to the graph, the section that represents savings begins to widen at about the income level of $13,500.

1 COMPREHENDING SOCIAL STUDIES MATERIALS

When you **comprehend** something, you understand what it means. For example, if you understand football and attend a game with someone who has never seen it before, you should be able to explain the game to that person. The ability to interpret written material or illustrations shows your understanding of the information.

On the Social Studies Test, you will have to show your comprehension of passages, quotes, graphs, charts, maps, and cartoons in at least three ways—by:

- summarizing the main idea

- restating information

- identifying implications

Summarizing the Main Idea

Summarizing the main idea in social studies materials means finding the key thought. Actually, you often hear lengthy information summarized into one key thought, or main idea. For example, you may have heard the president of the United States give a long speech on television and then later heard a newscaster summarize the speech in just a few sentences.

The main idea of a speech, article, or report is often stated near its beginning or its end, since the speaker or writer wants to give the idea the primary emphasis. Sometimes the main idea is not stated. The author gives the details, but the reader must *infer*, or read between the lines to determine what the key thought is. In some cases, a title may be a clue to identifying the main idea.

Read the passage below and in the question that follows circle the choice that best indicates the main idea.

On January 31, 1948, nearly a million people waited in the hot sun of India to mourn the assassination of Mohandas K. Gandhi, a thin brown man of seventy-eight who had died as he had lived—a poor private citizen without official title, position, or academic honors. Yet heads of state from all over the world were there to show respect for this friend of the oppressed, and the United Nations lowered its flag and interrupted its sessions in tribute. Gandhi had demonstrated to the world the effective strategy of nonviolent civil disobedience toward unjust laws. Humanity had lost an international symbol of nonviolence and mourned for itself as much as for the man.

The main idea expressed in the above passage is

(1)   the irony of life in general and one man's life in particular.
(2)   mankind's loss of a unique activist.
(3)   that Gandhi never held an official public title or position.
(4)   that Gandhi died a poor man.
(5)   a plea for more international understanding and love.

In answering this question, it would help to go back to the *last sentence of the passage:* "Humanity had lost an international symbol of nonviolence and mourned for itself as much as for the man." This concluding sentence summarizes the main idea of the passage, so choice (2) would be the correct answer. All of the other sentences show how unusual and well-respected Gandhi was.

Although there is irony in Gandhi's violent death, this is not emphasized in the passage, so (1) must be eliminated. The passage does state that Gandhi never held an official public title or position, choice (3), but this is not the key thought on which the entire passage focuses. Choice (4) must be rejected for a similar reason. While the author might be sympathetic to the need for international understanding and love, (5), he does not state this directly in the passage, nor does he imply it.

★ GED PRACTICE ★

Exercise 1

Directions: Read the passage below and circle the choice that best indicates the author's main idea or purpose.

"For a thousand days I would serve as counsel to the president. I soon learned that to make my way upward, into a position of confidence and influence, I had to travel downward through factional power plays, corruption, and finally outright crimes." These are the words of John Dean, who served in former President Richard Nixon's administration during the Watergate crisis. His testimony against his employer led to calls for the impeachment of former President Nixon.

President Nixon made his resignation speech on August 8, 1974, after three articles of impeachment had been voted against him by the House of Representatives. Only one other president in history, Andrew Johnson, had ever faced the prospect of impeachment proceedings. No president had ever resigned from office before. Though never convicted of a crime, or even brought to trial for one, to many U.S. citizens, former President Richard Nixon will remain a symbol of abuse of power.

1. The writer's main purpose in this passage is to

   (1) make a case for the elimination of the impeachment process as ineffective and outdated.
   (2) compare the corruption of Andrew Johnson's presidency with Richard Nixon's.
   (3) show sympathy for former President Nixon.
   (4) remind us of the abuse of power in former President Nixon's administration during his term as president.
   (5) point out that John Dean's testimony against Richard Nixon is what led to the former president's resignation.

2. *Impeachment* may be defined as

   (1) finding a public official innocent.
   (2) convicting a public official.
   (3) bringing formal charges against a public official.
   (4) executing a public official.
   (5) the resignation of a public official.

ANSWERS AND EXPLANATIONS START ON PAGE 285.

Summarizing the Main Idea in Illustrations

Newspapers, magazines, and social studies textbooks frequently make use of illustrations. Very often, these illustrations summarize or emphasize points being made in the text. Your ability to understand and use such illustrations will be tested on the Social Studies Test.

You will work with several major types of materials throughout this text. They are graphs, charts and tables, maps, and political cartoons. Each of these types of illustrations serves a particular purpose.

Graphs make comparisons of numbers or amounts by using lines, bars, circles, or pictures. Graphs are tools that are effective in showing patterns. Line, bar, and area graphs are particularly useful in showing trends at a glance. Circle graphs or pie graphs are effective in showing how parts of a thing relate to the whole. Picture graphs, or pictographs, use symbols representing the subject being studied.

Charts and *tables* are concise reference tools. They list information in orderly rows and columns with easily readable headings and captions.

Maps give information about specific geographic areas, highlighting such data as weather, population, politics, and routes for traveling.

Finally, *political cartoons* express opinions in a humorous and pointed way.

When you read a graph, chart, cartoon, or map, you will need to grasp the main idea of the picture quickly before you can use the information. To do this, you need to translate the picture into words. Look at the example below:

This is a circle graph. A circle graph looks like a pie that has been cut into pieces. The title of the graph is "Breakdown of Annual Budget for School District."

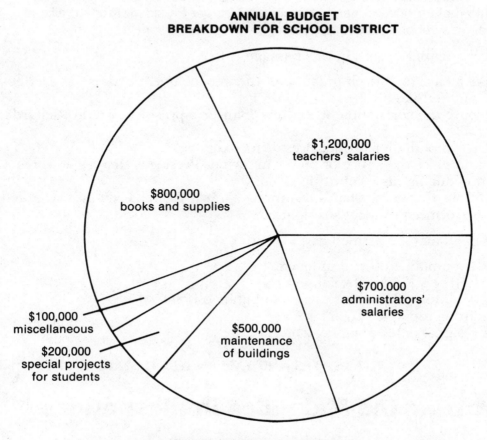

**ANNUAL BUDGET
BREAKDOWN FOR SCHOOL DISTRICT**

$1,200,000
teachers' salaries

$800,000
books and supplies

$700.000
administrators'
salaries

$100,000
miscellaneous

$200,000
special projects
for students

$500,000
maintenance
of buildings

Total = $3,500,000 annual budget

Looking quickly at this graph, you can see that the school district has many different expenses. Out of an annual budget of $3,500,000, the biggest chunk of money is spent on _____ , followed by _____ , _____ , and _____ .

Based on the information given, the main idea of this circle graph is that school dollars for this district are used in many ways, the largest amount ($1,200,000) going to *teachers' salaries*. The next largest amount spent is on *books and supplies*, followed by *administrators' salaries* and *maintenance of buildings*.

The following "skill builder" is a helpful hint in understanding circle or pie graphs. You will find "skill builders" throughout this section to help you strengthen your social studies reading skills.

Skill Builder
Interpreting Circle Graphs or Pie Graphs

Pie graphs show important pieces of information as *parts of a whole*. Each segment represents a percentage (or part) of the whole. To understand pie graphs, try restating, in a sentence, the figures represented. For example, based on the preceding graph, you could say, "Two hundred thousand (part) of all dollars in the annual budget for the school district (whole) is spent on special projects for students."

★ GED PRACTICE ★

Exercise 2

Directions: The circle graph below shows the amounts of money a business spends on various forms of advertising. Study the graph and choose the answer that best summarizes the main idea.

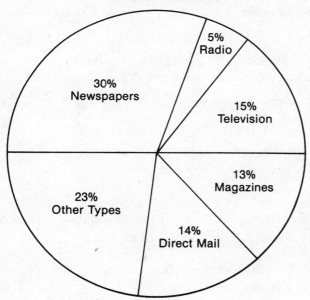

ADVERTISING SPENDING FOR ONE BUSINESS

5% Radio
30% Newspapers
15% Television
13% Magazines
23% Other Types
14% Direct Mail

The main idea of this graph is that this business

(1) does not use coupons as a form of advertisement.
(2) uses a variety of methods to get its message to consumers.
(3) spends the majority of its advertising dollars on marketing through magazines and newspapers.
(4) is spending too much money on advertising in newspapers.
(5) spends the least of its advertising money on radio commercials.

ANSWERS AND EXPLANATIONS START ON PAGE 285.

Restating Information

Restating information is "putting it into your own words," or paraphrasing. By paraphrasing the speaker's words, you are showing that you understand what has been said.

One situation in which restating information is useful is in client-centered therapy. Certain psychologists believe that a good way to help troubled patients work through their problems is to restate information that the patient offers. Through this method, the psychologist gives the patient a chance to understand his situation better. A typical dialogue between a doctor and a patient in which information is restated might go like this:

DOCTOR: What is troubling you today? You look worried.

PATIENT: *I haven't been sleeping well* lately.

DOCTOR: *You have had trouble with insomnia.*

PATIENT: Well, yes. I'm *afraid I'm going to lose my job.*

DOCTOR: *So, you are fearful of being unemployed.* Do you have a reason to be afraid?

PATIENT: Yeah, sorta. *I got really mad* the other day and told off a couple of people at work. One of them was my *boss.*

DOCTOR: *Oh, you were angry with your supervisor.* Can you tell me more about that?

PATIENT: My boss is so hard on me. I don't think he likes me, really, so he picks at everything I do, and I just got fed up.

What do you think this doctor would say next?

DOCTOR: _____

You probably wrote something like "So you feel *your boss is too critical of you.*" The psychologist would restate the patient's words.

Notice how the italicized words in the dialogue are restatements of the patient's ideas. When you *restate information,* the words and phrasing may be different, but the meaning is the same.

Read the passage on the next page and choose the correct restatements that follow.

BEFORE YOU READ: The title of the passage is "The Virginia Split." In the space below, write your prediction of what the passage will be about and then read to find out if your prediction was accurate.

_____

_____

THE VIRGINIA SPLIT

It is interesting how the geography of an area can influence its culture and politics. The south Atlantic region of the United States provides a good example. There are three important topographical features that were important to the development of the region—the Tidewater with low-lying land and large rivers, the Piedmont with gently rolling hills above the falls of the rivers, and the Appalachian Mountains.

The Tidewater and the Piedmont were settled primarily as plantations, but the mountains presented a barrier that was insurmountable for the Virginia gentlemen farmers. The mountains and the valleys west of them were settled instead by a people different from the farmers—in culture, religion, nationality, and economy. So different were they, in fact, that when Virginia seceded from the Union in 1861, western Virginia seceded from eastern Virginia and fought on the side of the small farmers and non-slave owners of the North.

Check to see if your prediction about the subject of the passage was correct.

Directions: Based on what you have read, place a check mark before the correct restatements of the ideas from the above passage. As you check off each restatement, underline the words and phrases in the passage that say the same thing.

_____ **(a)** The people who settled what is now West Virginia were from a different social and economic group from those who settled Virginia.

_____ **(b)** The Tidewater is a land of gently rolling hills above the falls of the rivers.

_____ **(c)** West Virginia is largely mountainous whereas Virginia is an area of gently rolling hills and low-lying river basins.

_____ **(d)** Virginia joined the Confederacy in 1861.

_____ **(e)** West Virginia seceded from the Union when the Civil War broke out in 1861.

You should have checked off: (a), (c), and (d). The words that are restatements of (a) are "The mountains and the valleys west of them were settled instead by a people different from the farmers—in culture, religion, nationality, and economy." The words that say the same thing as (c) are ". . . Tidewater with low-lying land and large rivers, the Piedmont with gently rolling hills above the falls of the rivers. . . ." The words that say the same thing as (d) are ". . . when Virginia seceded from the Union in 1861. . . ."

★ **GED PRACTICE** ★

Exercise 3

On the Social Studies Test, you will have to answer questions in a format similar to the one below.

Directions: Read the selection carefully. Answer the multiple-choice questions that ask for a restatement of information.

BEFORE YOU READ: Look at the title, "How to Be a Hostage." In the space below, write your prediction of what the passage will be about, then read to find out if your prediction was accurate.

HOW TO BE A HOSTAGE

The terrorist tactic of hostage-taking is becoming all too commonplace around the world, and a primary target is the American citizen. The U.S. Army considers this to be enough of a threat to its servicemen overseas that it has informally set policies to guide soldiers through such an experience. Some of the suggestions that might help ensure a hostage's freedom from captivity and preserve the country's and the victim's own personal dignity are:

- Remain calm, courteous, and cooperative.

- Do not provide any pertinent information to the terrorists, or even appear capable of providing information that could be used to their advantage.

- Do discuss unimportant personal information with the captors—family, favorite sports, fashions, etc.

- Do listen to the terrorists talk about their cause, their beliefs, and their reasons for taking hostages, but do not praise or debate their cause or any other issue.

- Form a chain of command among military and civilians present and sustain communication among hostages as much as possible.

Was your prediction about the passage correct?

1. Which of the statements below best describes a common practice of terrorists who seize hostages?

   (1) Terrorists are usually calm and courteous in such circumstances.
   (2) U.S. military servicemen are always harmed in such situations.
   (3) Terrorists ensure the release of hostages who follow certain guidelines.
   (4) Americans are being sought as hostages.
   (5) Terrorists never release their hostages.

2. Which of the following is recommended as proper behavior for hostages taken by terrorists?

    (1) Do not let the terrorists talk about their ideology to you.
    (2) Make sure to communicate as often as possible with other hostages.
    (3) Do not provide any personal background about yourself to the terrorists.
    (4) Give the terrorists any relevant documents or other information they may need to further their cause.
    (5) Do not cooperate with the terrorists in any way.

3. Which of the following is *NOT* recommended by the article?

    (1) Appear to be cooperative in unimportant ways.
    (2) Suggest to terrorists that you could provide helpful information if they don't harm any hostages.
    (3) Listen to the terrorists, but don't comment on their views.
    (4) Keep communication lines open among the hostages.
    (5) Discuss family and personal issues with the terrorists.

ANSWERS AND EXPLANATIONS START ON PAGE 285.

Restating Information from Illustrations

Giving directions is a form of restating information. Whenever you read road maps as the "navigator" on a trip, you are putting the information from the map into words for the driver. Look at the map shown in the example below:

In giving directions to someone driving from downtown Highland Park to the corner of Washington Street and Sheridan Road in downtown Waukegan, you might say, "Take Sheridan Road in Highland Park north to Walker Avenue. Turn left on Walker Avenue to get back on Sheridan Road. Follow Sheridan Road north as it curves into Witchwood Lane and continue north on Sheridan until you reach Washington Street in Waukegan."

In order to give these directions you would have to know that the direction north is at the top of the map, which means south is at the bottom, east on the right, and west on the left.

Which direction is Waukegan from North Chicago? _____

Which direction is Lake Bluff from Libertyville? _____

Which direction is Buffalo Grove from Mundelein? _____

On road maps, some streets are heavier and darker than others. On most maps that heavier, darker color indicates a U.S. interstate or state highway.

Name the interstate shown on this map. _____

A scale of miles is usually provided in the legend of a road map. A legend explains any symbols that are used in a map. A scale of miles may be shown in inches (one inch = 50 miles) or by marks spaced equally along a line.

Using the scale on the map above, about how many miles is it from

Lake Bluff to North Chicago? _____

From Riverwoods to Mettawa? _____

The distance between Lake Bluff and North Chicago is about 4 miles. The distance between Riverwoods and Mettawa is about 5 miles.

Exercise 4

Directions: Look at the same map and write instructions for the most direct way you can get from Lake Zurich to Wildwood.

_____

_____

_____

ANSWER AND EXPLANATION START ON PAGE 285.

Identifying Implications

So far you have practiced two ways to show your comprehension of passages and illustrations: by summarizing the main idea and by restating information. A third way to show that you understand information is by being able to identify implications.

Implications are ideas that are suggested or *implied* but not stated directly. A writer *implies* ideas; a reader *infers* meaning from ideas.

Advertisements in newspapers and magazines and commercials on television make suggestions all the time. For example, at election time you may have seen many commercials for political candidates. These commercials often show the candidate in a setting that implies a favorable background. The messages might show a politician at home in a happy family setting. The commercial does not have to *state* that this candidate is a stable, happy, family man. It *implies* this fact by *showing* a smiling family.

Read the following paragraph to identify its implications.

Equality and fairness in the U.S. military are twentieth-century concepts. In fact, it was not until after World War I and II were fought and won that technical expertise and a cooperative spirit in leadership were rewarded by promotions through the ranks in the military.

The implication in this paragraph is that the promotion system in the U.S. military before the twentieth century was _____ and

_____ .

The author has implied that, prior to the twentieth century, promotions in the U.S. military were based on criteria other than technical expertise and a cooperative spirit; therefore, promotions were *unequal* and *unfair*.

The writer states in the first sentence that equality and fairness are new to the military. He then describes the "new" promotion system as an example of fairness and equality.

★ GED PRACTICE ★

Exercise 5

Directions: Read the following passage and circle the best choice in each question below.

BEFORE YOU READ: Look at the title, "How the Other Half Spends." In the space below, write your prediction of what the passage will be about and then read to find out if your prediction was accurate.

HOW THE OTHER HALF SPENDS

Needs are defined as food, shelter, and clothing. Wants are defined as extras in life—vacations, television sets, jewelry, pleasure boats, etc. Wants and needs can mean different things to different people, but generally social scientists agree that economic groups can be fairly well classified by the amount of money they spend on needs versus wants.

The very poorest people in the world live at a bare subsistence level. At best, they have just enough food and shelter to stay alive. On a rung above this level on the economic ladder are the working poor, those who spend $9 out of every $10 on things they *need* and only $1 out of every $10 on what they *want* out of life. The middle income group spends about $8 out of $10 on needs and the remaining $2 on wants, and the upper income group spends only $4 out of $10 on needs.

Check to see if your prediction about the subject of this passage was correct.

1. The implication of the figures listed for needs versus wants in the various economic groups is that

    (1)   the wealthier a person is, the fewer needs he or she has
    (2)   people at the upper income level want more things than those at the lower end of the economic ladder
    (3)   the lower one's income, the more material things one needs to get by
    (4)   the middle income group is the only one that is able to keep a sensible balance of needs versus wants
    (5)   as one's income goes up, one has more money to spend on wants

2. This author has also implied that some of the very poorest people in the world

   (1) cannot even provide for all their own needs
   (2) are not concerned with providing for their own wants because they have none
   (3) should be given monetary assistance by the government
   (4) are uneducated and unable to deal with money
   (5) are not considered to be in any economic group

ANSWERS AND EXPLANATIONS START ON PAGE 285.

Identifying Implications in Illustrations

You can draw implications from illustrations as well as from written materials. Line graphs are particularly effective in showing trends from which we may draw implications. A quick look at a line graph can reveal increases, decreases, uneven movements, or leveling off of numbers. Look at this line graph.

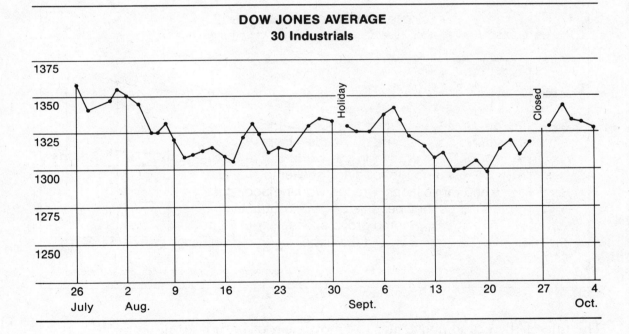

DOW JONES AVERAGE
30 Industrials

Notice that the graph has a *title*, "Dow Jones Average," and a *subtitle*, "30 Industrials." It has figures going up the *vertical* axis that represent the number of stocks traded and dates along the *horizontal* axis that show what period of time the graph represents.

Between July 26 and October 4, the line on this graph fluctuates between 1300 and 1350. The implication is that, over a given period of time, the number of stocks traded each day will vary. Looking at the graph, you can see that the line of the graph has moved up and down since early August, so the implication is that it will continue to fluctuate over time.

Skill Builder
Reading Line Graphs

1. The title and/or subtitle indicate the main idea and contents of the graph.

2. The *vertical* axis contains the information going *up the side* of the graph.

3. The *horizontal* axis contains the information going *across the bottom* of the graph.

4. *Trends* may be identified by describing the movement of the line from its beginning to its end.

★ **GED PRACTICE** ★

Exercise 6

Directions: Circle the letter of the choice that best answers the question below.

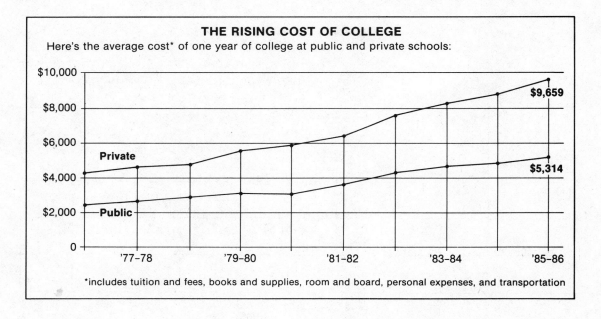

THE RISING COST OF COLLEGE

Here's the average cost* of one year of college at public and private schools:

Private — $9,659

Public — $5,314

'77–78   '79–80   '81–82   '83–84   '85–86

*includes tuition and fees, books and supplies, room and board, personal expenses, and transportation

The title of the graph above and the movement of both lines imply that

(1) the cost of attending college in the future will be too high for the average family.

(2) in future years, the cost to send a child to college will steadily increase.

(3) private schools are better than public schools.

(4) inflation is the reason for the steady rise in college costs.

(5) private schools have raised their costs at a more gradual pace than public schools have.

ANSWERS AND EXPLANATIONS START ON PAGE 286.

2 ANALYZING SOCIAL STUDIES MATERIALS

When you analyze something, you break it down into its basic parts or elements to understand better what makes up its whole. For example, if you've ever taken a high school biology course, you probably had to dissect, or take apart, a frog to examine its internal organs.

By analyzing the frog, you were able to understand better the function of each organ and to see how each related to the whole frog. Taking this a step further, you also should have been able to picture the similar placement of these organs in the human body.

In social studies, you must also analyze; however, you look at specific ideas—pieces of information—to understand better the point being made by a writer, graphic artist, or cartoonist. You can analyze information in the field of social studies in a number of ways. On the Social Studies Test, you will be tested on your ability to analyze material in at least five ways:

- identifying cause-and-effect relationships

- distinguishing facts from opinions and hypotheses

- understanding unstated assumptions

- drawing conclusions from supporting details

- drawing inferences from given material

Cause and Effect

When we analyze social studies material for causes and effects, we connect important events with the conditions that made them happen. Without thinking about it, you connect causes with effects every day. For example, in recent winters, the U.S. experienced such extremes in temperatures that the frost line reached Florida, damaging the state's orange crop. Many oranges were lost. On the television news, it was predicted that consumers would soon be forced to pay more for orange products at the store.

A number of results stemmed from this single cause: sudden cold temperatures. A couple of them are listed below:

Cause   **Effect**

1. freezing temperatures   ——————➤   damaged orange crop

2. damaged orange crop   ——————➤   fewer oranges harvested

What effect might come from the cause shown below? Write one.

Cause   **Effect**

3. fewer oranges harvested ————————➤ _____

You may have written, "higher prices for orange products," since a short supply of a commodity leads to higher prices. You can probably think of other causes and effects stemming from this event. For example, *higher prices for orange products* (Cause) might mean that *fewer orange products will be bought* (Effect). Also, *a damaged Florida orange crop* (Cause) might mean the *sale of more California oranges* (Effect).

As you see, events can sometimes lead to a chain of cause-and-effect relationships. Analyzing cause and effect helps us to understand everyday events and to plan our actions in accordance with them.

Effects normally *follow* causes in time. However, sometimes an effect appears in a sentence *before* the cause, even though the effect follows the cause in time. The statement below is an example of this inverted relationship:

effect
America finally turned its attention to the exploration of space largely
cause
because of the Soviet Union's launching of Sputnik in the late 1950s.

 ## Skill Builder
Recognizing Cause-and-Effect Relationships

The cause-and-effect relationship is frequently signaled by key words such as *because, since, therefore, as a result, consequently, accordingly, if...then, the reason was, led to, brought about, the outcome was, the end result was,* and *was responsible for.*

Exercise 1

Directions: Underline the *cause* and the *effect* in each sentence below and write a *c* above the word or words that indicate cause and an *e* above the word or words that indicate effect. Some sentences may include more than one cause or effect.

1. In addition to extreme overpopulation, extended drought has contributed to severe famine in Ethiopia and other parts of Africa.

2. Population growth in the Sunbelt states has come from many companies relocating to that area.

3. The emigration of the first pilgrims from England to the New World was prompted by religious persecution in their homeland.

4. Unfair employer practices brought about the establishment of labor unions.

Exercise 2

Directions: Frequently, you will be asked to trace causes and their effects in an article or a passage. Read the passage below. Match the effects listed in the column on the right with their causes listed on the left by writing the appropriate letter in the space provided.

Tornadoes, or "twisters," are among the smallest but more violent storms. They are caused by air masses that reach rotational speeds of about 300 miles per hour. Tornadoes often occur in series, like the ones in April of 1965 that caused havoc in Iowa, Wisconsin, Illinois, Indiana, Michigan, and Ohio, killing 271 people and damaging $300,000,000 worth of property. Forty years earlier, in March of 1925, another series had killed 740 persons in Missouri, Indiana, Illinois, Kentucky, and Tennessee.

"Tornado Alley" is a belt that runs through the Great Plains and southeastern portion of the United States. The Chicago area holds the greatest potential for tornado damage because of the combination of its location, its density of population, and its development. However, less populated southwestern Oklahoma has the highest incidence of tornadoes. Though Chicago has only half the incidence of tornadoes as Oklahoma, the need for disaster aid in Chicago is greater than anywhere else.

Cause	Effect
_____ 1. tornado series of 1965	(a) 740 people killed in 5 states
_____ 2. plains location, population density, and development in the Chicago area	(b) small violent storms
_____ 3. rotating air masses of about 300 mph	(c) the greatest potential for tornado damage
_____ 4. tornado series of 1925	(d) $300,000,000 in property damage

Exercise 3

Directions: Read the two passages below. Circle the letter of the choice that best completes the statements that follow each passage.

A troublesome problem in the American economy is reduced competitiveness with other industrial nations. This is especially true regarding automobile production and sales between the United States and Japan.

Japanese auto makers can produce smaller cars more cheaply than many of the American Big Four auto makers. Also, for many years, the American market has been open to Japanese car manufacturers. Because of this, car sales for GM, Chrysler, Ford, and American Motors have suffered.

Because of pressure from American government and business leaders, Japan has voluntarily reduced the number of cars exported to the United States. This self-imposed quota has allowed U.S. auto makers to improve quality, increase automation, and reduce manufacturing costs.

Unfortunately, American car buyers have not significantly increased their purchase of domestic cars. They choose, instead, to pay more for the fewer Japanese imports, and they have responded to the limited export of Japanese cars by buying more European imports.

1. According to the passage, one result of Japan's voluntary restraint on auto exports to the U.S. has been that

   (1) American cars have become scarce and highly priced.
   (2) American automobile manufacturers have demanded stronger protectionist policies.
   (3) Americans have been refusing to buy Japanese automobiles.
   (4) the Japanese have been buying more American cars.
   (5) American auto makers have become more competitive.

2. According to the passage, an effect of the reduced numbers of Japanese cars exported to the U.S. has been

   (1) a decreased demand for Japanese imports by Americans.
   (2) an increase in the number of European imports sold in the U.S.
   (3) a decrease in the cost of Japanese imports.
   (4) an increase in the number of American cars sold in Japan.
   (5) a greater commitment by Americans to "buy American."

In 1978, voters in the state of California revolted against high taxes by passing Proposition 13. This action severely limited revenue from property taxes that is vitally important in supporting public schools. One result of this was that educational programs in the state suffered. However, after 1978 the federal report *A Nation at Risk*, was released. This report focused on the "rising tide of mediocrity" engulfing American schools.

Now, California leads states that have raised taxes to enable schools to improve programs.

3. What is suggested as the reason for the change in feeling by the voters of California?

    (1) Homeowners weren't paying their fair share of taxes.
    (2) The public recognized the need for money to improve quality of schools.
    (3) Voters decided property taxes were not the proper source of revenue for schools.
    (4) A federal report convinced citizens that schools misused funds.
    (5) Taxpayers in California were paying a proportionally lower amount for school support than those in any other state.

4. As a result of raising taxes, California

    (1) had less revenue.
    (2) had mediocre educational programs.
    (3) was featured in *A Nation At Risk*.
    (4) had the first tax revolt.
    (5) will be able to improve educational programs.

ANSWERS AND EXPLANATIONS START ON PAGE 286.

Cause and Effect in Illustrations

Graphs, maps, charts, and cartoons can also show cause-and-effect relationships. The illustration below is a pictograph.

What is the topic of the pictograph? _____

Which car companies are being represented? _____

What does each white car in the pictograph represent? _____

What does each black car in the pictograph represent? _____

You should have written that the topic is *New Car Sales*. The car companies being compared are *GM, Ford, Chrysler,* and *AMC*. The white cars represent the number of cars sold in August 1984, and the black cars represent the number sold in August 1985.

According to this graph, the cause of such a dramatic rise in car sales from one year to the next is

(1) fierce competition among the domestic auto makers to be tops in sales.
(2) a rise in the rates of financing along with rebates to buyers of new cars.
(3) a lowering of interest rates combined with rebates on cars purchased.
(4) a virtual halt in import sales due to severe restrictions on the number of imports.
(5) a general growth in the U.S. economy in general and the automobile industry in particular.

The cause of the increased car-buying from 1984 to 1985 was (3), a lowering of interest rates combined with rebates on cars purchased. This can be determined by comparing the number of cars sold at higher interest rates during 1984 with the number of cars sold in 1985 at lower interest rates combined with rebates. The key for this information is shown at the top of the graph. Choices (1), (4), and (5) suggest causes that are not dealt with on this graph. Choice (2) mentions a rise in interest rates, which is the opposite of the information the graph gives you.

Skill Builder
Understanding Pictographs

Pictographs use symbols to stand for the subject being measured. Some common symbols are cars, houses, and dollars. Whole symbols and partial symbols may be used in a pictograph. The *title* tells us the main topic.

★ **GED PRACTICE** ★

Exercise 4

Directions: Look at the pictograph again, then circle the choice that best completes the following statement.

According to the graph, the effect of the 1985 drop in interest rates on AMC car sales was

(1) not significant.
(2) great enough to put AMC ahead of other auto makers in car sales.
(3) enough of an increase in sales to temporarily halt the layoff of workers.
(4) a doubling of the number of cars sold in 1984.
(5) a lowering of the number of cars sold in 1984.

ANSWER AND EXPLANATION STARTS ON PAGE 286.

Distinguishing Facts from Opinions and Hypotheses

Different types of newspaper articles illustrate the difference between facts and opinions. Newspaper and magazine articles are based largely on facts. Editorials and featured columns, however, present a writer's opinions along with the facts.

Facts can be proved to be true. ***Opinions*** are the writer's feelings or ideas about a topic and are influenced heavily by one's background, values, and outlook on life. ***Hypotheses*** are assumptions that are made for the purpose of explaining an event. Hypotheses may be proved or disproved with the passage of time and the acquisition of more information about why or how events occur. Hypotheses, too, are based on facts but also are influenced by one's impressions and hunches about a subject. The examples below show how facts, opinions, and hypotheses differ.

- It is a *fact* that the West Coast of the United States has several mountain ranges running along it, that it borders the Pacific Ocean, and that it is warmer on the average than the East Coast. These are facts because they can be proved.

- It is an *opinion*, however, that the West Coast is the best part of the United States in which to live because that is a statement based on a person's values, background, and outlook on life.

- It is a *hypothesis* that erosion along the coast will make the western coastal area uninhabitable in years to come because more information will be needed to prove or disprove such a hunch.

 ## Skill Builder
Distinguishing Facts from Opinions and Hypotheses

1. Facts can be proved with data.

2. Opinions are beliefs that are influenced by feelings. Opinions can be debated.

3. Hypotheses may be proved or disproved with the passage of time and the acquisition of more information.

Classify each of the following as *fact*, *opinion*, or *hypothesis*, by writing *f*, *o*, or *h* on the line before each statement.

_____ The economic system of the U.S. is basically capitalistic, but modified with some aspects of socialism.

_____ If social welfare programs like Medicare were abolished, the economy might perform better.

_____ The socialistic schemes in our system should be removed because they are too expensive for the taxpaying citizens.

The first statement above is a *fact*, which can be proved by obtaining a definition of capitalism and socialism. The second statement is a *hypothesis* that could be supported by data and could even be proved to be either true or false in the future. The third statement is an *opinion* that is based on a person's beliefs.

As the example below shows, hypotheses provide reasonable explanations for occurrences.

Read the passage below. Place an *H* on the line next to the hypothesis or hypotheses that explain why the event occurred.

Over the period of one year, motor vehicle deaths in nineteen states decreased significantly over the previous year's. Research has shown that the two most important factors that determine the survival of a victim in a serious traffic accident are (1) whether the victim is restrained in the car and (2) whether medical attention is immediately available.

Based on the information in the above passage, which of the hypotheses listed explain why traffic fatalities were reduced?

_____ **(1)** The states instituted tough drunk driving laws.

_____ **(2)** The states hired more highway patrolmen to catch speeders.

_____ **(3)** The states increased the number of trauma centers and paramedics to handle victims of traffic accidents.

_____ **(4)** The states adopted laws requiring passengers to wear seat belts.

_____ **(5)** The states required more frequent driver examinations for senior citizens and teenagers.

Only (3) and (4) are reasonable explanations of the reduction in motor vehicle fatalities. Both of them address the two criteria upon which survival for victims of traffic accidents is based. None of the other choices have a direct relationship to the immediate access to medical care and the restraint of passengers in the vehicle. Choices (3) and (4) may be proved by comparing the number of motor vehicle fatalities both before and after the number of trauma centers and paramedics were increased and before and after seat belts were required.

Skill Builder
Hints for Identifying Opinions

Phrases like *should be* or *I believe/think/hope/want,* and those filled with emotionally charged words like *evil, wonderful, terrible* often indicate that a writer is presenting his or her opinion.

★ **GED PRACTICE** ★

Exercise 5

Directions: Read the passage below and answer the questions that follow.

Some jobs are more stressful than others, and air traffic controllers are considered to have one of the most stressful. This belief has been backed up by the fact that controllers have a high incidence of stress-related disorders like chronic anxiety and alcoholism. Many people believe, too, that the reason for the high level of stress is the responsibility that controllers have for the safety of passengers. However, such reasoning does not explain the low rate of stress disorders among airline pilots, who have much more direct responsibility for people's safety.

Recent studies have attempted to explain this discrepancy by naming poor labor/management relations as the main source of the controllers' stress.

Controllers who were interviewed complained that their recommendations for providing safety backups and other measures were not being considered by their employers or the Federal Aviation Administration. Interestingly, too, the studies concluded that the most conscientious of the workers were the ones most prone to experience stress—because of their high level of concern for safety.

1. Which of the following is a hypothesis that may be drawn based on the information in the passage?

   (1) Shortening the hours of air traffic controllers will reduce stress-related disorders.
   (2) Providing proof that management is implementing the controllers' recommendations will reduce stress.
   (3) Providing counseling services for victims of stress will reduce stress levels.
   (4) Ensuring that all planes are no more than twenty years old will lower stress levels among air traffic controllers.
   (5) Reducing the number of daily scheduled flights will reduce stress levels among air traffic controllers.

2. Which of the following is a fact about air traffic controllers that the author could support with data?

   (1) There is a relatively high rate of alcoholism among air traffic controllers.
   (2) There is a low incidence of stress disorders among the controllers.
   (3) Pilots suffer from more anxiety than controllers do.
   (4) The only source of air traffic controllers' stress is poor labor/management relations.
   (5) The controllers are not taken seriously by the Federal Aviation Administration.

3. According to the passage, air traffic controllers have which of the following opinions?

   (1) Some jobs are more stressful than others.
   (2) An air traffic controller's job is more stressful than a pilot's.
   (3) Neither airline company executives nor the FAA is paying attention to controllers' safety recommendations.
   (4) The more conscientious workers experienced the most stress.
   (5) Airline executives have no concern for safety.

ANSWERS AND EXPLANATIONS START ON PAGE 286.

Facts, Opinions, and Hypotheses in Illustrations

Political Cartoons

The real purpose in a political cartoon is to express an opinion of the cartoonist—a view of a political or social issue as the artist sees it.

Look at the political cartoon above. Notice that there are four people in the picture, each representing different groups as shown by their labels. Three of these people (the parents, the teachers, and the courts) are arguing over a book labeled "prayer issue." The boy labeled "students" is alone at the blackboard, being ignored by the other three, while he is incorrectly doing a math problem. This picture illustrates the opinion that:

Students' education is being _____ while the prayer issue is being debated by the people who should be helping them to _____ .

The completed statement should read: Students' education is being *ignored* or *neglected* while the prayer issue is being debated by the people who should be helping them to *learn*.

Skill Builder
Keys to Understanding Political Cartoons

Political cartoons are often based on politicians or statesmen, shown as caricatures (cartoon figures). The caricatures usually exaggerate a feature of the person being illustrated. For example, Reagan's dark hair, Nixon's nose, and Carter's smile have been widely caricatured.

Political symbols are often used as well. For example, the donkey represents the Democratic Party; an elephant, the Republican Party; a bearded man dressed in stars and stripes (Uncle Sam) represents the United States; a dove represents peace; and a hawk, war. Often, a family or person is shown to represent how a social problem is affecting the average person. Cartoonists often use humor or sarcasm to express their opinions on important issues.

★ GED PRACTICE ★

Exercise 6

Directions: Circle the number that best completes the statement about the cartoon below.

TOM FLANNERY
Courtesy Baltimore Sun

The American Dream House

It is the opinion of this cartoonist that the American dream to own a home is

(1) worth the struggle and sacrifice that it demands.
(2) threatened by increasingly high costs.
(3) becoming less desirable than apartment living.
(4) as attractive and as popular as ever.
(5) a realistic goal for most people.

ANSWER AND EXPLANATION STARTS ON PAGE 286.

Pictographs

Graphs, like the pictograph below, can also express facts and support hypotheses.

U.S. EXPORTS TO THE MAJOR WARRING NATIONS				
$ = $100 million		¢ = $10 million		
Nations	**1914**	**1915**		**1916**
MAJOR ALLIED POWERS				
United Kingdom	$ $ $ $ $ $	$ $ $ $ $ $ $ $ ¢ '		$ $ $ $ $ $ $ $ $ $ $ $ $ $ $ ¢ ¢
France	$ $	$ $ $ $		$ $ $ $ $ $ ¢ ¢ ¢
Czarist Russia	¢ ¢ ¢ '	¢ ¢ ¢ ¢ ¢		$ $ $ ¢
MAJOR CENTRAL POWERS				
Germany	$ $ $ ¢ ¢ ¢ ¢	¢ ¢ ¢		(
Austria-Hungary	¢ ¢	(		'
Turkey	(	'		—

Based on the pictograph, it is a *fact* that the United Kingdom received almost $600 million in imports from the U.S. in 1914, over $900 million in 1915, and over $1,500 million in 1916. It is a *hypothesis* (at least from the information on this graph only) that the U.S. was a close ally of Great Britain during this time period. With more data this could possibly be proven, but based on this graph this would just be a good hypothesis.

★ GED PRACTICE ★

Exercise 7

Directions: Looking at the pictograph above on U.S. Exports to the Major Warring Nations, circle the answer that represents the most accurate hypothesis that may be made.

In April 1917, the U.S. entered the war against the Central Powers. A hypothesis that can be made, based on the graph above, is that the U.S. entered the war because

(1) economically, the U.S. had already aligned itself with the Allied Powers.
(2) the Central Powers were quite depressed economically and would, therefore, be easy to defeat.
(3) the United Kingdom was receiving almost five times as much aid as Czarist Russia.
(4) the Central Powers did not need help financially, while the Allied Powers did.
(5) the cause of the Allied Powers was more just than the cause of the Central Powers.

ANSWER AND EXPLANATION STARTS ON PAGE 286.

Unstated Assumptions

When someone makes an *assumption* about something, that person takes a fact or an idea for granted. In newspaper or television editorials, the writers or speakers often take for granted certain ideas that may or may not be true. By doing this, they attempt to influence your opinion.

For example, in a familiar commercial, an individual with dandruff is shown as a social outcast until he uses a particular shampoo to get rid of the problem. The unstated assumption is that dandruff-free people are popular, while those with dandruff are not. A further assumption is that the use of a certain product will increase your popularity. It is important to be able to know when this kind of subtle persuasion is being used. If you can clearly understand unstated assumptions in what you read or hear, you will be better able to make informed decisions.

Read the statement below carefully to discover the underlying, unstated assumption made by the writer.

All people caught and convicted of DUI (driving under the influence) should be sent to mandatory Alcoholics Anonymous meetings.

The unstated assumption in this statement is that all DUI drivers are _____

_____

The blank should be filled with the word *alcoholics*. For the writer to state that all DUI drivers should be sent to AA meetings assumes that they are alcoholics. In fact, while they may be drunk at the time they are caught, they may not necessarily be alcoholics.

Exercise 8

Directions: Read the statements below. In the space provided, write what the underlying unstated assumption behind each statement is.

1. The United States should use its power to prevent small, developing countries from turning from capitalism to socialism.

    The writer assumes that socialism is _____

    _____

2. In the televised presidential debates, John F. Kennedy looked better on television than Richard Nixon. JFK's win in 1960 signaled the beginning of the "media sell" of the U.S. president.

    The writer assumes that Kennedy won the presidency in 1960 because

    _____

    _____

3. Finally, the people of mainland China can enjoy the benefits of Westernized society and escape, at least partially, the dreariness of their past existence.

    The writer assumes that, before westernization, China _____

    _____

4. The dress was punk, the music was 50,000 watts, the style was slamdance, but there would be no trouble at this rock concert. This concert was a Christian rock festival.

    The writer assumes that there is usually trouble at _____

    _____

5. If society would make those on welfare do volunteer work in the community, it would have no more problem with welfare cheats.

    The writer assumes that there are _____ in the welfare system.

Exercise 9

Directions: Unstated assumptions are often buried in editorials and newspaper columns. These are types of writing that express a person's point of view. Read the passage below to find unstated assumptions the writer makes and complete the exercise that follows.

> Public housing was supposed to be part of the solution, not part of the problem of poverty in the cities. Instead of being a springboard out of unemployment and crime, it has become a breeding ground for the worst of inner-city ills.
>
> The high-rise dwellings are unattractive, dangerous, and, in general, depressing to live in. New units need to be built, with fewer elevators in which to trap victims, with cleaner sewerage systems to keep out disease-carrying insects and rodents, and in areas with good schools to provide better educational opportunities for the youth. Most importantly, drug dealers and pimps must be identified and outlawed from any and all public housing residences.

Check off the statements below that the author has assumed *but not directly stated.*

_____ **(a)** Public housing breeds inner city ills.

_____ **(b)** The sewerage systems in public housing units are to blame for the insect and rodent problem.

_____ **(c)** If better facilities are provided, public housing residents will improve their lives.

_____ **(d)** The unattractiveness and uncleanliness of the public housing units is the fault of no one but the dwellers themselves.

_____ **(e)** Drug dealers and pimps are not presently identified and outlawed from public housing residences.

Exercise 10

Directions: Read the passage below and answer the questions that follow.

The Corrections Corporation of America was formed in 1983. It is an investor-owned corporation established to make a profit by running prisons as businesses. Excesses are eliminated, bureaucracy is avoided, employees are trained and paid adequately, and costs are constantly monitored. Though the corporation does not set policy, it runs everything else and manages the facilities toward the goal of turning a profit.

This ever-present concern for the bottom line bothers some of the critics of this bold new idea. Mark Cunniff, executive director of the National Association of Criminal Justice Planners, says pointedly, "The private sector is more concerned with doing well than doing good." For this reason, CCA may be a short-lived company despite the fact that people like Tennessee governor Lamar Alexander call the idea of a privately run prison "bold" and "impressive." He points out that private contractors have been running hospitals for years and have shown they can do it without cost overruns. "If private management is good enough for our sick mothers, it's good enough for our murderers and rapists," he concludes.

1. An unstated assumption made by Governor Alexander is that

    (1) private companies are more concerned about sick people than they are about prisoners.
    (2) private corporations are quite capable of setting government policy.
    (3) even though private contractors have done a good job of running hospitals, they may not do so well with prisons.
    (4) running private prisons would require similar management skills as running private hospitals.
    (5) cost overruns are unavoidable in institutions such as hospitals and prisons.

2. Mark Cunniff, executive director of the National Association of Criminal Justice Planners, is quoted in the passage. He says, "The private sector is more concerned with doing well than doing good." From the quote it is evident that he thinks that

    (1) private companies are concerned with performing social service.
    (2) private companies are more concerned with producing a profit than performing good deeds.
    (3) private citizens are more concerned with their own health than that of others.
    (4) private citizens are more concerned with having good hospitals than good prisons.
    (5) private organizations provide most of the country's social services.

ANSWERS AND EXPLANATIONS START ON PAGE 287.

Unstated Assumptions in Illustrations

The information that goes into tables, charts, graphs, and other illustrations is sometimes obtained on the basis of underlying, unstated assumptions. For this reason, it is a good practice to question how valid or true some data are.

Tables and Charts

A table or chart is an organization of many facts into a small space. Tables and charts are used to keep scores in games, list train schedules, assign work tasks, compare weather reports, and so on.

The chart below reports the results of a survey. The title, "Paying What the Job's Worth," gives us an idea of what the survey was about. Notice that occupations are listed along the left side of the chart and the headings "paid too little," "paid about right," and "paid too much" are on the right. Percentages across from each listed occupation tell us how many of the people surveyed viewed the pay scale for that job as too little, too much, or about right according to the contribution it makes to society.

PAYING WHAT THE JOB'S WORTH

843 respondents were asked how they feel "about the amount of income that different kinds of people receive for the contribution they make to society."

Occupation	Paid too little	Paid about right	Paid too much
Movie stars/top entertainers	0.5%	18.8%	80.7%
Professional athletes	2.9%	18.2%	78.8%
Top executives	1.3%	24.3%	74.4%
Physicians	2.4%	27.5%	70.1%
Government officials	4.7%	25.1%	70.2%
Landlords	5.1%	41.8%	53.1%
Skilled blue-collar workers	8.7%	48.3%	43.1%
Union factory workers	14.4%	55.8%	29.9%
Scientists	22.7%	55.8%	21.4%
Middle-level managers	21.1%	69.2%	9.6%
Owners of small business	43.5%	52.5%	4.0%

Source: American Journal of Public Health

One assumption the interviewer must have made is that the people responding to the survey knew *how much money* each job pays. Another assumption the interviewer must have made is that the respondents had some idea of what

_____ each job makes to society.

Here you should have recognized that the respondents had to know what *contributions* each job makes to society in order to be able to answer the question effectively in this survey.

Skill Builder
Reading Charts and Tables

1. The *title* tells the major topic.

2. A *caption* further explains the data (how it was obtained, who obtained it, when it was obtained, etc.).

3. *Columns* and *rows* are arranged so they can be read across or down and are labeled with *headings* to classify the information in the table.

Political Cartoons

Political cartoonists assume a great deal in representing their ideas in pictures. Such cartoons are usually found on the editorial pages of newspapers because cartoons are really editorials in picture form. Just as a table or chart makes a statement, a cartoon's picture and its few words can be thought-provoking.

Reprinted with permission from the *Minneapolis Star and Tribune*

'GO AHEAD AND OPERATE. JUST DON'T DRAW BLOOD!'

The cartoonist seems to assume that ecology programs adopted to protect our environment will necessarily take a chunk out of the economy, since the cartoon shows a surgeon, labeled _____, about to operate on a patient, labeled _____. The cartoonist also seems to assume that the patient (economy) cannot afford the programs since the patient is asking the surgeon (ecology) not to draw blood.

Exercise 11

Directions: Look at the cartoon below and answer the questions that follow.

LOU ERICKSON
Courtesy Atlanta Journal

Which of the following is an un-stated assumption made by the cartoonist?

(1) America started out with too many personal freedoms for its citizens.

(2) The growth of government in America made it a freer, safer place to live.

(3) Big government has eroded personal freedoms over the years.

(4) The security afforded by big government is worth the price of fewer personal freedoms.

(5) Expansion of the government was an inevitable result of modern problems.

ANSWERS AND EXPLANATIONS START ON PAGE 287.

Drawing Conclusions

On the Social Studies Test, you will be asked to analyze materials to determine what conclusions the author wants you to draw from the facts supplied. You probably draw conclusions from details every day. If you have ever put together a jigsaw puzzle, you had to draw conclusions. For example, while working a puzzle, you might conclude that the blue pieces fit together, then the brown and white ones, and then the green, until finally the pieces fit together in such a way as to lead you to the conclusion that this is a picture of a snow-capped mountain surrounded by blue sky and green grass.

Read the paragraph below. Draw the necessary conclusion to complete the final sentence.

In 1977, capital punishment was restored by the legislature in California. By September 1985, the California State Supreme Court had reversed thirty-five out of thirty-eight appealed death penalty convictions and had commuted the sentences to lesser punishments, such as life imprisonment.

This paragraph supports the conclusion that, although the California state legislature supported capital punishment, the state's supreme court questioned

the _____ of the death penalty in many cases where it has been applied.

You may have put together the following facts:

a. The state legislature passed the law allowing capital punishment and, therefore, must have supported it.

b. The state supreme court reversed almost all the decisions for the death penalty that had been appealed over an eight-year period of time.

You can draw the conclusion that the courts must have questioned the *legality* of the use of the death penalty.

Like pieces in a jigsaw puzzle, the pieces of information fit together to lead you to a conclusion.

Exercise 12

Directions: Read the paragraphs below. Circle the letter of the choice that best indicates the conclusion that may be drawn from the information given.

1. Prior to the 1980s, the U.S. home finance system was stable, easy to understand, and acceptable to lenders and home buyers alike. The basic home loan, or mortgage, was for a thirty-year period, during which time the rate of interest for the mortgage was fixed and unchangeable. Now, home buyers applying for mortgages are often confronted with the choice of a high fixed interest rate or a rate that can fluctuate monthly during the life of the loan.

    A conclusion based on this paragraph is that borrowers looking for a mortgage these days must be prepared to

    (1) choose between different mortgage options.
    (2) settle for a 15-year mortgage.
    (3) finance the purchase with cash.

2. Adults have obligations to the children they bring into this world. Infants are incapable of caring for themselves and will not develop normally without proper love and discipline. Society sets up laws, therefore, to assure the normal growth of its young. Parental neglect is generally considered to involve the disregard of the physical, emotional, and moral needs of children under the age of eighteen and is punishable in most states by imprisonment, fines, or removal of children from the home.

    It can be concluded that this writer thinks that

    (1) punishment for adults guilty of parental neglect are too severe.
    (2) parents have the ultimate responsibility for the proper development of their children.
    (3) society needs to do more to protect the welfare of its children.

3. The creative uses of futuristic computers in such movies as *Star Wars* and *2001* have made many people think about their seemingly limitless capabilities. The impact of computers on such industries as grocery stores, banks, gas stations, design and machine shops, and education has been obvious to many. Despite this fact, we are amazed by each new enhancement of computers' capabilities. For example, psychologists and counselors are presently working with programmers to develop a program that will enable computers to perform routine counseling tasks in the areas of career and personal advisement.

    We can conclude that in the future computers will be

    (1) present in almost all aspects of society's workplace.
    (2) completely replacing psychologists and counselors for career and personal advisement.
    (3) able to make all our decisions for us.

Exercise 13

Directions: Read the following passages and in the exercises circle the choice that best represents a conclusion that may be drawn.

In possibly the first action of its kind, a coalition of union, community, and religious groups negotiated an agreement with the city of Vacaville, California, requiring certain employers to give a year's notice of plant closings or major cuts in operations. The agreement is limited to those companies attracted to the city by the offer of tax-supported financial aid.

1. From this paragraph we can conclude that

   (1) when union, community, and religious groups unite, they can demand anything they want from a city.
   (2) the city of Vacaville, California, has limited the number of companies that may move there.
   (3) cooperation among certain groups in Vacaville, California, has given some employees there a chance to plan their futures.
   (4) labor agreements between city and community groups must be limited to companies benefiting from tax breaks.
   (5) unions, communities, and religious groups often cooperate with each other to accomplish a common goal.

Economic researchers at the Federal Reserve and the Internal Revenue Service reported that during the 1980s America's super-rich became even richer. The richest 1 percent of American households (all of them at least millionaires) accounted for 37 percent of private net worth in 1989, up from 31 percent in 1983. In fact, by 1989 the top 1 percent of American households had a greater net worth than the bottom 90 percent of American households. This surge in wealth among the super-rich was the first significant rise in wealth concentration since the Roaring Twenties.

2. We can conclude from this passage that

   (1) the Roaring Twenties were boom years for the super-rich.
   (2) during the 1980s most Americans became wealthier.
   (3) more households were among the super-wealthy during the 1980s.
   (4) Reaganomics' "trickle-down" theory was a success.
   (5) the same households have been among the super-wealthy since the 1920s.

ANSWERS AND EXPLANATIONS START ON PAGE 287.

Drawing Conclusions from Illustrations

You have seen how conclusions can be drawn from reading a passage. Now let's look at how to draw conclusions in graphs and maps.

Bar Graphs

Look at the bar graph below. Notice that it has a title, "Number of Immigrants to the United States," a horizontal label (across the bottom axis of the graph) of "Years," and a vertical label (up the left axis) of "In millions." Bars of various heights represent variations in numbers of immigrants throughout the years.

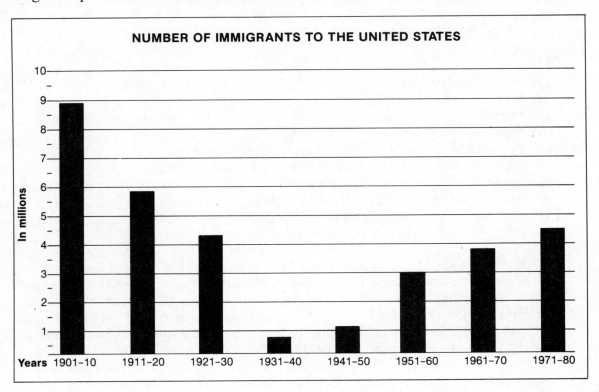

Keeping in mind all of the details the graph shows, place a check next to the correct conclusions that may be drawn.

_____ **(a)** During the 1970s the nationalities of the predominant immigrant groups changed from European to Indo-Chinese.

_____ **(b)** The decades from 1931 to 1950 mark the period when immigration to the U.S. was at its lowest.

_____ **(c)** A 1953 law called the Refugee Relief Act stopped the increasing trend of immigration to the U.S.

_____ **(d)** No significant changes in immigration patterns are foreseen for the coming decades.

_____ **(e)** The post World War II "baby boom" had no effect on U.S. immigration patterns.

_____ **(f)** Immigration to the U.S. was at its highest during the early twentieth century.

_____ **(g)** There were approximately the same number of immigrants to the U.S. during the twenties and the seventies.

Choice (a) above cannot be concluded logically from the graph because there is nothing in it that indicates the nationalities of the immigrants. Choice (c) would be incorrect because an increasing trend, though slight, seems to be occurring during the 1950s, not a decreasing one. Choice (d) cannot be concluded from the information on this graph. Too many events could occur to change the immigration patterns in the future decades to make a conclusion like this one. Choice (e) is incorrect because it is impossible to conclude from this graph that the baby boom had an effect on immigration.

Choices (b), (f), and (g), however, can be supported by the information in the graph. A look at the bars representing the period from 1931 to 1950 reveal that immigration was at its lowest, the number of immigrants hovering about or just below the 1 million mark, (b). Similarly, a glance at the period from 1901 to 1910 (the early twentieth century) reveals that immigration to the U.S. was at its highest—a figure of nearly 9 million immigrants, (f). In comparing the figures for the decades of the twenties (1921–30) and the seventies (1971–80), you can see that the number of immigrants to the U.S. was similar, (g).

 ## Skill Builder
Reading Bar Graphs

1. The *title* tells the main topic.

2. The *horizontal axis* gives information along the bottom of the graph.

3. The *vertical axis* gives information up the side of the graph.

4. *Bars* of differing heights or lengths show how subjects compare in relation to the main topic.

Weather Maps

Maps are other illustrations from which we can draw conclusions. You may have noticed weather maps in newspapers or on television. Maps can give us a variety of information about a place. In the map on page 62, for instance, you determine what the weather will be like on one day in different regions of the country.

 ## Skill Builder
Reading Weather Maps

1. Weather maps can give us temperature ranges, levels of precipitation, or other features of the climate in an area.

2. The title tells us what the map's focus is.

3. Symbols stand for information shown in the map.

4. A key or legend explains the symbols.

Exercise 14

Directions: Look at the map below. Study the symbols for snow, rain, flurries, and showers. Write *Y* for yes or *N* for no before each conclusion listed below. Write *Y* only if the conclusion can be based on the map.

= rain   = snow   = flurries   = showers

_____ 1. This was a forecast for a winter day in the U.S.

_____ 2. Most of the country is free of precipitation on this day.

_____ 3. As you head south in the U.S., the weather gets warmer.

_____ 4. There is snow in the Pacific Northwest.

_____ 5. The East Coast should be prepared for flooding.

_____ 6. Central Pennsylvania is experiencing periods of showers.

_____ 7. All of Florida will be in the 70 degree range.

ANSWERS AND EXPLANATIONS START ON PAGE 287.

More on Drawing Conclusions from Maps

The map below is different from the weather map just analyzed. It covers the whole world and is on a different topic, population distribution of the world. But there are similarities, too. They both use symbols (showing weather conditions on a forecast map and number of people on the population distribution map). Both also show outlines of countries drawn to scale—in proportion to their actual size—with north at the top of the map. These are all typical characteristics of any map.

POPULATION DISTRIBUTION OF THE WORLD

EQUATOR

EACH DOT REPRESENTS 750,000 PEOPLE

WORLD'S LARGEST URBAN AREAS

New York, N.Y.	16,206,841	Moscow	7,300,000
Tokyo, Japan	11,324,417	L.A.-Long Beach	7,032,075
Shanghai, China	10,820,000	Calcutta	7,031,382
Paris, France	9,250,647	Chicago	6,978,937
Mexico City, Mex.	8,589,630	Bombay	5,970,575
Buenos Aires	8,352,900	Seoul, Rep. of Korea	5,536,377
Osaka, Japan	7,838,722	Essen, West Germany	5,425,000
Sao Paulo, Brazil	7,693,000	Cairo	4,961,000
Peking	7,570,000	Philadelphia	4,817,914
London	7,418,020	Rio de Janeiro	4,658,000

Exercise 15

Directions: For each statement below, write *S* if the information on the map is sufficient to draw a conclusion. Write *I* if there is insufficient information from which to draw a conclusion.

_____ **1.** London, England, is one of the most pleasant cities on earth in which to live.

_____ **2.** The earth's deserts, rain forests, tundras, and ice caps are virtually uninhabitable.

_____ **3.** The more populated areas tend to be the more prosperous ones economically.

_____ **4.** Since most highly populated areas are north of the equator, there must be difficult living conditions in the Southern Hemisphere.

ANSWERS AND EXPLANATIONS START ON PAGE 288.

Drawing Inferences

You draw *inferences* or figure what is being implied by circumstances every day. You see a man wearing dark glasses cross the street using a white cane. The man is led by a large dog. You *infer* that the man is blind.

In making that inference you considered the details that you could see: dark glasses, white cane, large dog. To these details you added knowledge from your past (blind people often use white canes and guide dogs when walking).

You can also *infer*, or guess, what an author's point of view is by the words he uses.

Read the passage below to infer what the author's attitude is.

> By noon the temperature is 118 degrees. By 1:00 P.M. you can't move. The food is monotonous and disease is rampant, but the *professionals* working here wouldn't be anywhere else. This is Ethiopia and the workers are anthropologists from all over the world searching for hints about prehistoric human existence. Like *skilled detectives*, these *scientists* piece together bits of information about the lives of our earliest ancestors to *increase our knowledge* about mankind.

What is the author's attitude toward anthropologists?

_____

_____

To answer this question, look at the details of the passage. The writer refers to the anthropologists as "professionals," "skilled detectives," and "scientists." He also mentions that they "increase our knowledge."

These details show a positive, or respectful, attitude.

Exercise 16

Directions: Read each of the following quotations and write an inference that best describes the speaker's attitude toward the subject. Watch for words and phrases that indicate positive or negative feelings.

1. "Either you cry out and act, or you become part of the injustice."
   How does this person feel about missionaries who are active in opposing oppressive regimes in Central America?

   _____

   _____

2. "Efficiency in operations permits the Japanese to price their cars about $1,500 cheaper than their American competitors."
   What does this speaker most likely think of Japan's ability to produce cheaper cars?

   _____

   _____

3. "Thanks to Six Flags Great America Amusement Park, the relatively crime-free village of Gurnee now has the highest crime rate of any town in Lake County, Illinois, and the fourth highest in the entire Chicago region."
How does this person feel about Six Flags Great America Amusement Park?

_____

_____

★ **GED PRACTICE** ★

Exercise 17

Directions: Read the passage below. In the exercise that follows, circle the choices that represent the most accurate inferences that can be made from the information provided.

In 1957, Senator Strom Thurmond of South Carolina talked for more than twenty-four hours to purposely delay the vote on the first civil rights law to be proposed since shortly after the Civil War. Fortunately, Thurmond's filibuster did not prevent passage of the bill, and the Civil Rights Act became law that year.

1. What can you infer about the author's point of view on Senator Thurmond's filibuster of 1957?

    (1) It was a waste of the senator's valuable time.
    (2) It would have been a shame if it had prevented passage of the bill.
    (3) It fortunately helped to get the Civil Rights Act passed.
    (4) It was a brave and lonely act for the one senator.
    (5) It resulted in the unfortunate defeat of the Civil Rights Act.

2. What can you infer to be the meaning of *filibuster*?

    (1) a twenty-four-hour delay of a vote to give legislators a chance to discuss a bill
    (2) an opportunity to propose a bill on a topic that has been long ignored
    (3) a monologue aimed at convincing legislators to vote for passage of a bill
    (4) political lobbying to get others to vote either for or against a bill
    (5) marathon talking for the sole purpose of delaying the vote on a bill

ANSWERS AND EXPLANATIONS START ON PAGE 288.

Drawing Inferences from Illustrations

Most visual materials—graphs, charts, maps, cartoons, etc.—require the use of inference skills in order to get across their meanings. When you see a billboard along the highway with a picture of a ruggedly handsome cowboy smoking a cigarette while riding his horse into the sunlit horizon, you should be able to infer that this advertisement is trying to influence your feelings about cigarettes. By making it appear that "All-American" individualists like cowboys smoke this brand of cigarette, the advertisers are trying to develop a positive feeling from the public toward their cigarettes. When you see a political cartoon like the one shown below, you should also be able to infer the author's main idea and point of view.

HECK OF A WAY TO RUN A RAILROAD

KARL HUBENTHAL
*Courtesy Los Angeles
Herald-Examiner*

This cartoon has a title, "Heck of a Way to Run a Railroad." The people and objects are labeled according to what they symbolize. The engineers who are running the "Social Security" train are labeled "Senate" and "House" to symbolize the U.S. Congress. To the dismay of the elderly couple on the "Social Security" train, this "railroad's" workers are tearing apart the same train that they are trying to keep running.

In drawing such a comparison, the cartoonist is implying that the Social Security system is being _____ by the Congress of the United States and probably will not _____ much longer.

Looking at the expression on the faces of the elderly couple, you can infer that what is happening to the Social Security system is _____ to our senior citizens. If you did not know it already, you could also infer that the elderly _____ on Social Security to support themselves financially.

You should have inferred that the sentence above would be completed this way: ". . . the Social Security system is being *destroyed* or *dismantled* by the Congress of the United States and probably will not *last* much longer." In the faces of the older man and woman you can see fright and disbelief, or puzzlement, so you can infer that the situation is *frightening* to them, probably because of how important Social Security is to them financially. You can infer that the elderly *depend* on Social Security for financial support.

★ **GED PRACTICE** ★

Exercise 18

Directions: Choose the answer that best completes the following statement.

CRAIG MACINTOSH   Reprinted with permission from the *Minneapolis Star and Tribune*

Apparently, the cartoonist thinks that nuclear waste disposal is

(1) no longer a problem.
(2) being handled carefully by trained technicians.
(3) of concern only in out-of-the-way places.
(4) getting too close for comfort.
(5) the responsibility of all citizens.

ANSWERS AND EXPLANATIONS START ON PAGE 288.

3 APPLYING SOCIAL STUDIES CONCEPTS

Have you ever taken a first-aid course and had to use your knowledge to help an injured child, friend, or co-worker? Have you ever taken a driver's education class and then had to apply that knowledge behind the wheel in real traffic and again during the written test for your license? If so, you were applying your knowledge to real situations.

One of the most important ends of learning is an ability to *apply* what you have learned. On the Social Studies Test you will have to demonstrate this ability by:

- applying given theories, ideas, or facts in a different situation

- applying remembered ideas in a different situation

Applying Given Ideas

When you were in school, a teacher may have given you an explanation of a theory or principle and then asked the class to provide an example.

For instance, the teacher may have explained the economic principle of supply and demand like this:

How much a society has of something (the supply) together with how much the people in that society want it (the demand) influences the cost of the product.

If there is a low demand for something, but a large supply, the price will be low. On the other hand, if there is a great demand for a product but a small supply, the price will be high.

An initial low price can sometimes influence more people to buy a product. As a result, demand increases and the prices along with it. Also, other factors, like ease and cost of production, can affect prices. The basic principle of supply and demand, however, is the cornerstone of the U.S. economic system.

The teacher might then ask the class to give some examples of the supply-and-demand principle at work.

Of the statements below, decide which would be correct applications of the principle of supply and demand and which would not. Indicate *correct* applications by writing *YES* in the space and *incorrect* applications by writing *NO*.

_____ At the end of a season, when clothing stores have a surplus of stock on hand, they run clearance sales.

_____ Despite the fact that there were very few qualified applicants for the job and the job had to be filled, Henry was not able to get the high salary he wanted.

_____ When Congress set a limit on cars imported, the public's demand for them increased and the prices of Japanese cars went up.

_____ The Cabbage Patch Kids were hard to find and expensive during the Christmas rush but were readily available in July—and cheaper too!

_____ "I've noticed that a lot of companies charge low prices for stuff when it first comes out, but when it gets real popular, they jack the prices up."

All of your responses should have been YES except for the second example. In this case, the demand was high (the job had to be filled), the supply was small (there were few qualified applicants), but the price (Henry's salary) would not go up.

Exercise 1

Directions: Read the passage below. Indicate a correct application of the Supreme Court ruling by writing *YES* on the line before each statement and an incorrect application by writing *NO.*

> In 1954, the Supreme Court of the United States reversed an earlier controversial ruling. In 1896, the Supreme Court had ruled in the case of *Plessy* v. *Ferguson* that separate but equal facilities for blacks and whites were correct and legal. But the decision of 1954, called *Brown* v. *the Board of Education of Topeka*, ruled that blacks had equal rights to the *same* public schools because separate educational facilities were deemed inherently unequal. Public schools were ordered to desegregate "with all deliberate speed."

A correct application of the 1954 ruling would be

_____ **1.** busing children from black inner-city schools to white or racially mixed schools in the same district.

_____ **2.** the setting up of Afro-American history courses in high schools and colleges.

_____ **3.** the establishment of the United Negro College Fund to send poor, college-bound blacks to black colleges.

_____ **4.** the use of minority quotas in admissions policies at public universities and colleges.

Exercise 2

Directions: Read the passage below and complete the exercise that follows.

> Are females usually better with language skills than males? If so, is it because of a natural development of the brain, or because of the way the two sexes are raised from infancy?
>
> These questions are often explored and debated by psychologists and sociologists. This debate is often referred to as "the theory of nature versus nurture." Those who believe that nature determines differences in skills believe that males and females are born with inherent differences and these differences become more pronounced as sex hormones change the growing bodies.
>
> Those who believe that nurture plays the most important role in creating differences think that the environment in which a person is raised and nurtured is the determining factor.

For each of the examples below, write *nature* in the blank if the statement is an application of the nature theory of human growth and development and write *nurture* if the statement is an application of the nurture theory.

_____ In an experiment, researchers found that female infants are talked to more than male infants are.

_____ Nurses in a large hospital report that newborn female babies tend to coo, cry, and make other noises much more often than male babies.

_____ Experiments have shown that students who are not expected to do well in school do not do well, and teachers traditionally do not expect males to excel in language skills.

_____ Chemical analyses of male and female brains have shown definite differences between the sexes in the region of the brain that controls language development.

★ GED PRACTICE ★

Exercise 3

Directions: Let's look at how the skill of applying your knowledge and understanding will be tested on the Social Studies Test. Read the following passage and circle the choice that best answers the question that follows.

When people hear the word *monopoly*, probably the first thing they think about is the popular board game. A monopoly, however, is the exclusive control over a money-making activity.

In 1890, the U.S. government passed a law called the Sherman Anti-Trust Act that outlawed price-fixing (the agreement between companies to set their prices), underproduction of goods, market sharing, and any other form of monopolizing among producers of a similar product. However, public utilities such as gas, electric power, and water companies are exempted from these restraints. These government-sanctioned monopolies are permitted to exist so that essential services are not duplicated and natural resources are not wasted.

According to the Sherman Anti-Trust Act, an example of an illegal monopoly would be:

(1) the existence of only one power company in a city, giving consumers no choice of whom to obtain service from

(2) a computer company whose growth is well beyond that of any of its competitors

(3) a hamburger chain's restaurants, all of which belong to the same system of franchises

(4) the oil refineries in a state agreeing on a minimum price to set for gasoline

(5) a public university system in a state setting minimum and maximum tuition rates for the schools in its system

ANSWERS AND EXPLANATIONS START ON PAGE 288.

Special Item Type

The Social Studies Test will test your ability to apply given ideas in a different situation by using an item type similar to the one below. In this type of item, certain categories are defined and then specific situations are given. You will need to read the categories carefully to understand the differences between them. Then, read the situations below to match them up with the information given. If you have trouble with these questions, you might use a process of elimination. In other words, you may go through the categories and decide which ones do *not* fit. In this way, you may be able to narrow your choices.

★ GED PRACTICE ★

Exercise 4

Directions: Questions 1–3 refer to the following information.

Propaganda is a method by which information is provided in such a way as to influence or slant the opinion or feelings of the audience that receives the message. Listed below are five techniques used by propagandists.

name-calling—attaching an unfavorable name to an idea, person, or group of people in order to influence the attitude of the audience against the idea or position

glittering generalities—speaking in high-sounding but general and vague terms to influence positively the feelings of the audience toward a subject

bandwagoning—advising people to do something because "everyone" does it, because it is popular, or because it is the "in" thing to do

transferring—associating the respect, prestige, or power of one person or object with another person so that the audience is influenced favorably

card-stacking—choosing only specific, favorable points that support a cause and ignoring the unfavorable points

1. A manufacturer of laundry detergent introduces a "revolutionary new" product that dissolves grease faster than the "leading product on the market." The propaganda technique described is

   (1) name-calling.
   (2) glittering generalities.
   (3) transferring.
   (4) bandwagoning.
   (5) card-stacking.

2. A radio commercial suggests that all residents of Rapid Falls, Idaho, should subscribe to the *Rapid Falls Gazette*, since 85 percent of the households there subscribe to the paper. The announcer adds that, "40,000 households can't be wrong." The propaganda technique described is

    (1) name-calling.
    (2) glittering generalities.
    (3) transferring.
    (4) bandwagoning.
    (5) card-stacking.

3. While campaigning through the South, a candidate for the presidency of the United States appears in a church on the same platform with the leader of the "Moral Majority." The propaganda technique described is

    (1) name-calling.
    (2) glittering generalities.
    (3) transferring.
    (4) bandwagoning.
    (5) card-stacking.

ANSWERS AND EXPLANATIONS START ON PAGE 288.

Applying Given Ideas in Illustrations

On the Social Studies Test you also will be asked to apply given ideas or facts from illustrations like political cartoons.

Look at the cartoon below.

KEN ALEXANDER
Courtesy San Francisco Examiner

"If made into paper it could supply the entire federal government for 16 minutes."

Underline the words in parentheses that best answer each question pertaining to the cartoon.

Based on his statement, what is the ranger's tone? (serious, sarcastic, confused)

This tone may be inferred from the ranger's (understatement, exaggeration, or misunderstanding) of the facts about government's use of paper.

The cartoonist seems to think the federal government (has no regard for trees, needs a new source for paper, uses too much paper).

You should have underlined *sarcastic, exaggeration*, and *uses too much paper.*

Organizations like the U.S. government that use large amounts of paper do so because of record-keeping and management systems. The cartoonist thinks that the federal government is a large bureaucracy that uses an excessive amount of paper.

Which of the following systems would this cartoonist likely criticize? Circle the correct answer.

(1) the U.S. Army's insistence on all documents being copied and filed in triplicate

(2) a local grocer's system of having employees post on a chart items that are low in inventory

(3) a government agency's practice of filing its budget on a computer so that it can be readily retrieved and modified

(4) a mortgage company's action to simplify its loan application procedures by consolidating forms

(5) a large corporation's appointment of a chairman to coordinate a United Way Christmas drive

You should have chosen (1) because of the fact that the Army system requires so much paperwork. Choices (2), (3), and (4) are actually systems that reduce paperwork and bureaucracy. Choice (5) has nothing to do with paperwork or wastefulness.

★ **GED PRACTICE** ★

Exercise 5

Directions: Study the political cartoon below before answering the questions that follow.

According to the cartoonist, the Helsinki Agreement guaranteeing political freedom behind the Iron Curtain is not being adhered to. What do you think the cartoonist would choose as a good example of a violation of the Helsinki Agreement?

(1) A Soviet citizen makes an attempt on the life of the Soviet premier and is immediately arrested by government police.

(2) A Polish worker is arrested for protesting the government ban on unions.

(3) A Hungarian housewife is arrested for stealing a loaf of bread.

(4) A Bulgarian diplomat is accused of espionage in the U.S. and is deported to Bulgaria.

(5) A Czechoslovakian youth runs away from home but is forced by authorities to return to his parents.

'Don't believe everything you read'

ANSWER AND EXPLANATION STARTS ON PAGE 289.

Applying Remembered Ideas

You have practiced applying theories, ideas, and facts in reading passages and illustrations. Now you will apply knowledge you have gained from prior learning or experience, rather than from written passages.

For example, if you saw a movie about a Vietnam veteran going back to the site of his worst wartime experiences, you could understand his emotions much better if you had prior knowledge of the horrors of the Vietnam conflict. You could apply that prior knowledge to decide for yourself whether his performance was convincing. If you also had prior knowledge of World War II and its veterans' reactions to their experiences, you would be better able to understand the actions of the Vietnam veterans.

In exercises in this book, you will be expected to apply your prior knowledge of events, people, and ideas to new situations.

In some cases, in this book and on the GED tests, you may not be familiar with the person, place, or thing being discussed. First of all, keep in mind that the following sections of this book will give you a lot of information on social studies issues. Secondly, if you cannot recall what is being discussed in a test item, make the most reasonable choice and move on to the next item.

Suppose you read an article with a title like this: "From Selma to Johannesburg: Americans Are Marching Again, This Time Against Apartheid."

The magazine's editor expects the reader paging through the magazine to read the article because it deals with the issue of apartheid and how Americans are protesting it. The words *Johannesburg* and *apartheid* in the title are clues

that this article is about discrimination in _____ .

To fill in the blank above, you must have knowledge of world events and geography. Johannesburg is in South Africa. The fact that the title mentions apartheid may be another clue to that answer, but this again requires the knowledge that apartheid is the system of racial segregation in South Africa.

The title also includes the city Selma. The mention of this city, located in the

state of _____ in the United States, is an attempt to link the

marches against apartheid in South Africa to the _____ .

To be able to fill in the blanks, you must have had prior knowledge of the *civil rights marches of the 1960s* in the United States. They took place all over the country, but the site of one of the most famous was *Selma, Alabama*. That march was led by Dr. Martin Luther King, Jr.

Exercise 6

Directions: Now try doing an exercise in which you must apply prior knowledge. Read each paragraph below. Circle the number of the choice that best completes each statement.

1. In 1876, Rutherford B. Hayes was elected president of the United States even though he had received fewer votes from the citizens than his opponent. In 1888, the same situation occurred when Benjamin Harrison became president. In both cases these men became president, not through the popular vote, but through

   (1) cheating and bribery.
   (2) the Supreme Court system.
   (3) the electoral college system.

2. A case before the Supreme Court requesting a ruling on whether an Orthodox Jew in the United States Air Force should be allowed to wear the traditional religious skull cap represents another of the many conflicts of

   (1) church vs. state.
   (2) national vs. state's rights.
   (3) individual vs. state's rights.

3. "My mother always used to refer to England as home, although she was born here," said a middle-aged doctor, Ian Prior. "Then, after World War II, it was America we all looked toward. Now perhaps we are starting to feel ourselves a nation that can stand on its own feet. The Maori call it *tutangata*—to stand tall."

   Prior knowledge of world history would tell you that the doctor lives, along with the Maoris, in the country of

   (1) France.
   (2) New Zealand.
   (3) Austria.

ANSWERS AND EXPLANATIONS START ON PAGE 289.

Applying Remembered Ideas in Passages

On the Social Studies Test, you will be expected to apply remembered ideas (prior knowledge) in a multiple-choice format.

Read the passage below and choose the best answer to the question that follows.

Many Americans today complain that we are quickly becoming a bilingual country—the primary and secondary languages being English and Spanish. They resent the concessions made to the non-English speaking minority. Yet the first European settlers in the New World were Spanish. Christopher Columbus himself was sailing under the flag of Spain when he "discovered" the North American continent in 1492. Saint Augustine, Florida, was founded in 1566 by the Spanish and was the first European settlement in the United States or Canada. As early as 1630, Spanish padres of the Roman Catholic faith established missions in territories now known as the states of California, Texas, Arizona, and New Mexico. Perhaps, if more Americans were reminded of this Spanish influence on our country's history, they would be more tolerant of our non-English speaking minority.

This author would likely agree with the groups who

(1) are trying to get a law passed in the United States to make English the official language of the U.S.
(2) want to ban the use of Spanish in bilingual classes in public elementary and secondary schools.
(3) support the use of two languages—French and English—in Canada, where the French played a large role in founding the country.
(4) maintain that the native Indians of the Americas should be given free land and other special rights as original inhabitants of this part of the world.
(5) send teachers of English as a second language all over the world to help those who have the desire to learn our language.

You should have chosen (3) because it most closely resembles the situation described in the passage in which a controversy has developed in a country over the historical justification of officially using two languages. Choices (1) and (2) really express opposite opinions from the author's. Choice (4) does not address the problem of language usage. Choice (5) is on a different topic—the increasing influence of the English language around the world.

★ **GED PRACTICE** ★

Exercise 7

Directions: Read the passage below and in the question that follows circle the choice that shows the most accurate application of the idea described in the passage.

> Death Valley did not come by its name by whim or chance. Death Valley is an arid desert in southeastern California that was named in 1849 by one of eighteen survivors of an original party of thirty who had attempted to cross it in search of a shortcut to the California gold fields. The Rocky Mountains, too, are well deserving of their title, as are Crater Lake in Oregon and Salt Lake in Utah.
>
> In other parts of the world, cities, bodies of water, and land forms have been named for their physical characteristics. The Diamond Coast in southwestern Africa, for instance, gets its name from its valuable resource and Buenos Aires in Argentina for its "fair winds."

Which of the following would this author probably agree was named for its physical attributes as described in the article above?

(1) Cape Horn in Chile, South America, after its first successful navigator's birthplace in the Netherlands
(2) San Juan, capital city of Puerto Rico, named for Saint John by its Spanish founders

(3) the Hwang Ho (Yellow River) of China, for the color it develops as it picks up silt along its course

(4) the city of Philadelphia (City of Brotherly Love) in Pennsylvania, so called by its Quaker founders to reflect their highest hopes for the community

(5) New Delhi, the capital city of India that was built on a site three miles from the original city of Delhi

ANSWER AND EXPLANATION STARTS ON PAGE 289.

Applying Remembered Ideas to Illustrations

You will be expected to apply your knowledge of social studies events, places, and people in other ways on the GED test than in written form. One of these other methods may be through the use of political cartoons.

Look at the cartoon below.

"It says, 'Negotiations between Israelites, Egyptians, and Philistines are proceeding slowly.' "

The Christian Science Monitor
GUERNSEY LEPELLEY
Courtesy Christian Science Monitor

In the spaces below, fill in the words that best complete each statement. You will need to apply knowledge that you may have gained previously by reading newspapers or magazines, talking with friends, watching television, or going to school.

1. The men in the cartoon appear to be in an _____

   underground cave
   Israeli museum
   Egyptian tomb

2. The men in the cartoon are probably _____

archaeologists
politicians
students

3. The cartoonist is implying that war and negotiations to end hostilities

between the Israelites and Egyptians have been going on since _____

_____

the beginning of this century
the end of World War II
at least ancient Egyptian times

4. The cartoonist wants us to analyze this cartoon and apply our knowledge

of today's events to understand his opinion that _____

_____

hostilities in the Middle East probably will go on forever
interest in ancient Egyptian archaeological findings is increasing
peace in the Middle East will come soon

The blanks should have been filled with

1. *Egyptian tomb* (notice the hieroglyphics on the wall and the mummy in the background)

2. *archaeologists* (notice their appropriate dress and notepads)

3. *at least ancient Egyptian times* (reread the quote and think of where the characters are)

4. *the war in the Middle East probably will go on forever* (apply your knowledge of today's events in that part of the world and consider the cartoonist's implication that the war has been going on for thousands of years already)

★ GED PRACTICE ★

Exercise 8

Directions: Look at the cartoon below. Apply your knowledge to answer the questions that follow.

Leif Ericson Discovers The ~~New~~ Modern World

NORTH SEA SPILLS

SANDY CAMPBELL
Courtesy The Tennessean

1. Leif Ericson is one of several explorers to whom historians attribute

    (1) the blame for oil spills in the oceans.
    (2) the discovery of oil under the ocean floor.
    (3) the discovery of the New World.
    (4) the pollution of the New World.
    (5) the beginning of the environmental conservation movement.

2. The cartoonist is implying that, were he alive today, Leif Ericson would be

    (1) shocked at some of the environmental conditions of modern-day North America.
    (2) saddened by the pollution near modern-day Norway, his ancestral home.
    (3) confused by the modern technology used on the North American continent.
    (4) unhappy about the waste of time and money on underwater oil drills.
    (5) discouraged by the lack of modern progress along the North Sea coast.

ANSWERS AND EXPLANATIONS START ON PAGE 289.

4
EVALUATING SOCIAL STUDIES MATERIALS

When you must make a major purchase—like a car—you often *evaluate* your financial situation and your specific transportation needs before you start shopping. Once you are out in the marketplace, you continue to evaluate. You judge the vehicles you see as to how well you can afford them and how well they are made.

In social studies, you also have to evaluate information. You must be able to judge the value or logic of an idea. You also have to be able to understand how and why people make the decisions that they do. Perhaps most important, you need to be able to determine when a decision has been based on sound logic. In this section, you will learn how to evaluate material in social studies in four ways:

- judging the extent to which information satisfies criteria

- recognizing the role that values play in beliefs and decision-making

- judging the adequacy of facts

- identifying faulty reasoning

Judging Information

In order to judge the worth or value of something, you must have standards or reference points to go by. A typist's ability is judged by the *criteria* of speed and accuracy. The value of a movie is measured by its entertainment level, its cinematography, its acting and direction. A newspaper article is evaluated by its adequacy of facts, its style of writing, and its objectivity (omissions of opinions or biases of the writer).

If you know and understand the criteria by which something is judged, you are better prepared to *evaluate* it. For example, if you know the legal requirements for a good and binding contract, then you are better prepared to enter into one. Some of the criteria for a legally binding contract include:

1. a clear written offer by the buyer or buyer's representative

2. a clear written acceptance of the offer by the seller or seller's representative

3. a settlement of the deal agreeable and clear to both buyer and seller

4. a clear exchange of something valuable between the buyer and seller

5. no illegal activity involved in the deal by either the buyer or the seller

Judge whether the situation described below constitutes a legally binding contract according to the criteria listed above. If it does, write *YES* in the space next to it. If the situation does not, write *NO* in the space. If *NO*, write the number of the criterion above that the case does not satisfy.

_____ A husband and wife both shake hands with a neighbor in an agreement to purchase a used car for $5,995 from him, and the neighbor, in turn, agrees to hand over the title to the automobile upon receipt of the money.

You should have written *NO—1 and 2*. Though an offer to purchase the car is made, and the seller accepts the offer, neither the offer nor the acceptance is *in writing*. Therefore, no legally-binding contract exists.

Exercise 1

Directions: In the following cases, judge whether the situation described constitutes a legally binding contract according to the criteria. If it does, write *YES* on the line. If the situation does not, write *NO* on the line. For each *NO* answer write the number of the criterion that the case does not satisfy.

_____ 1. A private pilot agrees to pick up 100 pounds of marijuana in Mexico and deliver it to a buyer in Texas.

_____ 2. The attorney of a couple who are selling their home drafts an acceptance to a written offer along with a $5,000 check from an interested buyer.

_____ 3. After much discussion and haggling over price, an owner of a small bookkeeping business tells a computer salesman that he will seriously consider buying a personal computer only if he can get it for $500 less than the salesman's "final" offer.

_____ 4. A poor but diligent farmer signs a note promising to feed and house a laborer in his home in compensation for the work the laborer has agreed, in writing, to do on his land.

Exercise 2

Directions: Read the passage below. Be prepared to judge the theory described in the passage.

> In 1964, anthropologist Ashley Montagu edited a startling book entitled *The Concept of Race*. In the book, Montagu and nine other writers stated that the concept of race is a myth that leads to the perpetuation of error.
>
> According to Montagu, skin color and physical features are not necessarily accurate indicators of a person's ancestry. He believes that the term, *ethnic group* might be a better term than race.

For each of the facts below, write the number *(1)* in the blank if the fact should *help support Montagu's theory, (2)* if the fact should *dispute Montagu's theory,* and *(3)* if the fact should *have no bearing on Montagu's theory.*

_____ **1.** Ashley Montagu is a white man.

_____ **2.** Montagu has supported this theory since at least 1941.

_____ **3.** The use of the term race has had a long history and, in fact, is prevalent even today among all levels and aspects of society.

_____ **4.** There are obvious differences among groups of people in the world that seem fairly easy to define and categorize by "race."

_____ **5.** Ashley Montagu is one of America's most distinguished anthropologists, having taught at New York University, Rutgers University in New Jersey, Hahnemann Medical College, and the University of California.

_____ **6.** The book *The Concept of Race* contains contributions from nine other distinguished scientists besides Montagu who all support his theory.

★ GED PRACTICE ★

Exercise 3

Directions: Circle the correct answer.

Which of the facts below would tend to support Montagu's ideas that: (1) racial classification leads to perpetuation of error, and (2) skin color and physical features are not accurate indicators of a person's ancestry?

(1) American blacks are categorized in the same racial group as Africans from the continent of Africa.
(2) Because of their skin color, Hispanic Americans are often categorized as a race separate from other Caucasians of European stock.
(3) Canadians are considered Caucasian, as are other North Americans of European stock.

(4) Most of the people of the Soviet Union are Caucasian, but a minority belong to the Mongoloid race.

(5) Eskimos are considered to be of Asian ancestry.

ANSWERS AND EXPLANATIONS START ON PAGE 289.

Judging Information in Illustrations

In addition to having the ability to judge written materials by certain standards or criteria, you should be able to judge visual materials in the same way.

When evaluating a table or chart in social studies materials, you need to know what you are looking for; in other words, what the criteria are.

Look at the table and the explanation of it below.

YOUR LOSS IN PURCHASING POWER					
Your pretax income in:		Purchasing power after taxes and inflation:		Purchasing power is decreased by	
1972	1980	1972	1980		
$10,000	$19,860	$ 9,247	$ 8,998	—2.7%	
$20,000	$39,720	$17,640	$16,862	—4.4%	
$30,000	$59,580	$25,588	$23,708	—7.4%	
$40,000	$79,440	$32,972	$29,948	—9.2%	

Source: The Women's Guide to the Stock Market: How to Make Your Own Investment Plan—by Barbara Lee

1. "Purchasing power" is the amount of money you have available to

_____ . In the first column of this table a comparison is made between income in 1972 and income in 1980.

2. "Pretax income" represents the amount of money a person would receive

_____ taxes are taken out.

3. The second column of figures represents purchasing power after

_____ and _____ have reduced the spending power of a person's income.

4. In all cases, purchasing power went _____ between 1972 and 1980.

5. This fact is further highlighted in the third column of figures, which shows

the percentage of _____ in purchasing power.

6. The _____ signs in front of each percentage emphasize that these are decreases.

7. It can be concluded that Ms. Lee thinks that raises in income each year

are not necessarily enough to keep a person's _____

_____ increasing at the same rate as inflation.

The blanks above should be filled in accordingly:

1. spend, buy with, or purchase with
2. before
3. taxes and inflation
4. down

5. decrease or decline
6. negative or minus
7. purchasing power

★ **GED PRACTICE** ★

Exercise 4

Directions: There are many accepted methods for arriving at conclusions or formulating hypotheses. Of the five methods below, circle the one method by which Ms. Lee arrived at her conclusion. After reading the table, she concluded that yearly raises are not keeping up with rising inflation.

(1) Intuition: arrived at through imagination and guesswork
(2) Authority: arrived at by accepting other experts' opinions as true
(3) Tradition: arrived at by assuming information to be true because it has been long accepted as true
(4) Common sense: arrived at through casual observation sometimes combined with any or all of the above three methods
(5) Science: arrived at through careful and objective collection of data

ANSWER AND EXPLANATION STARTS ON PAGE 289.

Recognizing Values

What values and beliefs do you hold nearest and dearest to your heart? What would you die for? If you could be doing anything you wanted right now, what would it be? These questions all focus on your personal values.

Your beliefs and values influence the big decisions that you must make in life. In understanding social studies material, you must be able to recognize how an individual's values affect the the decisions he or she makes.

For example, former president Jimmy Carter is known to have put great value on human rights during his term in office. Because of his beliefs, he made decisions and statements about Soviet human rights policies during the Strategic Arms Limitation Talks (SALT) with the U.S.S.R. Thus, Carter's beliefs had an influence on his decision-making in the area of foreign relations.

Fill in the words that best summarize the values of the person described in the case below.

A senator does not believe that she could ever have an abortion because it is morally repugnant to her. A survey shows, however, that her constituency overwhelmingly is in favor of a law permitting abortion. The senator votes "yes" on the bill.
The senator apparently values _____

over _____ .

You should have written *her responsibility to her constituency* or *political expediency* over *her personal beliefs*. In other words, the feelings of those who elected her override her own personal feelings.

Exercise 5

Directions: For each statement, supply the most accurate words that reflect the values of the person described in each case below.

1. A young man wants very much to settle down and save enough money to get married and to buy a home, a good-running car, and some new clothes. However, he has been instilled with a strong belief in the responsibility of every American citizen to serve his country. His decision to join the U.S.

    Army was affected primarily by his sense of _____ .

2. A scientist is asked to work on a prestigious project to develop a neutron bomb, a weapon he despises because it is designed to destroy on impact living things, not buildings. When the scientist refuses the project, it shows that

    he values his _____ over his _____ .

★ GED PRACTICE ★

Exercise 6

Directions: Let's analyze a longer, more complicated passage to recognize the role that values play in decision-making. Read the passage below. Be prepared to answer the questions that follow.

The derogatory term *Yankee imperialist* has not always been applied to Americans. Prior to the Spanish-American War in 1898, the United States was strongly isolationist and did not concern itself with issues involving other parts of the world.

The Spanish-American War grew out of the American public's growing desire to expand American territory and interests and out of a general "war fever."

Several of the larger American newspapers began to capitalize on the Cuban struggle for independence from Spain, sensationalizing abuses Spanish military forces were committing against the Cubans.

Public outrage reached its peak with the sinking of the battleship *Maine*, which was sent to the Havana harbor to protect U.S. citizens and property in Cuba. Though the cause of the explosion was never discovered, President

McKinley approved a congressional resolution demanding immediate Spanish withdrawal from Cuba. A few days later, Spain declared war.

The congressional resolution stated that the U.S. was not acting to secure an empire. However, the terms of the Treaty of Paris that officially ended the war required that Spain cede the Philippines, Puerto Rico, and the island of Guam to the U.S. For good or ill, the U.S. became less nationalistic. It had become a world power, admired by some who felt the U.S. now had an altruistic concern for smaller nations. Others detested the U.S. for what they believed to be imperialistic bullying of countries in its way.

1. According to this writer, what values of Americans most directly triggered the U.S. decision to enter the war against Spain in 1898?

    (1) a desire to help and protect the less economically fortunate in this world
    (2) a belief that democracy is the only fair form of government and that military rule is unjust
    (3) an overriding desire to maintain peace and harmony in the Western Hemisphere
    (4) an abhorrence of social injustice and a belief in their responsibility to the oppressed
    (5) a sense of outrage about dangers to American lives and property abroad

2. What change in American values resulted from the Spanish-American War?

    (1) The public became more wary of electing indecisive candidates for high public office.
    (2) Nationalism increased as Americans found ways to strengthen their internal society and economy.
    (3) The U.S. abandoned a policy of isolation and became involved in international conflict.
    (4) The U.S. adopted a materialistic policy of acquiring property and increasing capitalistic ventures inside and outside the U.S.
    (5) The public developed a cautious, wait-and-see attitude toward getting involved in further conflicts with other world powers.

3. Those who use the term *Yankee imperialist* against the U.S. would most likely be the same ones who would agree that

    (1) the Peace Corps was established to help Third World countries develop their own independent economic bases.
    (2) Puerto Rico should be made a colony of the United States.
    (3) the U.S. had no right to invade the island of Grenada in 1983.
    (4) the Philippines can blame its economic woes on the U.S. decision to grant it independence in 1946.
    (5) the U.S. entered the Vietnam conflict because of its concern for the well-being of Southeast Asia.

ANSWERS AND EXPLANATIONS START ON PAGE 289.

Recognizing Values in Illustrations

When a professional photographer decides to specialize in wedding and family portraits instead of nude layouts for pornographic magazines, his values have come into play. Similarly, you can tell the difference between the values and attitudes of the artist who has painted protestors at the scene of a march as rowdy, mean, and ugly and one who has painted them as serene, youthful, and beautiful.

So, too, in other illustrations, like political cartoons, the values of the artists influence their choice of topics and the way the topics are treated.

Look at the cartoon below.

DICK LOCHER
Courtesy Chicago Tribune

This cartoon brings out one side of a debate that has been running since labor unions were first formed in western Europe in the late eighteenth and early nineteenth centuries and in the U.S. in the early twentieth century. This debate pits those who favor unions because of their help to the workers *against* those who think the unions have been a factor in lowering the productivity of industries. Ultimately, this debate often comes down to a difference in the values that affect one's beliefs.

The creator of the above cartoon believes that union wages are

_____ . He also believes that these wages have been responsible for driving _____ into the ground.

The cartoonist thinks wages are *too high* (notice how huge the rocket labeled "union wages" is). He thinks these wages have forced *productivity* down. (Notice that the rocket's label has changed to "productivity" and is driven into the ground.)

★ GED PRACTICE ★

Exercise 7

Directions: Choose the answer that best completes the following statement.

Based on the cartoon, you can see that the cartoonist believes that

(1) the living standards of workers are more important than profit and efficiency for a company.

(2) productivity is too important to industry to be sacrificed to union wage demands.

(3) workers' pride in their accomplishments is more valuable than either wages or productivity.

(4) productivity should be sacrificed for the sake of higher wages for workers.

(5) production lines should be used in favor of individual craftsmanship in large industries.

ANSWER AND EXPLANATION STARTS ON PAGE 290.

Judging the Adequacy of Facts

Have you ever told one of your favorite jokes to a friend, only to have him appear bewildered after you delivered the punch line? If you considered why the joke failed, you may have learned that you omitted an important detail. Anytime facts are lacking in a story, confusion or misinterpretation of the story is likely to result.

When important facts are omitted, you cannot make an informed decision. Suppose, for example, you overheard a debate about the purchase of a new fleet of buses for your city's transit system. One group supports the buying of American-made buses. These buses cost more than the foreign-made buses that another group wants. To be able to judge how you feel about the issue you need to know all the facts. You need to know:

1. how much of a difference in cost there is between the buses

2. what shape the city's finances are in

3. the level of quality of the bus each company manufactures

You may also need to know what impact the purchase of a foreign product over an American product is likely to have on American jobs.

All of these considerations may have some influence on what your final position will be. Similarly, when you read social studies materials, you must be able to determine whether the facts are adequate to support the writer's conclusion or point of view.

Certain information is missing in each case below. On the line provided, indicate what facts are needed to answer each question.

CASE 1

Intelligence (IQ) tests were improved dramatically by French psychologist Alfred Binet when he found a way to measure judgment, comprehension, and reasoning skills. In what ways could Binet have made his test bias-free, also?

_____

You should have written: *How are the tests biased?* In order to answer the question, you need to know in what ways the IQ test is biased.

CASE 2

The number of registered black voters in Leflore County, Mississippi, increased by 50 percent during the last election. However, the defeated black candidate for the U.S. Congress did not benefit directly from this increase in the number of registered voters. In fact, he lost the election by the same margin of votes as he did the last time he ran. Why didn't the candidate get more votes if the number of black registered voters increased by 50 percent?

_____

You should have written the question *How many of the black registered voters in the county actually voted in the election?* The fact that the information tells you the number of *registered* voters increased by 50 percent does not mean that they came out and voted. The important fact that is missing is *the number of black registered voters who actually voted.*

★ GED PRACTICE ★

Exercise 8

Directions: On the Social Studies Test you will have to answer questions about adequacy of facts in a multiple-choice format. Read the passage below and circle the letter of the choice that best answers each question that follows.

"Equality of rights under the law shall not be denied or abridged by the United States or by any state on account of sex." So reads the Equal Rights Amendment proposed in 1972. Opponents of the amendment insisted, however, that it meant that anti-family, pro-abortion, pro-homosexual, and anti-privacy laws would be passed.

As a result, the amendment was defeated in 1982. Ten years had passed since the first of thirty-five states ratified it. Thirty of these states had approved the amendment within the first year of its proposal. By law, three-fourths of the state legislatures, or thirty-eight states, had to approve it to make it part of the U.S. Constitution.

If there had been more time, the amendment probably would have been ratified. In two major opinion polls just a few weeks before the ERA's defeat, it was reported that the majority of American citizens supported the amendment.

1. Which of the statements in the article is not adequately supported by facts?

    (1) A majority of Americans supported the ERA at the time of its defeat.
    (2) Thirty-eight state legislatures needed to ratify the amendment to make it law.
    (3) The ERA might have passed if it had had more time.
    (4) Its opponents were fearful of the ramifications of the ERA.
    (5) A majority of the states approved of the ERA.

2. Which of the following statements is supported by the information provided in the passage?

    (1) Organizations working for the ERA had more popular support than governmental support.
    (2) As a result of the defeat of the ERA, men are given more consideration in parental custody cases than they were before.
    (3) Since the 1982 defeat of the ERA, single-parent, female-headed families have become more numerous and more poverty-stricken.
    (4) Gay rights groups supported the ERA and worked for its ratification.
    (5) More female citizens were in favor of the ratification of the ERA than males.

ANSWERS AND EXPLANATIONS START ON PAGE 290.

Judging the Adequacy of Facts in Illustrations

There are many ways to represent facts in social studies. You have evaluated the adequacy of facts given in written materials. Now you will do much the same thing with maps.

As you have seen, maps are used to represent information visually. They are often the most efficient method to get across certain facts. "One picture is worth a thousand words," says the old expression. Of course, different kinds of maps are used to illustrate different kinds of facts.

Let's look at a map and see how adequately it shows facts about one of the world's continents.

Study the map of Asia shown on page 92. Place an *X* in the spaces below to indicate whether the information on the map is adequate or inadequate to support each fact. If the information on the map is not adequate, write what kind of map would best show that kind of information. You may refer to the skill builder on page 94 that reviews the types of maps.

Asia is the world's largest continent and covers over one-third of the earth's surface.

_____ adequate _____ inadequate: _____ map would show this better

You should have marked that the information on the map was *inadequate* and that a *world* map would show this better.

Exercise 9

Directions: Use the map of Asia to answer the following questions.

1. The continent of Asia extends north and south of the Arctic Circle.

    _____ adequate _____ inadequate: _____ map would show this better

2. China is a communist country.

    _____ adequate _____ inadequate: _____ map would show this better

3. Besides its famous mountains, Asia contains many plains, plateaus, and river basins.

    _____ adequate _____ inadequate: _____ map would show this better

4. Some parts of Asia receive more than eighty inches of rain a year.

    _____ adequate _____ inadequate: _____ map would show this better

5. Asia is bordered by three oceans.

    _____ adequate _____ inadequate: _____ map would show this better

6. The countries that have the largest population and the greatest land mass are in Asia.

    _____ adequate _____ inadequate: _____ map would show this better

7. The West Siberian Plain borders Russia on the continent of Asia.

    _____ adequate _____ inadequate: _____ map would show this better

8. Tokyo is Japan's most heavily populated city.

    _____ adequate _____ inadequate: _____ map would show this better

---

★ GED PRACTICE ★

Exercise 10

Directions: Use the map of Asia shown on page 92 to answer these questions.

1. Which of the following statements is supported adequately by the data provided by the map?

    (1) The former Soviet Union was located on the continent of Asia.
    (2) The Indus River empties into the Atlantic Ocean.
    (3) India and China are unfriendly neighbors.
    (4) The Himalayan Mountains are the highest in the world.
    (5) Japan's economic impact on the world is in direct proportion to its size.

2. Which of the following land features is *not* shown adequately by the map?

    (1) the location of plateaus in Asia
    (2) the distance from one end of Asia to the other
    (3) the size of the Indian peninsula in Asia
    (4) the height of the Himalayan mountains
    (5) the course of the Mekong River

ANSWERS AND EXPLANATIONS START ON PAGE 290.

Skill Builder
Review of Types of Maps

1. *Topographical* maps show geographic land features of an area.

2. *Population* maps explain distribution of people in an area.

3. *World* maps compare various facts about many locations all over the world.

4. *Weather* maps can show current or forecasted weather, as well as climate.

5. *Political* maps can outline borders between countries or states, show trade relationships among countries, and indicate systems of government.

Identifying Faulty Reasoning

You have practiced drawing conclusions from supporting details in a passage. An extension of that skill is the ability to identify faulty conclusions or fallacies in arguments. We often hear people make illogical statements. Take the following example:

HUSBAND: I'm late because the traffic was bad. That's all.

WIFE: Two-and-a-half hours late because of traffic! You must think I'm an idiot! I know you stopped at a tavern.

HUSBAND: Now why would I have done that? I never stop at a bar after work. I don't even drink.

WIFE: I know you did because that's why my father used to be so late coming home.

Obviously, the wife is upset and not using her powers of logic. Just because her father used to do something does not mean her husband does the same thing. Her judgment is further shown to be unreasonable by the husband's reply that he does not even drink.

Read the following story. Underline the two *illogical* or *faulty* conclusions that appear.

Marlena Jackson is a typical working wife and mother. She works because she needs to help support her family financially. Her days are very hectic because she has to keep both work *and* home schedules. Marlena shops primarily at one chain grocery store because it sponsors games with prizes for customers. The prizes provide extras for the house, such as towels, cookware, and small appliances.

The food at this grocery store generally costs more than that at a discount store a few miles away. This fact, however, just proves to Marlena that the more expensive store has better food.

Marlena drives an old, gas-guzzling car that is always in need of repair. Her husband, Donnell, knows how to fix it, though, so the repair costs are low. Insurance costs on the car are not high either, so Marlena assumes that the car is safe.

Despite all the money they spend on gas and repairs for the old car, it is still cheaper to keep it than it would be to buy a newer, smaller, more fuel-efficient car.

In the second paragraph above, the faulty conclusion is that *a more expensive store is a better store.* The cost of food can be affected by quality, but it can also be affected by other things, such as more lavish surroundings, higher-paid clerks, or more games and gimmicks that draw in customers (but boost costs!).

In the third paragraph, the faulty conclusion is that *lower insurance costs indicate safer cars.* That *could* be a reason for the lower premiums, but other factors, like lack of comprehensive coverage or lower replacement cost on the vehicle, could also keep the cost low.

★ **GED PRACTICE** ★

Exercise 11

Directions: Read the passage below. Answer the questions that follow.

Some American blacks can claim ancestors who arrived on the continent before the Pilgrims landed at Plymouth Rock. Unfortunately, this just means that racial bias has always existed in the Americas, for most of the first African arrivals were slaves.

Slavery and indentured servitude were both employed initially because of an acute shortage of labor in the Americas. But there were glaring differences between the two systems from the beginning. Most indentured servants were white, and most served only four or five years. Most slaves were black, and most served for their entire lives. In addition, servile status for slaves was made inheritable through the mother, and intermarriage between slaves and white servants was prohibited by law. The few free Negroes living in those early years had their liberties restricted severely, a practice sanctioned by the law. If it had not been for such laws, white Europeans immigrating to the U.S. would not have become so biased against blacks.

1. Which of the following is an illogical conclusion that is contained in the story?

    (1) Laws restricting the freedoms of the nonslave blacks in the early years of this country fostered the bias against them by the European immigrants.
    (2) Some American blacks can claim ancestry on the continent for many more generations than American whites can.
    (3) Slavery and indentured servitude were both reactions to an economic need in the early development of the U.S.
    (4) The most glaring difference between indentured servants and slaves is that the servants usually served for just four or five years, whereas slaves served a lifetime.
    (5) Intermarriage between blacks and whites was made illegal in the early years of the country because of a fear of the owner that the slave would run away.

2. The conclusion at the end of the passage is illogical because it

    (1) is the opposite of what is shown to be true.
    (2) compares events of different generations.
    (3) is not based on facts to support it.
    (4) is unrelated to the topic being developed.
    (5) is true for only a limited number of cases.

ANSWERS AND EXPLANATIONS START ON PAGE 290.

Identifying Faulty Reasoning in Illustrations

You have practiced your skill at identifying faulty reasoning in a written passage. Now you will apply that skill to identifying poor reasoning based on visual materials. You have probably seen situations in which graphs were used to "prove" a person's point. Often, it is not the data included in the graph that are questionable, but the *interpreter's use of the data* that causes the problem. After all, graphs and other illustrations do not usually appear on their own but are tied to an article or other written material. In the example below, however, we will analyze a graph that stands on its own.

Look at the graph below.

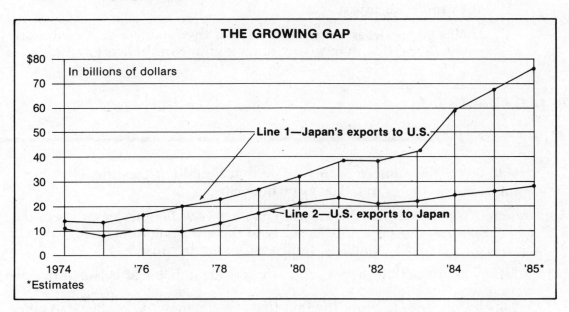

THE GROWING GAP

In billions of dollars

Line 1—Japan's exports to U.S.

Line 2—U.S. exports to Japan

1974   '76   '78   '80   '82   '84   '85*

*Estimates

The title of this graph is _____

It refers to the gap in exports between _____ and

_____ in billions of dollars.

Line 1 on the graph stands for _____ .

Line 2 on the graph stands for _____ .

The graph shows that the gap has been _____ over the years.

    You should have answered: *The Growing Gap, Japan and the United States, Japan's exports to the U.S., U.S. exports to Japan, getting larger or increasing.* A *logical* conclusion that can be drawn is that, unless something is done to stimulate the Japanese's interest in American goods, or to reduce exports of Japanese goods to the U.S., the gap will probably keep getting bigger.

    An *illogical* or *faulty* conclusion would be that the Japanese are more concerned about keeping their people employed in manufacturing industries than Americans are. This conclusion is faulty because no data in the graph support it.

Exercise 12

Directions: Based on the graph "The Growing Gap," indicate whether each of the statements below is based on logical reasoning or on faulty reasoning. If the statement is based on logical reasoning, write *L* on the line before it; if based on faulty reasoning, write *F* on the line.

_____ **1.** The widening gap between the exports of the two countries indicates that U.S. products must have been getting increasingly more expensive and, therefore, less desirable.

_____ **2.** The trend shown on the graph indicates that Americans were getting more receptive to buying Japanese goods over the years.

_____ **3.** If it were not for a pro-Japanese lobby, there would be more American exports to Japan.

_____ **4.** The large gap in exports indicates that the Japanese exported more goods to the U.S. than to any other country in the world.

★ **GED PRACTICE** ★

Exercise 13

Directions: Circle the number of the choice that best completes the following statement based on the graph "The Growing Gap."

Someone has concluded that the growing gap between Japanese exports to the U.S. and U.S. exports to Japan is due solely to the lower manufacturing costs of Japanese producers. This would be faulty reasoning because

(1) it falsely assumes that there is a growing trade imbalance between the two nations.
(2) it fails to take into account the fact that the Japanese do not have to abide by U.S. trade laws.
(3) it falsely assumes that lower manufacturing costs are the only factor causing increased Japanese imports.
(4) it fails to take into account the American policy of allowing Japanese exports to enter the U.S. on an unrestricted, import tax-free basis.
(5) it fails to take into account the effect of quality circles in Japanese manufacturing.

ANSWERS AND EXPLANATIONS START ON PAGE 290.

▦ 5
U.S. HISTORY

"Those who cannot remember the past are condemned to repeat it," said the philosopher George Santayana. Was he right?

World War I was supposed to be "the war to end all wars," but of course, it was not. Twenty-one years after it ended, World War II began.

A no-win situation in a limited, undeclared war in Korea apparently was not reminder enough to keep the U.S. from becoming involved in Vietnam.

Today, many people believe that the U.S. will never again get involved in such an unwinnable war in a foreign land because of what we learned from Vietnam. Yet, others see evidence of such involvement all over the world.

We study history to help chart our future by studying the past. Sometimes we learn from our mistakes, but many times we do not. In this chapter, you will study U.S. History. As you read, try to keep in mind events today that parallel those of yesterday. You may find that, indeed, history repeats itself.

A New Nation in a New World

Exploration, Discovery, and Colonization

In some ways Christopher Columbus can be considered a failure. He originally set sail in 1492 to find a new, easier passage to the Far East to make trade cheaper and more convenient. However, he did not find that route or any riches in the New World. He even lost in the "name game." America was named for another Italian explorer in service to Spain, Amerigo Vespucci, who journeyed to the New World later and wrote a very good account of that trip.

But Columbus was a great success in other ways. He believed in the revolutionary idea that the world is round, he undertook a journey based on that idea, and he discovered a territory full of natural resources and new opportunities. He is also credited with starting the first colony that established Europe's ties to the New World, on the island now made up of Haiti and the Dominican Republic.

Once word of Spain's discovery spread, it was no longer the only European country interested in the New World. The map above shows the division of territory as it stood in 1689.

In claiming land in the New World, Spain was interested primarily in finding gold and sending in Christian missionaries. The French were interested especially in the seemingly endless abundance of furs in the interior territories of North America. However, the English who came were interested mainly in finding a new homeland. Many were persecuted for their religious beliefs back in Great Britain, and the British king was glad to let them leave.

In the mid 1700s, the French and English clashed again and again over claims of land "ownership." At the same time, English settlers were fighting the continent's native Indians over the rich farm acres beyond the Appalachian Mountains. In a treaty of lasting significance, the French and the English agreed to divide the land of North America as shown in the map above. The Appalachian Mountains marked the Proclamation Line of 1763, separating French from English territory. In this Proclamation, the British king forbade white settlers to go beyond the line shown on the map. However, the Proclamation of 1763 later proved to be meaningless.

★ GED PRACTICE ★

Exercise 1: The New World

Directions: Choose the *one* best answer to each question.

1. According to the map of the New World on page 100, which of the following conclusions can be drawn about the years from 1492 to 1689?

   (1) Spain became uninterested in the resources and possibilities of the New World.
   (2) France and England became rivals in the establishment of some settlements in the New World.
   (3) The Dutch were consistently driven out of areas that they tried to colonize in the New World.
   (4) Portugal's fortunes dwindled in the financing of exploration of the New World.
   (5) Much of North America was unclaimed by anyone.

2. According to the map of Colonial America in 1763, what was the result of the treaty between France and England in 1763?

   (1) Spain and England went to war over the competition for land in the New World.
   (2) The English became allies with the Spanish and Russians.
   (3) The Spanish gave up their search for gold in the New World.
   (4) The English gave up power in the New World.
   (5) The French lost virtually all claim to territory in the thirteen colonies.

ANSWERS AND EXPLANATIONS START ON PAGE 290.

Thirteen English Colonies

The English were not the first to establish a colony in the New World, but, when they came, they came in earnest. In 1607, Jamestown, Virginia, was settled as a business venture, and the colonists soon made a profit on tobacco. The Pilgrims and the Puritans came later for religious and political reasons and developed governing bodies soon after their arrival.

The English settled along the eastern coastline in three distinct geographic regions. The chart below highlights the characteristics of the regions.

THIRTEEN COLONIES IN THREE GROUPS
New England Colonies *Territory*—Massachusetts, New Hampshire, Rhode Island, Connecticut *Founding Purpose*—religious freedom *Land Features*—dense forests; good harbors and rivers; rocky soil
Middle Colonies *Territory*—New York, New Jersey, Pennsylvania, Delaware, Maryland *Founding Purpose*—fur trade and grain farming *Land Features*—coastal plains and river valleys; fertile farming soil; large, convenient harbors
Southern Colonies *Territory*—Virginia, North Carolina, South Carolina, Georgia *Founding Purpose*—large-scale farming *Land Features*—fertile soil; abundant rainfall; warm climate; long growing season

Exercise 2: Thirteen Colonies

Directions: Check off the statements that are supported by the chart above.

_____ 1. The New England Colonies had less desirable farmland than the Middle and Southern Colonies.

_____ 2. The Middle Colonies tended to be most closely tied to the British.

_____ 3. Colonists who sought religious freedom settled only in New England.

_____ 4. Both the climate and the founding purpose of the Southern settlers laid the basis for a plantation economy.

ANSWERS AND EXPLANATIONS START ON PAGE 291.

The Revolutionary War

Key Words

duty—a tax, usually placed on imported goods
sovereign nation—a nation free from outside control

War is expensive. So, soon after the end of the French and Indian War in 1763, England needed to finance its huge war debt. As a result, the British Parliament and King George III passed the *Stamp Act of 1765* and the *Townshend Acts of 1767.* The Stamp Act required all official documents in the colonies to bear a purchased British stamp. The Townshend Acts placed large duties on glass, lead, and tea.

By September 1774, the colonists had had enough. However, the first Continental Congress did not ask Britain for independence for the colonists; it demanded only their rights as British subjects. The purpose of the congress was to demand representation in the British Parliament so that colonists could have a say in what taxes they would have to pay. But by the time of the second Continental Congress in May 1775, hostile encounters had already taken place between the English soldiers and the colonists.

In the battles of Lexington and Concord, British soldiers had been surprised by the diligence and unorthodox tactics of the American militia. George Washington was named commander-in-chief of the colonists' army, and he immediately began reorganizing and strengthening his troops.

On July 4, 1776, the second Continental Congress adopted the *Declaration of Independence*, and thereafter the Americans fought as citizens of a sovereign nation who were expelling a foreign power, not as British rebels against their own king. This was important not only to boost their own morale but also to elicit the sympathetic support of the world for their fight.

★ **GED PRACTICE** ★

Exercise 3: The Revolutionary War

Directions: Choose the *one* best answer for each statement or question below.

1. The purpose of the first Continental Congress was to

    (1) ask the British king for the colonies' independence.
    (2) demand the colonists' rights as British citizens.
    (3) form a militia to fight the British soldiers.
    (4) name George Washington as commander-in-chief of the militia.
    (5) write the Declaration of Independence from Great Britain.

2. Actual battles between the British and the colonists began

    (1) after George Washington was named commander-in-chief.
    (2) before the second Continental Congress.
    (3) after the Declaration of Independence was written.
    (4) on the same day that the Declaration of Independence was written.
    (5) before George III became king.

3. The fight of the American colonists against Great Britain can be compared to which anticolonialist event of the twentieth century?

    (1) the attempted takeover of Europe by Hitler
    (2) the struggle of India for its independence from Great Britain
    (3) the attack on Pearl Harbor by the Japanese in 1941
    (4) the return of the Panama Canal to the country of Panama
    (5) the growth of communism in Latin America

Writing Activity 1

The American Revolution set the stage for many revolutions that followed. Revolutionaries in Haiti, France, and Vietnam were inspired by the American *Declaration of Independence*.

Why do you think the American Revolution captured the imagination of people around the world? Write two or three paragraphs explaining why the American Revolution was so inspirational.

ANSWERS AND EXPLANATIONS START ON PAGE 291.

Splitting into Political Groups

Great Britain recognized its former colonies as the United States of America on September 3, 1783. For more than five years afterward, the new nation struggled with heavy war debts and a weak central government operating under the *Articles of Confederation*, which had almost no authority over the separate states.

In 1786 and 1787, Daniel Shays, a former captain during the American Revolution, led a group of poor, debt-ridden farmers in violent rebellion against high taxes and an unjust legal system. The rebellions highlighted the need for a strong central government that could keep the peace when the country was not at war and could govern the states uniformly.

In 1787, a *Constitutional Convention* was called to strengthen the *Articles of Confederation*, but it did not take long before the delegates realized that the articles would have to be thrown out and a new constitution drawn up. The articles were lacking too many vital ingredients for effective unification. They did not empower the national government to collect taxes, defend the new country, pay the war debt, or even regulate trade and commerce.

But drawing up a new constitution that all the representatives would agree to was no easy task. A split soon developed between the Federalists, who wanted a strong central government with authoritative control over the states, and the anti-Federalists, who were afraid that the individual person and the individual states would lose their freedom and flexibility under one central government. Other disputes over how the new government should be set up arose. These arguments and the compromises that settled them are highlighted in the chart below.

Despite all the disagreements among the states, the *Constitution of the United States* was ratified by the required ninth state in July of 1788 and by all thirteen by May of 1790, a year after the new government had already started operating.

DISPUTES AND COMPROMISES AT THE CONSTITUTIONAL CONVENTION	
Dispute:	Should the states be governed by a strong central government (Federalists' view)? *or* Should the new government be based on the sovereignty of the states (anti-Federalists' view)?
Compromise:	1. President was to be elected by electoral college, the Senate by the state legislatures (this was later changed by the Twelfth Amendment, adopted in 1804) and House of Representatives by the people. 2. Bill of Rights—first ten amendments were added to the Constitution later to guarantee individual rights.
Dispute:	Should the makeup of Congress be based on each state's population (large states' view)? *or* Should all states have equal representation (small states' view)?
Compromise:	bicameral legislature (two houses in Congress) 1. Members of House of Representatives were based on each state's population. 2. Senate would have two delegates from each state. This was called the "Great Compromise."
Dispute:	Should slaves be counted in the population (southern slave states' view)? *or* Should slaves be excluded from the population count (northern industrialized states' view)?
Compromise:	1. Slave importation would be allowed until at least 1808. 2. Slaves would be counted as three-fifths of the population only for the purposes of representation and for assessing taxes; however, they were not permitted to vote.

Exercise 4: Federalists and Anti-Federalists

Directions: Read the quotes shown below. Write *F* (for Federalist) in the space provided if the speaker favors Federalism and *A* (for anti-Federalist) if the speaker advocates states' rights.

_____ **1.** "The territories themselves should determine whether slavery should exist."

_____ **2.** "I need assurance that my money will have value in Georgia as well as in New Jersey."

_____ **3.** "If this nation is to prosper, trade among states must be regulated uniformly.

———— **4.** "We need our own local standing militia to put down uprisings in the state's own territories."

———— **5.** "What right does Massachusetts have to make treaties with other nations?"

★ **GED PRACTICE** ★

Exercise 5: Disputes and Compromises————————

Directions: Choose the *one* answer that best completes each statement.

1. Alexander Hamilton was an early patriot who, from the first, stated that it would be impossible to govern one nation through thirteen separate sovereign states. It can be assumed that Hamilton was

   (1) a Federalist.
   (2) an anti-Federalist.
   (3) from a large state.
   (4) from a northern industrialized state.
   (5) a southern slave owner.

2. The "Great Compromise" of the Constitutional Convention involved

   (1) the settlement of trade laws across the states.
   (2) the mutual agreement by North and South on how to count slaves in the population.
   (3) the addition of a Bill of Rights to guarantee personal freedoms for the states' citizens.
   (4) the creation of a two-house federal legislature to allow for fairness in state representation.
   (5) the establishment of an electoral college so that the people could not directly elect the president of the country.

3. Counting slaves as only three-fifths of the population was detrimental to the southern states in

   (1) determining the number of seats for the House of Representatives.
   (2) deciding on the number of senators to represent those states.
   (3) figuring the amount of property for taxing purposes.
   (4) establishing trade laws between the North and South.
   (5) setting a date to abolish slavery in the nation.

4. Why was the Bill of Rights such an important addition to the Constitution, especially for the anti-Federalists?

   (1) It guaranteed the end of slavery by a certain date.
   (2) It set the rules for the process of amending the Constitution.
   (3) It would end the abuse of personal liberties many colonists had experienced.
   (4) It determined a fair process under which the president of the U.S. would be elected.
   (5) It gave the states supreme rights over the federal government.

Question 5 refers to the following quote:

"It appears to me, then, little short of a miracle, that the Delegates from so many different States (which States you know are also different from each other), in their manners, circumstances, and prejudices, should unite in forming a system of National Government, so little liable to well-founded objections."
George Washington to Marquis de Lafayette, February 7, 1788

5. From this quote we can assume that George Washington believed ratification of the Constitution by the United States

    (1) would be quick and easy.
    (2) would be hampered because of the southern states' resistance.
    (3) would be a long, tedious process, taking many years.
    (4) would never take place.
    (5) looked more likely than one would expect from such a diverse group of states.

 Writing Activity 2

The chart on page 105 cites the position of the southern and northern states about counting slaves as part of the population. Write a paragraph telling why you think the South wanted slaves counted and the North did not.

ANSWERS AND EXPLANATIONS START ON PAGE 291.

Domestic and Foreign Policy

The Western Frontier

> ### Key Words
>
> *Manifest Destiny*—the drive to extend the U.S. borders to the Pacific Ocean
> *implied powers*—authority suggested in the Constitution that is not specifically spelled out

Next to buying Manhattan Island from the Indians for $24 worth of kettles, axes, and cloth, the Louisiana Purchase was probably the United States' best bargain. The United States paid only $15 million to purchase the Louisiana Territory from France in 1803. This acquisition doubled the size of the country, expanding its territories from the Mississippi River westward to the Rocky Mountains. Moreover, the Louisiana Purchase fortified the nation's wealth and position in the world, intensified the expansion westward, and set a precedent for the president's use of implied powers. Implied powers represent authority a president has that is not specifically spelled out in the Constitution.

Because he was afraid of setting a precedent of going beyond constitutional powers, President Thomas Jefferson was at first opposed to the Louisiana Purchase. He thought a constitutional amendment would be necessary to make such a move possible, but time did not permit the long amendment process, and, besides, the idea of the "destiny" of expansion to the Pacific Ocean was already becoming a popular one in the U.S.

In 1804, Jefferson sent Meriwether Lewis and William Clark on an expedition to explore the newly purchased territory, which was virtually a mystery to its new owner. The two men started in St. Louis, went northwest toward the present-day Dakotas, and there took on the Indian guide Sacajawea. They eventually reached the Pacific Ocean and then journeyed back to St. Louis. They did not find an all-water route to the West as they had sought, but they did find several passes through the Rockies, establish friendly relations with the Indians in the West, and gather invaluable information about the life and resources in the new territory.

By 1853 the boundaries of the continental U.S. were set as they are now. "Manifest Destiny" had become a rallying cry in America and shaped the history and culture of the country. Manifest Destiny was the drive to expand the territory of the United States into the undeveloped areas of the West and South. It led directly to the annexation of Texas in 1845 and the acquisition of the Oregon territory in 1846. By 1848, the area comprising California, Nevada, Arizona, Utah, and New Mexico became part of the United States as the nation's boundaries stretched from the Atlantic to the Pacific Oceans.

★ **GED PRACTICE** ★

Exercise 6: The Western Frontier

Directions: Choose the *one* statement that best answers the questions below.

1. Which of the following expresses an opinion of Thomas Jefferson regarding the Louisiana Purchase?

    (1) It doubled the size of the U.S. territory and increased its wealth.
    (2) It helped increase the movement of settlers to the West.
    (3) It was not a move allowed by the Constitution as written.
    (4) It would start a cultural ideology known as "Manifest Destiny."
    (5) Its purchase and exploration would provide invaluable information to the country.

2. In what way did the American belief in "Manifest Destiny" shape the history of the U.S.?

    (1) The relationship between the settlers and the Indians improved greatly.
    (2) The Constitution of the U.S. was amended to allow for more purchase of land for expansion.
    (3) Rivers became an important method of traveling and formed boundaries between states and territories.
    (4) The settlement of the West became more rapid.
    (5) The U.S. soon obtained its first colonial territory in the Pacific.

3. Which of the following statements is best supported by evidence presented in the reading above?

    (1) President Jefferson's commissioning of the Lewis and Clark expedition was foolish considering the waste of time and money to the U.S.
    (2) The Louisiana Purchase and the Lewis and Clark expedition both detracted from President Jefferson's prestige at home and abroad.
    (3) The movement of settlers westward after the Louisiana Purchase raised hostilities between white men and the Indians.
    (4) Jefferson's authorization of the Louisiana Purchase established the idea that a president has powers not stated directly in the Constitution.
    (5) The Louisiana Purchase enabled the U.S. to buy all of the territory to the Pacific Ocean.

ANSWERS AND EXPLANATIONS START ON PAGE 291.

The War of 1812

Key Word

nationalism—pride in one's country, especially the elevation of one nation or group of people above all others

Had the Americans been successful in the War of 1812, Canada would now be part of the U.S. The takeover of Canada was a major aim of the American forces once they had decided to declare war against Great Britain. The War of 1812 was declared, in part, because the Americans blamed their motherland for interfering with trade with other nations and for inciting Indian uprisings in the West. In addition, there was proof of the British forcing American men into the British navy during the Napoleonic Wars.

Tecumseh, chief of the Shawnee Indian tribe, along with his brother Tenskwatawa, had worked tirelessly in the early 1800s to unite the North American Indians in a confederation against white customs, dress, products, and land encroachment. During the War of 1812, Tecumseh and his followers joined forces with the British. It was the great Indian warrior's death in this war that marked the end of the united Indian resistance in most of the Midwest and South of the United States.

Despite the fact that the U.S. did not really win this war, impressment of American men had stopped, the Indian/British alliance had been undone, and the U.S. dependence on Europe was broken. A new sense of nationalism soon developed as America entered the "Era of Good Feelings" and turned its focus inward.

★ **GED PRACTICE** ★

Exercise 7: The War of 1812 ——————————————

Directions: Choose the statement that best answers the following questions.

1. Which of the following British actions of which the colonists had proof contributed to America's declaration of war in 1812?

    (1) the passage of the Townshend Act
    (2) the forcing of American seamen to join the British navy
    (3) the British attempt to regain control of the former thirteen colonies
    (4) Britain's attempt to gain control over Canada
    (5) Britain's responsibility for America's economic depression

2. Which event that occurred during the War of 1812 had the most direct effect on its outcome?

    (1) the takeover of Canada
    (2) the impressment of American men into the British navy
    (3) the death of the British ally, Tecumseh
    (4) the economic depression in the American West
    (5) the incitement of Indian uprisings

3. Which of the following accounts for America's new sense of independence from Europe after the War of 1812?

    (1) The war had forced the U.S. to learn to do without Europe's economic and political help.
    (2) The end of the war had brought peace between the white settlers in the U.S. and the Indians.
    (3) The war proved that the American military could win a war against a larger, more experienced army.
    (4) The Treaty of Ghent that ended the war gave the U.S. its legal freedom from British rule.
    (5) Europeans shunned the U.S. after the war and forced Americans to depend on themselves for their needs.

ANSWERS AND EXPLANATIONS START ON PAGE 292.

The Monroe Doctrine

Key Words

colonization—the act of establishing colonies
Monroe Doctrine—a statement of U.S. foreign policy that prohibits foreign intervention in the Western Hemisphere

The feelings of nationalism that arose at the end of the War of 1812 were heightened by a "hands-off" policy initiated in 1823 by President James Monroe. The "Monroe Doctrine" announced to the world that the U.S. would no longer tolerate European intervention or colonization in the Americas and that the U.S. would not interfere in any political affairs in Europe. The map below illustrates the boundaries on which the Monroe Doctrine was based.

Exercise 8: The Monroe Doctrine

Directions: Place a check mark before each situation below that represents an attempt to enforce the principles of the Monroe Doctrine.

_____ **(1)** the dispatch of American soldiers to Grenada in the Caribbean to protect American citizens during an internal conflict

_____ **(2)** the opposition of the United States to Spanish domination of Cuba in the late nineteenth century

_____ **(3)** the sending of arms to Nicaraguan Contras of Central America to fight the leftist Sandinistas who took over the government

_____ **(4)** the American blockade of Cuba to prevent Soviet ships from entering and establishing missile bases

_____ **(5)** the sending of U.S. arms to El Salvador in Central America to fight the communist rebels who fought against their own government

ANSWER AND EXPLANATION STARTS ON PAGE 292.

Times of Internal Strife

Sectionalism and Slavery

Key Words

abolitionist—one who strongly favors doing away with slavery
secession—the breaking away of a part of a country to form its own nation

Though the nation had developed a sense of national pride and identity after the Monroe Doctrine was announced, sectional loyalty throughout the U.S. persisted. The first U.S. president elected to office as a result of these sectional differences was Andrew Jackson, a southerner. Jackson was considered to be a *populist*, a man who represented the interests of the common people. He opposed the establishment of a national bank because he feared eastern merchants and industrialists would control it. As the country expanded its borders and its population, resentments grew. New Englanders saw the West as an irresistible lure for the youngest, ablest, and most energetic of their population. The South was offended by the other sections' criticism of its dependence on slavery as a part of its economy and society.

As new territories were added to the U.S., the debate over slavery continued. Southern plantation owners believed that they should be able to run their businesses as they thought best, while some northerners believed slavery was wrong and should not be allowed in the new territories and states. However, these northerners did not believe that slavery should be prohibited from areas where it was already the established practice. It was only the abolitionists who believed slavery was evil and demanded that it be banned throughout the country. Compromises were attempted, but none resulted in a lasting solution to the problem of slavery in the country.

Secession and States' Rights

"This government cannot endure, permanently half slave and half free," President Abraham Lincoln proclaimed as he openly campaigned against the spread of slavery into the new territories.

Talk of secession from the Union started among influential southerners and came to a climax when Abraham Lincoln was elected president in 1860.

Almost immediately after the election, South Carolina withdrew from the United States. By February of 1861 six more states—Georgia, Florida, Alabama, Mississippi, Louisiana, and Texas—had also seceded. Jefferson Davis became president of these new Confederate States of America, and Montogomery, Alabama, was chosen as their capital. Soon, four more states—Virginia, Arkansas, North Carolina, and Tennessee—joined the Confederacy, and the capital was moved to Richmond, Virginia.

VOTE ON SECESSION IN THE SOUTH

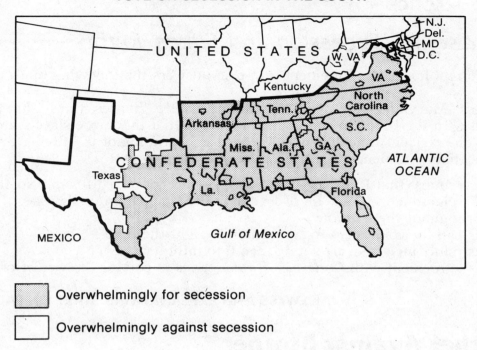

◫ Overwhelmingly for secession

☐ Overwhelmingly against secession

Exercise 9: The Vote on Secession

Directions: Refer to the map above to answer the following questions.
Write the letter of the description on the right that matches the state listed on the left.

_____ **1.** Virginia

(a) As a "border state," it remained in the Union despite being a slave state.

_____ **2.** Texas

(b) As a solid southern slave state, this one voted overwhelmingly to secede from the Union.

_____ **3.** Kentucky

(c) This state split in two over the issue of secession, with the western part loyal to the Union.

_____ **4.** Mississippi

(d) The entire state seceded from the Union despite the fact that only its eastern part voted to do so.

★ GED PRACTICE ★

Exercise 10: Secession and States' Rights

Directions: Choose the statement that best answers the following question.

Delaware, Maryland, Kentucky, and Missouri were "border states" that remained with the Union in spite of the fact that that they were slave states. Which of President Lincoln's positions at the beginning of the Civil War was most probably influenced by the status of these four states?

(1) his request that Robert E. Lee become chief strategist for the North
(2) his reluctance to issue an order for the emancipation of slaves throughout the country
(3) his call for volunteers for the Union to fight the rebels
(4) his reluctance to draft young men into military service
(5) his agreement with Congress to raise taxes to pay for the war effort

ANSWERS AND EXPLANATIONS START ON PAGE 292.

Brother Against Brother

Key Word

emancipate—to free from bondage

The Union underestimated the Confederacy's zeal even after the South had captured Fort Sumter in South Carolina in April of 1861. Initially, President Lincoln had ordered seventy-five thousand untrained volunteers to stop the "rebellion" of the Confederates.

On July 21, 1861, nearly 28,000 ill-prepared Union soldiers followed by picnic basket–toting spectators marched from the North toward the Confederate capital at Richmond. At Bull Run, Virginia, they met with nearly 33,000 equally unskilled Confederate soldiers. After five hours, 2,900 Union soldiers were dead, wounded, captured, or missing and 2,000 Confederate casualties were recorded.

After this confrontation, the status of the conflict changed from a rebellion to a civil war. The war lasted four years—four years of state fighting against state, friend fighting against friend, and often brother fighting against brother.

The South began with a greater familiarity with battle sites, a burning desire to win, and strong leadership provided by outstanding generals. Among these was Robert E. Lee, a graduate of West Point and former officer in the U.S. Army. His superior military ability, however, was overcome by the Union's larger population, its abundance of natural resources, and its excellent transportation system.

In 1862, President Lincoln issued the *Emancipation Proclamation.* The document ordered the freeing of all slaves in the Confederate states. As a result of this proclamation, the Union Army's ranks were swelled by 180,000 former slaves who fought against the Confederacy.

In 1863, Congress approved a law to begin drafting males into the military to maintain its ranks. Although riots broke out in protest, the North overcame this and other setbacks.

Women stepped into many work settings as the army took the men away to fight. Expenses for the war effort were financed through war bonds, taxes, duties on imports, and the printing of paper money. A network of government agencies was established to support the Union Army, and private industry changed and grew to meet the demands of these new agencies.

In the South, however, changes were not as quick or as successful. Since there were not as many businesses and industries, selling bonds and taxing profits were not as rewarding as in the North.

Cotton and tobacco farming were the big industries of the South, and these took lots of land and manpower. Because these crops were not as important to the war effort as food was, the region's two biggest industries were nearly abandoned. As the men went off to fight, the women took over the plantations. This resulted in weaker control over the system of slavery and contributed to the end of the institution that had built the South.

Confederate general Robert E. Lee surrendered to Union general Ulysses S. Grant at Appomattox Court House, Virginia, on April 9, 1865. By this time, the people of the South were bitter and alienated. The severe difficulties and changes they had experienced made readmission into the Union difficult.

Exercise 11: North vs. South

Directions: In the spaces below, write *N* if the description applies to the North, *S* if it applies to the South, and *B* if it applies to both. Base your answers on the passage above.

_____ **1.** greater population

_____ **2.** outstanding field generals

_____ **3.** burning desire to win

_____ **4.** abundance of natural resources

_____ **5.** cash crops abandoned in favor of food crops

_____ **6.** better transportation network

_____ **7.** forces boosted by Emancipation Proclamation

_____ **8.** women assumed bigger role as men went to war

_____ **9.** war debt financed in creative ways

_____ **10.** greater familiarity with battle sites

★ **GED PRACTICE** ★

Exercise 12: Brother Against Brother

Directions: Choose the *one* best answer for each statement or question below.

1. The effect of the Emancipation Proclamation on the outcome of the war was that

    (1) the South gained a reliable source of soldiers in the freed slaves.
    (2) the border states that held slaves turned against the Union and joined the Confederacy.
    (3) it officially ended the war, since the question of slavery for which the war was fought was no longer an issue.
    (4) it made President Lincoln one of the most unpopular presidents in American history.
    (5) it gave the Union a military advantage, since many former slaves fought on the side of the North.

Questions 2 and 3 are based on the following quote:

"It is clear enough that the Civil War was a watershed experience for America. . . . To understand that part of our past we need to understand the present, because today we are grappling with the commitment that was made for us a century ago. The ultimate meaning of that war depends on what we do now. We are still involved in it. When we move to make a living reality out of the great ideal of the equality of all Americans; when we take our stand anywhere in the world for freedom, and for just dealing between all races and conditions of man; when we work for an enduring unity among human beings, whether at home or abroad—when we do any of these things we are simply trying to meet the obligation that was laid upon us a century ago at a price higher than any other price we ever paid."

Bruce Catton, Civil War historian

2. Based on the quote above, it is likely that Bruce Catton would support the actions of which group in recent years?

    (1) The Ku Klux Klan of the fifties
    (2) The Civil Rights workers of the sixties
    (3) The anti-ERA demonstrators of the seventies
    (4) The Vietnam War protestors of the seventies
    (5) The antiabortionists of the eighties

3. It is the opinion of Bruce Catton that

    (1) the Civil War was the most important event in U.S. history.
    (2) the Civil War experience obligates us to promote freedom throughout the world.
    (3) the cost of the Civil War in lives and money was too high.
    (4) the Civil War could and should have been avoided.
    (5) writing about the Civil War is his obligation.

4. The Civil War forced women to become equal partners in the work force. What other event in U.S. history led to a similar adaptation?

  (1) The Vietnam War
  (2) World War II
  (3) The Great Depression
  (4) The Women's Suffragist Movement
  (5) Prohibition

ANSWERS AND EXPLANATIONS START ON PAGE 292.

Reconstruction and Healing

Key Words

carpetbaggers—northerners who moved to the South during Reconstruction to take advantage of business and political opportunities

impeachment—the bringing of charges against a public official for misconduct

Reconstruction—the reestablishment of the Confederate states as part of the Union after the Civil War

scalawag—white southerners who supported the efforts of the North in rebuilding the South

After the Civil War, the South was faced with the difficult task of picking up the pieces and going on. Strangers from the North who moved to the South to work in business and politics were called carpetbaggers by the southerners. They were despised by the former Confederates, who believed that these men came to exploit the region and its citizens. Even more hated were the scalawags, southern citizens who were perceived as helping the carpetbaggers.

The Freedmen's Bureau was set up in 1865 to provide food, schooling, and work for many former slaves and poor whites. The same year, Lincoln announced his "Ten Percent Plan," by which Confederates could become U.S. citizens again by taking an oath of loyalty to the Union. States could reenter once 10 percent of their citizens had taken the oath. One month later, however, Abraham Lincoln was assassinated by a Confederate sympathizer.

Vice President Andrew Johnson succeeded Lincoln as president. Johnson, a Tennessean, was the only southern senator not to join the Confederacy. Although Lincoln had trusted him, many in Congress believed him to be pro-South.

In 1867, Congress authorized federal army generals to head the policing of the South, which was divided into five military districts. It then demanded that the states set up new constitutions that would give blacks the right to vote and to hold office.

The same year, Congress passed the Tenure of Office Act to protect a certain member of Johnson's cabinet from being fired for agreeing with Congress's ideas on Reconstruction. When Johnson dismissed the cabinet member, Congress reacted by voting to impeach the president. Johnson, thus, was the first president to be impeached. He was acquitted by just one vote.

In 1868, Ulysses S. Grant was elected president, and in 1870 the Fifteenth Amendment guaranteed the right to vote to blacks and former slaves. It is viewed by many as a great victory for civil rights in general and Radical Reconstruction in particular.

★ GED PRACTICE ★

Exercise 13: Reconstruction and Healing

Directions: The following definitions apply to questions 1 and 2.

Thirteenth Amendment—abolished slavery
Fourteenth Amendment—gave full citizenship to freed slaves
Fifteenth Amendment—guaranteed voting rights to all races
Freedmen's Bureau Act—provided food, education, and work in the reconstructed South
Ten Percent Plan—proposed a plan by which confederate states could reenter the Union

1. Which is sometimes regarded as the authorization for the nation's first federal welfare system?

   (1) The Thirteenth Amendment
   (2) The Fourteenth Amendment
   (3) The Fifteenth Amendment
   (4) The Freedmen's Bureau Act
   (5) The Ten Percent Plan

2. Which of the following is used as the basis for abolishing discrimination in voting requirements?

   (1) The Thirteenth Amendment
   (2) The Fourteenth Amendment
   (3) The Fifteenth Amendment
   (4) The Freedmen's Bureau Act
   (5) The Ten Percent Plan

ANSWERS AND EXPLANATIONS START ON PAGE 293.

The Rise of Industrial America

The Industrial Revolution

> ### Key Word
>
> *industrial revolution*—the change in the economy from a manual means of production to a mechanical one

The U.S. emerged from the Civil War only to experience another major upheaval in the nation's way of life. America and the rest of the Western world entered an industrial revolution in which the economy relied less on animal power and more on machinery to produce goods.

As industries were founded, cities grew up around them. Mechanization of farming jobs caused some people to lose their jobs and move from farm to town. However, more commonly, the potential to earn more money and obtain modern conveniences lured workers to the cities. Jobs in industry paid much higher wages than farmhand work, and these wages bought luxuries never before dreamed of on the farm. The map on page 120 illustrates the amazing growth of American cities over a short, thirty-year period.

★ GED PRACTICE ★

Exercise 14: Industrial Revolution

Directions: Choose the *one* best answer for each statement or question below.

1. Eli Whitney's idea of using interchangeable parts for mass production was important to the Industrial Revolution because

   (1) it encouraged the invention of products that would have been impossible before.
   (2) guns could be produced on a larger scale than before.
   (3) purchasers of products could then assemble them themselves.
   (4) the quality of workmanship was no longer as important.
   (5) many industries took advantage of its application to the factory system.

2. By 1899, the U.S. had more miles of railroad than all of Europe and Russia combined. By the same year, the U.S. had been recognized as the industrial leader of the world. Which of the following implications may be drawn from this fact?

   (1) The railroad was a symbol of power and prestige.
   (2) The railroad system became the biggest industry in the U.S.
   (3) Industrialization is not possible without a large railroad system.
   (4) Industrialization depends on factories for mass production of goods.
   (5) Dependable transportation is a key to the mass production and sale of goods.

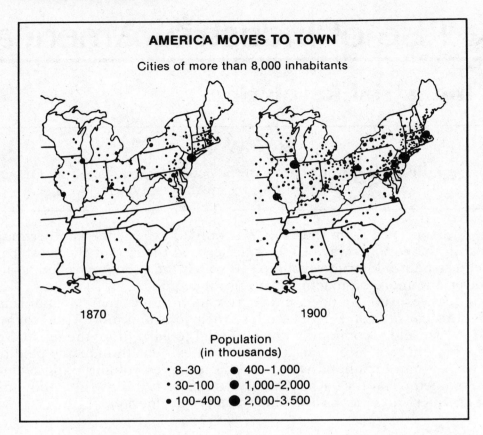

AMERICA MOVES TO TOWN

Cities of more than 8,000 inhabitants

1870

1900

Population
(in thousands)

· 8–30   ● 400–1,000
· 30–100   ● 1,000–2,000
● 100–400   ● 2,000–3,500

3. Which of the statements below is supported by the data provided in the maps and paragraphs above? During the period 1870–1900,

   (1) the U.S. experienced the loss of much of its farming areas.
   (2) there was more industry in the northern states than in the southern states.
   (3) there was a great influx of immigrants to the U.S.
   (4) there was a population loss in many areas in the U.S.
   (5) there was a bigger move to the South than in any other direction.

4. From the maps it appears that industries and the big cities that grew up around them were usually established near

   (1) the middle of the country.
   (2) national boundaries.
   (3) mountains and hills.
   (4) bodies of water.
   (5) farming areas.

ANSWERS AND EXPLANATIONS START ON PAGE 293.

Growth of Big Business

> ## Key Words
>
> **laissez-faire**—a government policy of noninterference in the affairs of business
>
> **urbanization**—the shift of population from the country to the city

In this climate of rapid expansion, big business grew without restrictions. The U.S. government observed a policy of laissez-faire, or "letting business alone" to do what it knows best. This policy often resulted in economic and social abuse as power became concentrated in the hands of a few.

Consolidation became a key to big business and industrial growth and power. Such men as Andrew Carnegie (Carnegie Steel), J. P. Morgan (U.S. Steel), and John D. Rockefeller (Standard Oil) created industrial empires through takeovers and trusts. These men became known as **Robber Barons** because of their unscrupulous business practices.

Several of these newly rich businessmen justified their prosperity as the result of "survival of the fittest," termed Social Darwinism. Social Darwinism held that the rich were richer because they were smarter than the poor.

As industrialization expanded, more and more people were lured to the cities in what became known as urbanization. The cities and factories became overcrowded and unhealthy. However, the Social Darwinists held that those conditions were due to the inferiority of the poor and not due to their exploitation by the wealthy factory owners.

Exercise 15: Laissez-faire Business Policies

Directions: Place a check mark before each of the following actions that represents economic activity without government intervention.

_____ **(1)** Major airlines engage in a price war, setting competitive prices for air fares.

_____ **(2)** A state does not have a usury law, a law that sets the maximum interest rate that can be legally charged for a loan.

_____ **(3)** A government commission determines the maximum wage increases for certain jobs.

_____ **(4)** Kansas wheat farmers are paid by Washington not to grow wheat on certain tracts of land.

_____ **(5)** Banks charge whatever rate of interest the market will bear on passbook savings accounts.

SOCIAL STUDIES TEST

★ GED PRACTICE ★

Exercise 16: Growth of Big Business

Directions: Choose the one best answer to the following question.

Which of the following is a conclusion that is supported by "The Growth of Big Business"?

(1) Sociologists do not understand business theories.
(2) Big business grew in the U.S. at the expense of the welfare of the public.
(3) Governments should not try to regulate private business.
(4) Only the best businessmen survived industrialization in the U.S.
(5) Congressmen received special favors to sponsor legislation favorable to big business.

ANSWERS AND EXPLANATIONS START ON PAGE 293.

The "New Americans"

The chance to escape oppressive conditions in their homeland lured an unprecedented number of immigrants to America in the late 1800s. These new immigrants from eastern and southern Europe were different from their predecessors. The Italians, Austrians, Hungarians, Poles, Serbs, and Russians were Catholic or Jewish rather than Protestant. Their customs and ways of life were foreign to naturalized Americans, and, as a result, prejudice based on the immigrants' ethnic background became a problem.

This great influx of immigrants gravitated toward the cities where the jobs were, presenting new problems for the young nation. In 1890, half of New York City's population was housed in tenement houses. Open drainage gutters polluted water supplies with human and industrial sewage. Working conditions worsened as owners put more money into modern machinery and invested less in comfort and safety measures for the employees. At the same time, the "new Americans" competed with established Americans for jobs, a competition that caused increasing friction in the workplace.

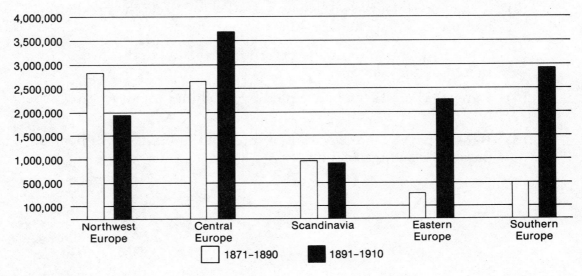

SOURCES OF IMMIGRATION TO THE U.S., 1871–1910

★ GED PRACTICE ★

Exercise 17: The New Immigrants

Directions: Choose the *one* best answer for each statement or question below.

1. According to the bar graph, the trend at the beginning of the twentieth century was for immigrants to the U.S. to come here

    (1) in much fewer numbers than during the 1870s and 1880s.
    (2) in about the same numbers as during the 1870s and 1880s.
    (3) from eastern, central, and southern Europe in greater numbers than twenty years earlier.
    (4) from northwest and central Europe in greater numbers than twenty years earlier.
    (5) from northwest and central Europe more so than from eastern and southern Europe.

2. Of the regions listed below, which one experienced the greatest reduction in the numbers of immigrants coming to the U.S.?

    (1) Scandinavia
    (2) Central Europe
    (3) Northwest Europe
    (4) Eastern Europe
    (5) Southern Europe

Writing Activity 3

How do today's "new Americans" compare to the "new Americans" of the nineteenth century? Do we naturalized Americans accept immigrants more readily than did our ancestors? Write two or three paragraphs comparing these "new Americans" of the late 1800s with today's "new Americans." You might compare their homelands, language barriers and the willingness to overcome them, competition with native Americans for jobs, and discrimination toward them by mainstream society.

ANSWERS AND EXPLANATIONS START ON PAGE 293.

Labor Organizations and Political Machines

Key Words
labor union—an organization formed by workers as a means to correct economic and social injustices caused by unfair labor practices
graft—the acquiring of money in dishonest or questionable ways
muckraker—a writer or cartoonist who exposed a public official's misconduct
political machine—a means by which powerful politicians were able to control votes and reap profits from city government

Friction also surfaced between the employers and the employed. Workers formed labor unions as a means to fight unfair employer practices. One of the first unions was the Noble and Holy Order of the Knights of Labor, founded in 1869.

In 1881, the American Federation of Labor (AFL) was founded to represent skilled workers who were organized by specific crafts. These workers readily acknowledged the need for strikes and boycotts. By 1904 there were over a million laborers in the AFL under the leadership of Samuel Gompers.

Efforts to organize workers and labor disputes often resulted in violence. One of the most famous was the Haymarket Square riot in Chicago in 1886 in which seven policemen and ten workers were killed and 117 people were injured.

Another phenomenon that grew out of the industrialization of the cities was the political machine. "Political bosses," controllers of machines, commonly offered jobs for votes. Many of these politicians came from the ranks of the immigrants and sought to help their brethren even as they profited from them.

The most notorious of the city "bosses" was Boss Tweed of New York. Boss Tweed was often caricatured by the famous political cartoonist Thomas Nast. Nast and other political writers were called muckrakers because of their ability to scrape up dirt about political corruption. These writers helped to formulate the attitudes and methods of the middle-class reformers of what came to be known as the Progressive Era in U.S. politics.

★ **GED PRACTICE** ★

Exercise 18: Political Machines

Directions: The quote below is from a famous political boss, George Washington Plunkitt, who was a ward boss for the corrupt political machine in New York City, Tammany Hall. Read the passage and answer the questions that follow.

"Everybody is talkin' these days about Tammany men growin' rich on graft, but nobody thinks of drawin' the distinction between honest graft and dishonest graft. There's all the difference in the world between the two. Yes, many of our men have grown rich in politics. I have myself. I've made a big fortune out of the game, and I'm gettin' richer every day, but I've not gone in for dishonest graft—blackmailin' gamblers, saloonkeepers, disorderly people, etc.—and neither has any of the men who have made big fortunes in politics.

"There's an honest graft, and I'm an example of how it works. I might sum up the whole thing by sayin': 'I seen my opportunities and I took 'em.'

"Just let me explain by examples. My party's in power in the city, and it's goin' to undertake a lot of public improvements. Well, I'm tipped off, say, that they're going to lay out a new park at a certain place."

"I see my opportunity and I take it. I go to that place and I buy up all the land I can in the neighborhood. Then the board of this or that makes its plans public, and there is a rush to get my land, which nobody cared particular for before."

"Ain't it perfectly honest to charge a good price and make a profit on my investment and foresight? Of course, it is. Well that's honest graft."

from *Plunkitt of Tammany Hall*

1. Which of the following judgments could be made based on the above passage?

   (1) There is a real difference between "honest" and "dishonest" graft.
   (2) Taking advantage of an opportunity is not the same as graft.
   (3) Graft is the "American way" in big city politics.
   (4) He who does not take advantage of an opportunity is a fool.
   (5) Political bosses appeared to have no sense of right and wrong.

2. Another name for "honest" graft as described by George Washington Plunkitt might be

   (1) accepting bribes.
   (2) appointing friends and relatives to political office.
   (3) demanding payoffs from gamblers.
   (4) profiting from inside information on government purchases.
   (5) blackmailing tavernkeepers.

ANSWERS AND EXPLANATIONS START ON PAGE 294.

Progressive Reform

Key Words

progressivism—a reform movement demanding governmental involvement to bring about economic and political improvements for the poor and disadvantaged

capital—money, machinery, or any other resource used to produce goods

In response to the abuses that resulted from rapid industrialization and urbanization, the Progressive Movement began at the beginning of the twentieth century. Lasting for fifteen years, this reform movement had as its goal the stamping out of political corruption and the improvement of the quality of life for Americans.

President Theodore Roosevelt was considered the embodiment of Progressive Reform. Only forty-two when he became president, he brought energy and adventure to the office. He used the implied powers of the presidency to establish our national policy of conserving the nation's natural resources.

During the Progressive Era, the government abandoned its laissez-faire policy of noninterference in the affairs of business and produced legislative reforms that have an impact on Americans today. Some of these reforms are highlighted in the chart below:

PROGRESSIVE REFORMS

Passage of the Sherman Anti-Trust Act outlawed monopolies

Passage of Hepburn Act gave Interstate Commerce Commission increased authority to regulate the nation's railroads

Passage of the Pure Food and Drug Act set standards for production and sale of foods and drugs

U.S.D.A. (United States Department of Agriculture) inspected meat

Passage of Child Labor Laws prohibited child labor

Radical journalists wrote about the corruption and poverty that rapid industrialization had caused. These writers were called *muckrakers* because they attacked these conditions in their columns and books. Among these famous writers were Lincoln Steffens, Edward Bellamy, Jane Addams, Jacob Riis, and Upton Sinclair. In his book *The Jungle*, Sinclair exposed the unhealthy conditions in the meatpacking industry and is credited with helping to get the *Pure Food and Drug Act* passed.

Exercise 19: Progressive Reform

Directions: Choose the *one* best answer for each statement or question that follows the passage.

In 1890, the journalist Jacob Riis published a book titled, *How the Other Half Lives,* which contained photographs and detailed descriptions of the deplorable life in New York's tenement district. About this problem, Riis wrote: "The remedy that shall be an effective answer to the coming appeal for justice must proceed from the public conscience. Neither legislation nor charity can cover the ground. The greed of capital that wrought the evil must undo it, as far as it can now be undone."

1. With which of the following positions on today's poverty and discrimination would Riis likely agree?

(1) Each individual should pull himself up by his own bootstraps.
(2) Government's funding for social programs should be cut.
(3) The states themselves must pass legislation to correct the problem.
(4) A booming, growing economy will automatically solve the problem.
(5) Private industry is morally responsible for helping to correct social problems.

2. Based on the values expressed in the quote above, to which of the groups below would Riis likely have given support?

(1) New York's Four Hundred, the self-appointed social elite
(2) machine politicians who have the power to give jobs
(3) private citizens who established the cities' settlement houses
(4) a lobbying group to pass anti-poverty legislation
(5) businessmen who believed in the theory of Social Darwinism

ANSWERS AND EXPLANATIONS START ON PAGE 294.

The U.S. as a World Power

From Isolationism to Imperialism

Key Words

imperialism—one nation extending its authority over other territories or nations
isolationism—the policy of noninterference in world affairs
jingoism—extreme nationalism marked by the frequent use of warlike rhetoric

Immediately after the Civil War and up until the U.S. entered the industrial revolution, the nation pursued a foreign policy of isolationism. America's rapid industrialization, however, soon forced the country to seek foreign markets for its manufactured goods, a cheaper labor supply to produce those goods, and new sources of raw materials. These three goals became accessible as the U.S. moved toward a policy of imperialism.

The new technology of the industrial revolution made many products, including newspapers, more readily available than before. Newspaper "wars" erupted among publishers. The "yellow press" emerged with exaggerated stories and became popular with the reading public.

When Cuban rebels revolted against Spain's presence on the island, the belligerent "jingo press" played a big part in stirring up anti-Spanish sentiment in the U.S. And, when it was reported that Spain sunk the U.S. battleship *Maine* in Havana Harbor, the U.S. declared war in 1898, handily winning the Spanish-American War four months later. Conceded to the U.S. under the terms of the Treaty of Paris were the territories of Guam, Puerto Rico, and the Philippines. This acquisition, along with President McKinley's annexation of Hawaii, positioned the U.S. well as a world power.

These moves, however, were criticized by anti-imperialists such as Mark Twain, former president Grover Cleveland, and Andrew Carnegie, who believed that the U.S. had no business controlling nations overseas. Supporters of American imperialism maintained not only that it was good for commercial and military reasons, but some also felt that it was America's "burden" to bring Christianity to "heathen" lands. The debates between the imperialists and the anti-imperialists that began in the aftermath of the Spanish-American War continue today.

★ GED PRACTICE ★

Exercise 20: Imperialism vs. Isolationism————

Directions: Choose the *one* best answer for each statement or question below.

1. Which of the following is an example of American imperialist policy?

    (1) the sending of food and medical assistance to drought-stricken Ethiopia
    (2) the purchase of Alaska from the Soviet Union in 1867
    (3) the American blockade of Cuba to prevent Soviet ships from entering the Western Hemisphere
    (4) the control of most of the Panama Canal Zone by the U.S. until 1979
    (5) the United States's bombing of Libya in retaliation for terrorist acts

2. President Grover Cleveland refused to annex Hawaii to the U.S. after learning that a majority of the natives preferred being ruled by their queen, Liliuokalani. In making this decision, he was abiding by the principle of rule by "consent of the governed" put forth by

    (1) the *Declaration of Independence.*
    (2) the Monroe Doctrine.
    (3) the *Treaty of Ghent.*
    (4) the *Emancipation Proclamation.*
    (5) the idea of Manifest Destiny.

ANSWERS AND EXPLANATIONS START ON PAGE 294.

World War I

The rivalry between William Howard Taft and Theodore Roosevelt for president in 1913 helped elect Democrat Woodrow Wilson. One of Wilson's first moves was to pass the Federal Reserve Act in 1913. The law remedied many of the ills in American banking at the time. The Wilson presidency is probably better known, however, for the United States's entrance into World War I.

In Europe, the assassination of Austrian Crown Prince Ferdinand, by a Serbian nationalist, touched off a war between the rival Central Powers, which included Germany and Austria-Hungary, and the Allied Powers (Great Britain, France, and Russia).

The U.S. tried to remain neutral during the early years of the war but was angered by the German submarine attack on the passenger ship, the *Lusitania*. Other threats to U.S. neutrality drew the U.S. into the war. On April 6, 1917, the U.S. declared war on Germany and joined the Allied Powers.

The U.S. servicemen played a vital role in World War I. They arrived just as the Europeans were tiring on all fronts. As the Allies broke through the German lines, the Germans conceded defeat.

President Wilson capitalized on Europe's exhaustion from four years of war and on November 11, 1918, proposed a "peace without victory." The fourteen point plan presented at the Paris peace conference was not accepted in its entirety, and the harsher Treaty of Versailles ended the war.

Wilson's attempt to establish a League of Nations to prevent war did succeed. However, isolationist sentiment in the U.S. Congress prevented the U.S. from joining, thus contributing to the organization's decline.

Exercise 21: World War I

Directions: Place a check mark before the events that directly contributed to the U.S. entering the war on the Allied side. You may check more than one.

_____ **(1)** the assassination of the Austrian prince

_____ **(2)** the arrest of the Serbian nationalist

_____ **(3)** the involvement of its old ally, Great Britain

_____ **(4)** Germany's attack on the passenger ship, the *Lusitania*

_____ **(5)** threats to U.S. neutrality

ANSWER AND EXPLANATION STARTS ON PAGE 294.

The Roaring Twenties

Return to Normalcy

Key Words

free enterprise—freedom of private businesses to organize and compete without unnecessary government interference

individualism—a belief that the interests of the individual should prevail

The United States had just experienced an exhausting world war, and weary Americans overwhelmingly supported President Harding's "return to normalcy."

The twenties were anything but normal, however, as Warren Harding's administration became tainted by the Teapot Dome Scandal. This bribery scandal disgraced the Harding Administration and characterized it as one of the nation's most corrupt presidencies.

Under President Calvin Coolidge (Keep Cool with Cal), the country prospered as it never had before. Business efficiency experts, advertising executives, and public relations people replaced the reformers of the Progressive Era as America's spokespersons of the twenties.

In 1929, Herbert Hoover won the presidency on the promise that good times would continue under the Republicans. He praised protective tariffs, Prohibition, individualism, and free enterprise. He won easily over Al Smith, a Catholic and big-city liberal politician, in spite of the fact that Smith polled twice as many votes as had the Democratic candidate in the previous election. It became obvious that changes in attitudes were developing slowly and that the voices of labor, immigrants, and minorities were demanding to be heard. The Democratic Party, if it were to be successful, would have to embrace these groups.

Also, during the twenties, taxes were cut, especially for the rich, with the belief that the remaining capital would "trickle down" in wages and other benefits to the poorer segments of society. Social programs were similarly cut, again hurting the poor and middle class to the benefit of the wealthy. Agencies that had been established by the Progressives were rendered ineffective by the appointment of antagonistic individuals to lead them.

 Writing Activity 4

How does today's social and economic climate compare to that of the twenties? Write two or three paragraphs comparing the twenties to the eighties in the areas of tax cuts or social programs. How are the eighties different from the twenties? How are they similar?

ANSWER AND EXPLANATION STARTS ON PAGE 294.

The Jazz Age and the Lost Generation

Key Word

prohibition—the legal forbidding of the manufacture, sale, and transportation of alcoholic beverages

The twenties could not be described as "normal" in other areas as well. It was an era marked by the glorification of youth. Young men and women thumbed their noses at conventional American behavior. This defiance of accepted behavior was expressed frequently in dance and music. Jazz emerged as the medium that best expressed this youth worship and alienation from the larger society.

Prohibition, which took effect in 1920, was largely ignored because speak-easies offered illegal liquor along with free-wheeling fun. Many were run by members of organized crime who trafficked in drugs as well as prostitution.

In reaction to what many of them considered to be smugness and an emphasis on the material in American life, American writers such as Ernest Hemingway, T. S. Eliot, and F. Scott Fitzgerald retreated to Paris and became members of the "lost generation."

Exercise 22: The Jazz Age and the Lost Generation

Below is one observer's opinion of the Jazz Age and its effects on American life.

A new breed of Americans is emerging in our cities. Were I not so frightened by this phenomenon, I might be amused.

Young people are throwing all caution to the wind; their only interest seems to be outdoing one another in outlandish behavior, dress, and dance. The so-called "flappers"—women whose outrageous antics exceed the men's—are the worst offenders.

"Jazz" seems to be the "music" for this younger generation, and it certainly expresses a disdain for American conventions. It is sensuous, spontaneous, and startling. Some are blaming it for an increase in sexual promiscuity, an increase in divorce rates, and a breakup of families.

In reaction to this obvious breakdown in the American moral fabric, our best writers are retreating to Paris to escape their social responsibility for decrying this ugly aspect of American life. As if the "Jazz Age's" scornful sneering at American ideals were not enough, we are being deprived of our most imaginative minds when we need them the most.

Directions: Check off the statements listed below that reflect assumptions by the writer of the above piece.

_____ **(1)** The "lost generation" could have reversed the negative effects of the Jazz Age if it had chosen to do so.

_____ **(2)** Their art was more important to the "lost generation" than concern about their country's moral climate.

_____ **(3)** American society was benefited when young artists and writers flocked to Paris.

_____ **(4)** Young people's striving for individuality and self-expression is a positive sign for our society.

_____ **(5)** Writers have a social responsibility that outweighs their responsibility to themselves as creative artists.

ANSWER AND EXPLANATION STARTS ON PAGE 294.

The Crash and Resulting Depression

Key Words

speculation—buying or selling with the expectation of profiting from a change in market conditions

conservatism—the belief that the existing order should be maintained and that any change should be gradual

depression—a low period of economic activity marked by high unemployment

"I have no fears for the future of our country. It is bright with hope." These were the words of Herbert Hoover at his inauguration in 1929. But a decade of tax breaks for the rich, antagonism toward labor unions, high protective tariffs, and laissez-faire policies intensified the problems developing in the stock market.

Speculative buying had reached sky-high limits, and much of it had been financed by loans. When the banks called the loans in, the borrowers could not pay. The prices of stocks fell rapidly. Though the stock market had wavered for two months, no one was prepared for the frenzied selling of October 23, 1929.

President Hoover's conservative policies did not help. His policy of noninterference in business affairs would not allow the drastic measures the country needed.

Investments fell at a staggering level. Banks closed their doors to shut out the demands of customers wanting their money.

The number of unemployed workers rose from four million in 1930 to eleven million in 1932. Depression was an apt word for the country's economic condition, for it described not only the financial situation, but also the mood of the country.

Exercise 23: The Crash and Depression —————

Directions: Choose the one best answer for the following question.

Based on the preceding reading, which of the following was *not* a cause of the Great Depression?

(1) the enforcement of high protective tariffs
(2) speculative buying financed by loans
(3) Hoover's pursuit of conservative policies
(4) the unemployment of 11 million workers by 1932
(5) the steep decline in investments

ANSWER AND EXPLANATION START ON PAGE 295.

The Thirties and Forties

The New Deal

The election of 1932 gave the Democrats the chance to come back and they did so in full force. Elected president in 1932, Franklin Delano Roosevelt promised Americans a "New Deal." Four days after his inauguration in March 1933, he presented a draft of banking legislation that passed the Senate and House in just eight hours.

Within his first "Hundred Days" in office, Roosevelt used his executive authority to get Congress to approve an unprecedented number of bills to deal with the nation's economic crisis. Roosevelt's legislation created an "alphabet soup" of agencies, many of which remain part of the federal government today.

Frequently criticized for abuse of his executive powers, Roosevelt, through his actions, reversed the economic and emotional climate of the country. Voters showed their approval by reelecting the president by the largest margin (up to that time) in U.S. history.

During Roosevelt's second term, the nation's priorities shifted away from New Deal politics to the brewing trouble in Europe. The social revolution of the New Deal, however, had altered the lives of Americans in every corner of the nation.

★ GED PRACTICE ★

Exercise 24: The New Deal vs. the Reagan Revolution

President Ronald Reagan is frequently compared to President Franklin D. Roosevelt. In the passage below, the writer discusses both men.

Directions: Read the passage and answer the questions that follow.

During the presidential campaign of 1980, Ronald Reagan lauded Franklin Delano Roosevelt as his political hero. On the face of it, this fact is hard to believe, given the sharp political differences between the two.

President Roosevelt, a liberal Democrat, founded the social security system to provide a worry-free retirement for the nation's elderly. President Reagan, a conservative Republican, was criticized for trying to weaken the program. President Roosevelt's New Deal legislation provided for the regulation of banks and other financial institutions; under the Reagan administration these institutions were greatly deregulated. President Roosevelt's administration set the minimum wage law; President Reagan's administration favored changing it. Labor organizations were encouraged under the Roosevelt administration and thrived; labor organizations were weakened and threatened under the Reagan administration.

Despite these differences, there are striking similarities between the two men. Roosevelt, an extremely popular leader, became president in the midst of economic despair. Reagan, an equally popular leader, became president when the country was suffering from a *malaise* and economic problems.

Roosevelt was a persuasive politician and a strong communicator; Reagan's nickname is the "Great Communicator" because of his skill in handling the media. Both men were reelected to the presidency by huge landslides. The legislation of the New Deal affected the lives of many Americans, and we now see that the "Reagan Revolution" has had a profound effect on the lives of many Americans.

Roosevelt, a man from a wealthy background who became a champion of the "little people," is considered one of America's few great presidents. Will Ronald Reagan, a man from a modest background who became the "champion of big business," be accorded the same honor? Opinions are sharply divided.

1. The purpose of the passage is to

   (1) show how President Reagan and Roosevelt are alike.
   (2) show how Reagan and Roosevelt are different.
   (3) compare and contrast two modern American presidents.
   (4) prove that history repeats itself.
   (5) persuade the reader that Reagan was a better president than Roosevelt.

2. The author expresses the opinion that

   (1) it is mere coincidence that Reagan's rise to power parallels Roosevelt's.
   (2) Reagan and Roosevelt have less in common than most people think.
   (3) Roosevelt was a better president than Reagan was.
   (4) Reagan deliberately patterned his presidency after Roosevelt's.
   (5) the verdict is still out on Reagan's stature as president.

3. From the passage it is obvious that the author is

   (1) impartial.
   (2) an admirer of Roosevelt's policies.
   (3) an admirer of Reagan's policies.
   (4) a critic of Roosevelt's personal style.
   (5) a critic of Reagan's personal style.

 Writing Activity 5

Why did the American people choose two such different men for president in times of national hardship? Choose either Franklin Roosevelt or Ronald Reagan and write two or three paragraphs telling why you think that individual appealed to American voters.

ANSWERS AND EXPLANATIONS START ON PAGE 295.

World War II

A month before FDR's second inauguration, Adolf Hitler, chancellor of Germany, was on a collision course with Britain and France as he sought to expand his power in western Europe.

Japan, too, displayed military aggression, especially toward China. Elsewhere in Europe, Spain was experiencing a bloody civil war, and Italy had invaded Ethiopia.

The U.S. attempted to remain neutral, but Roosevelt knew that the nation could not remain neutral forever.

By 1940, Italy and Germany had joined forces as the Axis Powers in an effort to control the rest of the continent.

The Pacific was anything but peaceful during this time. The Chinese government under Chiang Kai-shek had been resisting the Japanese invasion. By 1941, the U.S. imposed an embargo on essential materials for Japan and entered into negotiations to avoid armed conflict. Later in the same year, Japan, now an Axis power, intensified its invasion of Indochina and on December 7, 1941, bombed American bases at Pearl Harbor. The U.S. declared war, joining the Allied forces, which included Great Britain and France. The Allied forces made the decision to stop Hitler in Europe before dealing with Japan in the Pacific.

On June 6, 1944, the Allies landed on the beaches of Normandy, France, and soon spread throughout the country. In August, Paris was liberated from German control, and in September the Allied Powers crossed the German border, forcing Germany's surrender.

The Allies turned their attention to the Pacific. By this time, Japan had captured Guam, Wake Island, Hong Kong, Singapore, Java, and the Philippines in addition to maintaining its stronghold in China.

The Pacific was primarily an American concern and therefore an American responsibility. In an unprecedented action, Harry S Truman, Roosevelt's successor, gave the go-ahead to drop the atomic bomb on the city of Hiroshima. It devastated the city, killing almost 80,000 people. The after-effects of nuclear warfare were just beginning to become fully measurable when a second bomb was dropped at Nagasaki. On September 2, 1945, Japan surrendered.

As a result of World War II, the United Nations was formed. The purpose of the organization is to arbitrate international disputes in an effort to maintain world peace.

Exercise 25: The World at War

Directions: Write *T* in the space if the statement is true, *F* if it is false.

_____ 1. Territorial aggression by the Axis Powers was the leading cause of World War II.

_____ 2. The Axis Powers were Great Britain, France, and the U.S.

_____ 3. Japan's bombing of Pearl Harbor ended the United States's neutrality.

_____ 4. The U.S. did not use negotiation to avoid war with Japan.

_____ 5. The United Nations is a league of nations determined to defend its members in the face of war.

Exercise 26: World War II

Directions: Choose the best answer for each statement or question below.

Question 1 is based on the brief passage below:

Two days after Japan attacked Pearl Harbor, FDR made the following statement: "In the past few years and most violently in the past few days, we have learned a terrible lesson. We must begin the great task that is before us by abandoning once and for all the illusion that we can ever again isolate ourselves from the rest of humanity."

1. In the above statement, Roosevelt is expressing the ideas of

    (1) an isolationist.
    (2) an imperialist.
    (3) a jingoist.
    (4) an internationalist.
    (5) an anti-imperialist.

Questions 2 and 3 are based on the passage below:

"The S.S. had given the order to destroy us and burn the camp. April 11, 1945: We were to be shot at 3 P.M.; the British arrived at 11 A.M."
The writer of these words, Fania Fenelon, was a survivor of the German concentration camp at Auschwitz-Birknenau. She was one of the lucky European Jews of World War II. Six million others were slaughtered by the Nazis for no other reason than that they were Jewish and thus considered to be racially inferior to Germans. The dimensions of this Holocaust were not fully understood until after the invasion of Germany by the Allied forces. The shock waves caused by such a revelation of man's inhumanity to man are still being felt today.

2. The above passage describes which belief of the Germans taken to the extreme?

    (1) isolationism
    (2) imperialism
    (3) progressivism
    (4) jingoism
    (5) racism

3. The author of this piece exhibits which of the following?

    (1) racism
    (2) humanitarianism
    (3) nationalism
    (4) sectionalism
    (5) materialism

Writing Activity 6

Was President Truman justified in permitting the hydrogen bomb to be dropped on Hiroshima? Some believe that his action was justified because it saved American lives. Others maintain that the massive civilian casualties and the use of nuclear weapons can never be justified. Write two or three paragraphs defending your position.

ANSWERS AND EXPLANATIONS START ON PAGE 295.

The Atomic Age

The Truman Era

> ### Key Words
>
> *Cold War*—the term applied to the breakdown in U.S./Soviet relations fueled by the threat of nuclear war
> *communism*—a system of government in which the state owns the means of production and personal liberties are severely restricted

While relations with Germany and Japan improved as the 1940s waned, President Truman quickly saw that alliances with the communist Soviet Union were deteriorating.

The Soviets' goal to become a world power became apparent as they established footholds in such eastern European countries as Poland, Czechoslovakia, and Rumania.

The perceived threat to take over Greece and Turkey, however, led to the historic Truman Doctrine in which Truman announced to the world that the United States would support free peoples who resist attempted control by armed minorities or outside pressures. Thus, a U.S. policy on containment of communism was put into words, and Truman granted military and economic aid to those European countries he believed to be threatened by Soviet domination.

By 1951, the Marshall Plan, proposed by Secretary of State George C. Marshall, was adopted to help western European countries resist Soviet oppression.

In response, the Soviets tried to force the Western powers out of Berlin by blockading the city. The West circumvented the blockade. After its success, in 1949, the U.S., Britain, France, Italy, Belgium, the Netherlands, Denmark, Norway, Portugal, Luxembourg, Ireland, and Canada formed the North Atlantic Treaty Organization (NATO), an alliance of nations that promised to unite in defense if one of its member nations was attacked. The U.S. took immediate steps to build up its military strength. The Cold War between the U.S. and the Soviet Union had begun.

Though Truman led the country through perilous times in foreign policy, he was not favored to win the 1948 election. But to the amazement of the political pundits, he defeated his opponent, Thomas Dewey, in one of the narrowest victories in American presidential politics.

Exercise 27: The Truman Era

Directions: Place a check mark before each modern-day situation below that represents an attempt to enforce the principles of the Truman Doctrine.

_____ (1) the sending of American troops to prevent communist takeover of South Vietnam

_____ (2) the providing of weapons to Afghanistan enabling it to protect itself against Soviet domination

_____ (3) the American blockade of Cuba to prevent ships of its ally, the Soviet Union, from entering the Western Hemisphere

_____ (4) the ordering of American troops into South Korea to repel the advances of communist North Korea

_____ (5) the U.S.'s pressure on Baby Doc Duvalier to leave Haiti

ANSWER AND EXPLANATION STARTS ON PAGE 295.

The Korean War

The Korean War was the world's first example of a Cold War that heated up. The thirty-eighth parallel had been set after World War II as the dividing line between U.S. and Soviet interests in Korea. By 1949, the U.S. had helped establish the Republic of South Korea and withdrawn from the country.

At the same time, the Soviet Union set up its own North Korean government and in 1950 sent its troops across the thirty-eighth parallel.

President Truman made the decision to commit U.S. troops to help the South Koreans and also asked for U.N. troop support.

When the UN troops, under General Douglas MacArthur, crossed the thirty-eighth parallel, the Chinese Communist forces drove them back. President Truman, deciding that this was "the wrong war, at the wrong place, at the wrong time, and with the wrong enemy," advised MacArthur to stick to the original objective of regaining South Korea up to the thirty-eighth parallel. When MacArthur publicly advocated an attack on Red China, he was relieved of his command.

As a result of the Korean War, a communist "witchhunt" and blacklisting began with the case of Alger Hiss, a former State Department official accused of espionage. This was followed by an accusation by a little-known senator from Wisconsin, Joseph R. McCarthy, that many communists were employed by the State Department. Though his charge was unfounded, the atmosphere of fear created by the Korean conflict allowed him to carry his crusade to extremes.

President Truman declared, "Liberty can be endangered by the 'Right' as well as by the 'Left'." Nonetheless, the Korean conflict, the question of communism, and the suspicion of corruption within the administration forced him to withdraw from consideration as a 1952 candidate for president.

The Eisenhower Years

The voters chose World War II hero General Dwight D. Eisenhower as president over Democrat Adlai E. Stevenson. The United States, under President Eisenhower, signed an armistice ending the Korean War on July 27, 1953. By that time, more than 23,000 Americans had lost their lives in battle. Communism had been contained in Korea, and the strength and authority of the United Nations had met the challenge. However, the Cold War between the United States and the Soviet Union escalated.

During the early years of his administration, Eisenhower believed that communism could be contained only by threats of military retaliation against the Soviet Union. At home, domestic issues demanded attention as inflation rose, driving prices up, and economic growth declined as the country experienced a recession.

Above all other issues, however, loomed the problem of segregation. President Truman had tried to push through a civil rights program in 1948 but was unsuccessful. The NAACP (National Association for the Advancement of Colored People) bypassed the executive and legislative branches and took the issue to the courts. On May 17, 1954, the Supreme Court ruled, in *Brown* v. *the Board of Education*, that "separate educational facilities are inherently unequal." Resistance to this decision climaxed in Little Rock, Arkansas, in 1957 when Eisenhower sent federal troops to the high school to allow black students to enter the building. Subsequently, the Civil Rights Act of 1957 established the Civil Rights Commission to investigate disturbances in voting rights on the basis of race, color, national origin, or religion.

Traumatic as the civil rights conflicts were, however, other events signaled the end of the Eisenhower Era. Relations with nations like Japan and Venezuela reached such a low that American leaders were warned not to visit. The Battista regime in Cuba was overthrown in 1958 and 1959, and Fidel Castro came to power. Scandals in the highly regarded administration became known to the shocked public. Voters were ready for a change.

★ **GED PRACTICE** ★

Exercise 28: The Eisenhower Years

Directions: Choose the *one* best answer for each statement or question below.

1. The undeclared war in Korea most closely resembled the situation in

    (1) World War I.
    (2) World War II.
    (3) the Spanish-American War.
    (4) the Vietnam War.
    (5) the Civil War.

2. The *Brown* v. *Board of Education* decision is significant today because

    (1) it sanctioned segregated schools.
    (2) it allowed Eisenhower to send troops to Little Rock.
    (3) it serves as the legal basis for school busing to achieve desegregation in some cities.
    (4) it permitted blacks to attend private schools.
    (5) it helped to increase Eisenhower's personal popularity.

3. Which of the following hypotheses best explains Dwight Eisenhower's great popularity?

    (1) He was a war hero who represented American strength.
    (2) He established the Civil Rights Commission.
    (3) His policies started a recession.
    (4) His administration was free of scandal.
    (5) He defeated Adlai Stevenson for the presidency.

ANSWERS AND EXPLANATIONS START ON PAGE 296.

The New Frontier

John F. Kennedy, the youngest man and the first Roman Catholic to be elected president, was indeed a change for the country. No president since Roosevelt had so roused the country with his enthusiasm, vigor, and idealism.

Kennedy's challenge to the nation is best summed up by the quote delivered at his inauguration: "Ask not what your country can do for you, ask what you can do for your country."

Youth rallied to his call by joining his newly established Peace Corps. He declared war against poverty, illiteracy, and ill health among the nation's poor and elderly. The space program added excitement to this period as the Mercury Seven astronauts ushered in the era of manned space flights. Thus, the rivalry between the U.S. and the Soviet Union shifted to another arena.

The situation in Vietnam became increasingly troublesome, and JFK sent military advisors there in 1961. These advisors sent home glowing reports of American successes, but these proved later to be untrue. By 1963, the tiny Asian country was in turmoil.

In April of 1961, tensions between the United States and Cuba worsened as Cuba, under communist leadership, developed friendly relations with the Soviets. In October of 1962, President Kennedy quarantined the waters around Cuba to prevent Soviet shipments of nuclear missiles to Cuba. He demanded the dismantling of the missile site already established and the removal of the missiles, warning that any attack on the U.S. from Cuba would be considered a Soviet attack. After a week of international tension, Moscow removed the bases and missiles.

During the Kennedy years, executive action toward guaranteeing civil rights that began during the Eisenhower era continued. In 1962 the President sent federal troops to protect the right of James Meredith, a black student, to attend the University of Mississippi. A Civil Rights Commission, which was appointed in 1963, found that the citizenship of blacks was seriously hampered in the U.S. by the illegal denial of the right to vote. The same year Dr. Martin Luther King, Jr., led a series of nonviolent protests through the South, culminating in the march on Washington that August.

Legislation to support blacks was to be the triumph of a different president, however, as was legislation providing for Medicare, aid to education, and other social programs. On November 22, 1963, John Fitzgerald Kennedy was killed in downtown Dallas, Texas, by a sniper's bullet. Americans eventually would recover from the shock, but the country had lost the innocence and the youthful optimism that the Kennedy years had brought.

★ GED PRACTICE ★

Exercise 29: The New Frontier

Directions: Choose the best conclusion for each of the following statements.

1. The Kennedy administration was characterized by

   (1) a return to conservative politics.
   (2) growing commitments at home and abroad.
   (3) a loss of national optimism and idealism.
   (4) illegal denial of the vote to black Americans.
   (5) the passing of legislation to provide medicare to the elderly.

2. From reading the passage "The New Frontier," it may be assumed that

   (1) the Soviet Union sought to control Cuba.
   (2) the Soviet Union planned an attack on the U.S. from Cuba.
   (3) Cuba and the U.S. enjoyed friendly relations.
   (4) Cuba, a communist nation, was an ally of the Soviet Union.
   (5) Cuba planned to attack the U.S.

 ## Writing Activity 7

Was President Kennedy justified in quarantining the waters around Cuba? Why or why not? Defend your position in two or three paragraphs.

ANSWERS AND EXPLANATIONS START ON PAGE 296.

The Great Society

Lyndon Baines Johnson had quite an act to follow, but he pursued the course of fulfilling his predecessor's dreams. LBJ was a skillful politician and legislator whose influence pushed bills through Congress in numbers that had not been seen since the New Deal.

The Economic Opportunity Act of 1964 was the chief weapon in the "war on poverty" envisioned by Truman, reformulated by Kennedy, and finally carried out by Johnson.

The war on poverty was directed toward urban areas where most Americans then lived. A "head start" program provided early education to urban preschoolers, a Job Corps helped high school dropouts, Upward Bound brought bright but poor youth to college, and VISTA (Volunteers in Service to America) connected energetic middle-class workers with the cities' poor.

The Civil Rights Act of 1964, Johnson's most noteworthy achievement, forbade racial discrimination in circumstances where federal funds were used. Johnson also established the Equal Employment Opportunity Commission.

In 1965, voting rights were enhanced by law, federal aid to education and Medicare were enacted, immigration laws were liberalized, and the National Foundation on the Arts and Humanities Act was passed.

In foreign policy, Johnson was not so successful. Decisions on action in Latin America undid all the trust-building so carefully constructed by Roosevelt's Good Neighbor policies and Kennedy's Alliance for Progress. And the Vietnam War, an inherited problem, was escalated in 1965.

In that year, American combat troops were committed for the first time, and by 1967 the number of soldiers there reached half a million. The administration justified the action as a response to the larger threat of the spread of Chinese communism. Critics argued that the war was essentially a civil war in which outsiders did not belong. As a result of the winless war in Vietnam, Lyndon Johnson chose not to seek reelection in 1968, and his former vice president, Hubert Humphrey, lost to Republican Richard Nixon.

★ GED PRACTICE ★

Exercise 30: The Great Society

Directions: Choose the *one* best answer for each statement or question below.

1. According to the passage, President Johnson's chief contribution to society was

    (1) the active pursuit of world peace.
    (2) a commitment to social justice for blacks and the disadvantaged.
    (3) the successful containment of communism throughout the world.
    (4) the attainment of economic prosperity for all Americans.
    (5) the withdrawal of troops from Vietnam.

    Questions 2 and 3 are based on the passage below.

By 1967 over 10,000 young Americans had died in the small land so far away, and they had died for a cause that no one seemed to understand. In the midst of great poverty and problems at home, $20 billion had been spent on the unpopular war in 1967 alone.

In ever-increasing numbers, senators, statesmen, and citizens opposed U.S. involvement in the war. Protest marches, demonstrations, sit-ins, and love-ins continued through the sixties and into the seventies.

"Make love, not war" became a favorite slogan of American youth. The thoughtful criticism of the Kennedy years had soured into an open confrontation between generations and a complete disaffection with modern American society. Experimentation with drugs, attraction to hard rock music, and exploration of mystical religion were some of the ways in which American youth reacted against the Vietnam War.

2. The purpose of the passage is to

(1) defend American involvement in Vietnam.
(2) compare the nation's mood under the Kennedy and Johnson administrations.
(3) pay tribute to those who died in the Vietnam War.
(4) explain why the war was unpopular.
(5) show how an unpopular war disrupted American society.

3. Which of the following statements is best supported by the evidence in the passage above?

(1) The Vietnam War was the most unpopular and expensive war America ever fought.
(2) The American government should not have wasted money and lives in Vietnam.
(3) Most elected officials were afraid to speak out against the war lest they lose their jobs.
(4) The Vietnam War had repercussions that went well beyond Vietnam itself.
(5) America's purpose in Vietnam was clear and well supported by the American people.

ANSWERS AND EXPLANATIONS START ON PAGE 296.

The Nixon Era

The Vietnam War was still extremely unpopular in the U.S. when President Richard Nixon took office. His ordering of troops into Cambodia and other military moves did not help his personal popularity. But he did gradually withdraw troops and negotiated a pullout by the end of March 1973. It was not a victory, but the war was over after two decades of U.S. military and monetary support, the loss of 56,000 young American lives, and the deaths of hundreds of thousands of Vietnamese, Cambodians, and Laotians.

Riding the crest of popularity after the Vietnam pullout, Nixon was at the peak of his political career. *Détente*—the easing of tensions between nations—with the Soviet Union was more successful than it had ever been. Friendly relations with the communist People's Republic of China had been established for the first time in many years, and President Nixon visited there in 1972. In the Middle East, the U.S. had become a major peace-keeping influence. Four vacant Supreme Court slots had been filled by Nixon with justices who held his conservative philosophy.

Nixon won the election with one of the largest margins in modern history. But the illegal break-in of the Democratic National Committee Headquarters at the Watergate Hotel in June of 1972 and the subsequent attempt at a cover-up forced him from office in August 1974. Thus, former president Richard Nixon became the only U.S. president to have resigned from office to escape impeachment. Vice President Gerald Ford succeeded Nixon and finished his term. In his reelection bid, Ford lost to Democrat Jimmy Carter in 1976.

★ **GED PRACTICE** ★

Exercise 31: Nixon and Watergate

Directions: Choose the *one* best answer for each question below.

1. Of President Nixon's foreign policy initiatives, for which will history likely credit him most?

   (1) the ordering of troops into Cambodia
   (2) negotiating peace in the Middle East
   (3) reestablishing relations with the People's Republic of China
   (4) the bombing of Hanoi to end the war
   (5) ending the Cold War with Russia

2. Which of the following opinions is best supported by the evidence presented in the passage, "Nixon and Watergate"?

   (1) Political spying is a common practice in American politics.
   (2) Nixon's military strategy brought about victory in Vietnam.
   (3) Nixon's aides broke the law for the good of the country.
   (4) A serious character flaw cost Nixon the presidency.
   (5) The president of the United States is not above the law.

ANSWERS AND EXPLANATIONS START ON PAGE 296.

Closing the Twentieth Century

Carter and the Middle East

The nation's distrust of Washington government officials created a thirst for honest leadership. The American people found it in a little-known peanut farmer from Georgia, James Earl (Jimmy) Carter, who ran on an anti-Washington platform.

Jimmy Carter had been a successful governor of Georgia from 1971 to 1975, but he was virtually unknown nationally when he won the presidency in 1976. He had used his obscurity to an advantage in the years when the American people were wary of politicians. He promised decency, honesty, and humanitarianism in Washington, and voters welcomed his smiling face and small-town handshake.

He was not so welcome in Washington, however. He surrounded himself with Georgia friends. He advocated restraint in the use of natural resources, emphasis on education for personal and national betterment, and the safeguard of human rights and peace throughout the world. He was also a driving force in establishing full diplomatic relations with mainland China, concluding a second SALT (Strategic Arms Limitation Talks) treaty with the Soviet Union, relinquishing U.S. control of the Panama Canal, and framing a peace treaty between Egypt and Israel.

Carter was less successful with his domestic policy, however. He could not reform the nation's tax structure or simplify the unwieldy federal civil service system. He was also unable to quell the raging inflation rates.

Carter's biggest disappointment, however, was his frustrated attempts to bring fifty-two American hostages home from Iran. These foreign service employees were seized at the American Embassy in Iran on November 4, 1979, to punish the U.S. welcoming for the exiled shah of Iran. After 444 days, the hostages were released on January 20, 1981—the day Ronald Reagan took his oath of office.

Reagan and the New Conservatism

At the age of sixty-nine, Ronald Reagan was the oldest man to be elected president of the United States. Reagan was a conservative Republican who had twice served as governor of California.

Ronald Reagan won the election against Carter on the platform of making America strong again and improving the inflation-wracked economy.

Under the Reagan administration, conservatism became a national drive in many areas of American life. The Democratic spending policies of the sixties were blamed for the predicament of the American economy. To reduce federal spending, President Reagan cut many of the social programs implemented during the sixties. The "Reagan Revolution" soon became as well known for cutting social programs as Roosevelt's New Deal had been for establishing them.

American foreign policy focused on anticommunism as the administration supported the efforts of anticommunists in El Salvador, Nicaragua, and elsewhere throughout the world.

Bush and the "New World Order"

Vice president under Ronald Reagan for eight years, George Bush was elected president in 1988. Bush promised to carry on many of Reagan's conservative policies and made a "no new taxes" campaign pledge that later proved impossible to keep.

Bush became known as a "foreign-relations president." It was during his administration that communism collapsed in Eastern Europe (in 1989) and in the Soviet Union (in 1991), giving rise to Bush's phrase "a new world order." The apparent end to the Soviet empire forced the United States to rethink its Cold War policies.

Foreign relations again became paramount during the 1990–1991 crisis in the Persian Gulf, when Iraq's Saddam Hussein invaded neighboring Kuwait. Along with the United Nations, the United States used economic sanctions and then military force to oust Iraqi troops from Kuwait. The ground war, known as Operation Desert Storm, lasted a mere 100 hours—from February 23 to February 27, 1991. Hussein's troops were overthrown, although Hussein himself remained in power in Iraq. During the Persian Gulf War, President Bush's popularity was at an all-time high.

Economic troubles in the United States soon affected Bush's public approval rating, however. As the economy dipped into recession in the early 1990s, the public perceived Bush's attention to foreign affairs as a neglect of domestic problems. The deepening recession seemed to defy attempts to resuscitate the economy and became a major issue in the 1992 presidential campaign.

★ **GED PRACTICE** ★

Exercise 32: Closing the Twentieth Century

Directions: Choose the best answer for the questions below.

1. For which of the following actions will Jimmy Carter probably be remembered most favorably?

    (1) formally recognizing the African nation of Zimbabwe
    (2) establishing a friendship with the shah of Iran, who was accused of human rights violations by his people
    (3) negotiating for peace between Egypt and Israel
    (4) providing support for Nicaraguan dictator Anastasio Somoza Debayle during a bloody civil war against him
    (5) failing to gain the release of the fifty-two American hostages from Iran

2. Which of the following actions exemplifies the main thrust of Reagan's foreign policy?

    (1) giving aid to anticommunist rebels in Nicaragua, Angola, and Afghanistan
    (2) setting up summit talks with Soviet leader Mikhail Gorbachev
    (3) refusing to intervene in the Philippines' election of 1986 between dictator Ferdinand Marcos and his opponent, Corazon Aquino
    (4) helping dictator Jean-Claude "Baby Doc" Duvalier to flee from Haiti
    (5) initiating the "Star Wars" strategic defense system

3. Which of the following statements is best supported by the evidence in the passage about Bush?

    (1) The public should not blame the president for economic problems.
    (2) The president should not react to public opinion polls.
    (3) The performance of the economy has a major effect on the president's popularity.
    (4) The president should focus on domestic issues first.
    (5) Breaking a campaign promise will hurt the president's approval rating.

ANSWERS AND EXPLANATIONS START ON PAGE 296.

6 POLITICAL SCIENCE

"Man is by nature a political animal," said Aristotle over two thousand years ago, and it is just as true today. As long as humans feel the need to live in groups, organization will be necessary for order and efficiency. Organization requires formal rules. Rules determine the basis for forms of government.

The form of government a society adopts has to fit the needs of its people, or it will not last long. Many different types of government have been tried throughout civilization. **Political scientists** study the different forms of government and the process by which governments operate.

Types of Government

Key Words

democracy—a system of government in which "the will of the majority" rules; citizens elect representatives in free elections

dictatorship—a system of government in which one person has absolute authority to govern

monarchy—a system of government in which a single person rules by inherited power

oligarchy—a system of government in which a small group of people exercise total control

The Monarchy

A king or queen is at the head of government in a monarchy. If his or her position is severely limited by a constitution or other system of laws, it is called a **constitutional monarchy**, as exists in Great Britain today.

A ruler who has the absolute and final say in governmental decision-making is called an **absolute monarch**, a rarity today. In the past, many absolute monarchs claimed their authority was bestowed upon them by God. This belief was called the doctrine of **Divine Right**.

In either case, the monarch rules for life and passes the power to someone within his or her family, usually the oldest male child.

The Democracy

The leader of a democracy is elected by the people that he or she directs. All power to govern comes from the people, and decisions must meet their approval. The equality of all citizens is a principle that forms the basis of a democratic government, too.

Often, when a democracy is established within a country that once had been governed by a monarch, the new government is structured as a **parliamentary democracy**. In a parliamentary democracy, an elected legislature, a cabinet of executives, and a prime minister replace the absolute power of the king or queen. The king or queen maintains ceremonial authority as head of state and is considered to be a figurehead.

Most democracies today are representative, not direct or pure democracies. Only nations or states with very small populations can let *all* the citizens make *all* the decisions. For this reason, a nation with over 260 million people like the United States must function as a representative democracy in which we elect others to represent us.

Dictatorship

In a dictatorship, only one person has total control of the government. For this reason, it is often called a **totalitarian government**. Total control means the complete domination of the citizens' lives as well as the sole power to govern. The most basic of citizens' rights are taken away in order to guarantee absolute authority to one person. Revolution is often the means by which a dictatorship begins and ends.

Oligarchy

Though in *theory* communist countries are governed by the workers, or **proletariat**, in *practice* they are governed by a few party leaders. Such a "government by few" is called an oligarchy and is similar to a dictatorship in that government officials are not elected and often come to power after a revolution.

Exercise 1: Types of Government

Directions: In the space provided, write *M* if the situation describes a monarchy, *DE* if it describes a democracy, *DI* if it describes a dictatorship, and *O* if it describes an oligarchy.

_____ 1. The People's Republic of China claims that this system is most efficient and fair, since decisions are made by a few top men in the government's only political party.

_____ 2. This system works well for the tiny kingdom of Tonga because it retains respect and power for a ruler who inherited his throne by the will of the gods.

_____ 3. King John of England and his predecessors ruled by this system for many generations before the Magna Carta changed it to more democratic ways.

_____ 4. Canada patterns its system after the British one, with a prime minister who heads a cabinet and an elected parliament.

_____ 5. Generalissimo Franco used this system because it gave him absolute control over the country of Spain after a bloody takeover.

ANSWERS AND EXPLANATIONS START ON PAGE 297.

Blueprint for a New Nation

A Separation of Powers

Key Words

federalism—a system of government in which the states yield supreme authority to a central government

republic—a government in which voting citizens delegate to elected representatives the authority to govern

The U.S. Constitution is the "law of the land," or the base upon which all laws in the United States rest. It is the oldest written constitution in existence, and republics throughout the world have modeled their own constitutions after it.

The U.S. Constitution is based on the principle of federalism. It provides for a central government made up of three branches: the **legislative,** which *makes* the laws; the **executive,** which *carries out* the laws; and the **judicial**, which *interprets* the laws.

This separation of powers was proposed to keep each center of power in check and to prevent the abuses that the former colonies experienced under British rule.

The Legislative Branch: Maker of Laws

Article One of the Constitution concerns the legislative branch of the national government. The legislative branch, called **Congress**, is comprised of two houses: the House of Representatives and the Senate.

In the **House of Representatives**, each state's number of representatives is based on its population; in the **Senate**, each state is equally represented with two senators each.

Representatives are chosen by popular election and serve for two years. Senators are chosen by popular election also, although under the original constitution they were chosen by the state legislatures. Senators serve six-year terms.

Some of the important powers of Congress are:

- to levy and collect taxes
- to borrow money
- to regulate commerce
- to coin money
- to declare war

- to approve presidential appointments
- to provide and maintain an army and navy
- to ratify treaties—Senate only
- to impeach the president—House only
- to admit new states to the union

In addition to the powers of Congress that are stated specifically, the framers of the Constitution allowed for powers not spelled out. The **elastic clause** allows the legislative branch to make all laws "necessary and proper" to execute the powers granted by the Constitution. This clause enables Congress to stretch its authority to meet the needs of a changing nation without having to go through the laborious process of amending the Constitution.

Exercise 2: Making Laws

Directions: Based on the reading above, write *C* in the space if the action listed below is an example of a power stated in the U.S. Constitution. Write *E* in the space if it is an example of an application of the elastic clause that gives Congress certain necessary and proper powers.

_____ **(1)**   Congress declared war on Japan in 1941.

_____ **(2)**   The Senate approved Nixon's appointment of John Mitchell as attorney general in 1969.

_____ **(3)**   Congress established the United States Air Force in 1947.

_____ **(4)**   The House of Representatives impeached Andrew Johnson in 1868.

_____ **(5)**   In 1986, Congress enacted the law moving the beginning of Daylight Savings Time from the last Sunday in April to the first Sunday in April.

_____ **(6)**   Congress approved economic sanctions against the apartheid regime of South Africa.

_____ **(7)**   Congress annexed Alaska as the forty-ninth state of the Union.

_____ **(8)**   Congress raised the amount of money allocated to pay soldiers.

Exercise 3: The Legislative Branch ———————

Directions: Based on the facts and the definition of gerrymandering below, check off logical conclusions that could be drawn from the map of three congressional districts in suburban Chicago.

Gerrymandering takes place when the political party in power redraws congressional district boundaries to its advantage and to the disadvantage of the opposing party. To prevent this political abuse, the Supreme Court ruled (in the case of *Baker* v. *Carr* in 1962) that redrawn legislative districts must be kept as proportional to population as possible.

Congressional District Map of Northeastern Illinois

9th Congressional District

11th Congressional District

CHICAGO

4th Congressional District

_____ **(1)** The 9th Congressional District is the most densely populated of the three districts shown on the map.

_____ **(2)** Suburban districts are more politically desirable than urban districts.

_____ **(3)** If these districts had been drawn to equalize land area, population apportionment would not have been fair.

_____ **(4)** The 4th Congressional District has more voters from the political party in power than the other two districts shown.

_____ **(5)** The 9th Congressional District is too small.

ANSWERS AND EXPLANATIONS START ON PAGE 297.

The Executive Branch: Enforcer of the Laws

Key Words

electoral college—a body of electors who elect the president and vice president of the United States

precedent—an earlier action that serves as a justification for a later action

---

Most Americans believe they are electing the president and vice president when they cast their vote on election day, but they are not! The electoral college officially proclaims the president and vice president the December *after* the actual election. The Founding Fathers apparently had little confidence in the voting populace's ability to choose the holders of the highest office in the land, so they established the electoral college to certify the results of the popular election.

The candidates for president and vice president who receive a majority of the popular vote for a state almost always receive the state's electoral votes. However, in two instances in U.S. history candidates have received the majority of the popular vote but lost the election because of the electoral vote. This occurred in the elections of 1876 and 1888. Rutherford B. Hayes was chosen president in 1876 despite the fact that his opponent, Samuel Tilden, received the majority of the popular votes. And in 1888, although Grover Cleveland won the popular vote, Benjamin Harrison was chosen president by the electoral vote.

The president serves for four years and may serve a maximum of two terms as provided by the Twenty-second Amendment to the Constitution. The vice president also is elected for four years and serves if the president is unable to carry out the term.

As outlined in Section Two of the U.S. Constitution, the president:

- is commander-in-chief of the armed forces.

- has power to grant reprieves and pardons for offenses against the United States.

- has power to make treaties.

- may appoint judges to the U.S. Supreme Court and ambassadors.

- may nominate and appoint major executive officers.

- may veto bills sent by Congress.

In executing the nation's laws, presidents have often established precedents not specifically provided for in the Constitution. This exercise of implied powers was described in the "U.S. History" section of this book. In the example on page 108, President Jefferson entered into the Louisiana Purchase even though such an initiative was not written specifically into the Constitution. Other cases involving the establishment of a precedent based on the use of implied powers include:

- George Washington's setting up a cabinet of advisors

- James Polk's ordering U.S. troops into action before Congress had declared war against Mexico

- Abraham Lincoln's acting to free the slaves during the Civil War
- Theodore Roosevelt's mediating labor and international disputes

Thus, with each new president, the office changed to suit the personality and priorities of the man.

★ **GED PRACTICE** ★

Exercise 4: The Executive Branch

Directions: Read each paragraph below. Circle the letter of the choice that best completes each statement.

1. The Constitution originally specified that the president's term would be for four years, but it did not specify how many terms a president could serve. Until FDR's administration, each president followed Washington's example and stepped down after completing two terms. Doing something because a previous president did it is known as following a presidential

    (1) proclamation.
    (2) pardon.
    (3) precedent.
    (4) amendment.
    (5) priority.

2. Under the Kennedy and Johnson administrations, the executive branch of the government underwent an increase in the number of bureaucratic agencies. Based upon what you have read in the "U.S. History" section, this increase in the number of agencies was probably due to a precedent set by President

    (1) George Washington.
    (2) Harry S Truman.
    (3) Franklin Roosevelt.
    (4) Theodore Roosevelt.
    (5) Grover Cleveland.

Exercise 5: Setting Precedents

Directions: Match the presidential precedent shown on the left with the subsequent action of a later president shown on the right by writing the correct letter in the space provided.

Presidential Precedent

Subsequent Action

_____ 1. Polk's activation of troops in Mexico without waiting for Congress to declare war

(a) Carter's role in the Camp David accords between Egypt and Israel

_____ 2. Lincoln's expansion of executive power during a national emergency

(b) Johnson's military buildup in the undeclared Vietnam war

_____ 3. Teddy Roosevelt's mediation between two other disputing countries

(c) FDR's establishment of agencies during the Depression and World War II

Exercise 6: The Enforcer of Laws

Directions: Based on the information below, choose the one answer that best answers the question.

"Strong" presidents have been described as dominating the legislative branch and making the office of the presidency self-directing. "Weak" presidents have made the office more reliant on and subordinate to the legislature. Which of the following early presidents best fits the description of a "strong" president?

(1) President Madison, a statesman who declared war on Britain in 1812 only after popular demand called for it.
(2) President John Adams, who believed that the governing representatives should be "the rich, the well-born, and the able."
(3) President Thomas Jefferson, who opposed the Louisiana Purchase and the First Bank of the United States on the grounds that the Constitution did not provide for it.
(4) President James Monroe, who advanced the idea of the Monroe Doctrine on the advice of his secretary of state John Quincy Adams.
(5) President Andrew Jackson, who made unprecedented use of his veto power and who relied little on Congress and his cabinet in making his decisions.

Writing Activity 1

Should the president and vice president of the United States be elected by direct popular vote or by the electoral college system as is currently the case? Write one to two paragraphs defending your point of view.

ANSWERS AND EXPLANATIONS START ON PAGE 297.

The Judicial Branch: Interpreter of the Laws

Key Word

judicial review—the ability to decide on the constitutionality of a law

---

That the U.S. Constitution is a living document can be proven by the performance of the Supreme Court, which can and does reverse itself. You read in an earlier section of this book that the Supreme Court, in 1896, ruled that separate but equal facilities for blacks in the South were correct and legal. In 1954, however, the court reversed the earlier decision and ruled the opposite. This action by the court illustrates how this branch of government changes with the times.

Article Three of the Constitution describes the Supreme Court. The function of the Supreme Court is to decide whether or not certain laws are in keeping with the spirit of the Constitution. This ability to decide on the constitutionality of a law is called judicial review.

The Supreme Court is composed of nine justices appointed for life by the president. The head of the Supreme Court is called the *chief justice*.

The federal court system consists of the Supreme Court, eleven Circuit Courts of Appeal scattered throughout the country, and approximately ninety federal District Courts. In addition to the federal system of courts, each state has its own system. The diagram below illustrates the organization of the federal court system.

FEDERAL COURT SYSTEM

Supreme Court → court of final appeal

Circuit Courts of Appeal (11) → court that reviews decisions of district court

District Courts (90) → court in which case is first heard

Some of the powers vested in the Supreme Court are the powers to:

- rule on cases involving a state and citizens of another state
- rule on controversies between two or more states
- rule on cases between citizens of different states
- rule on cases between a state and a foreign state

The Supreme Court does not have the last word on all legal cases in the country. Only when a provision of the Constitution, an act of Congress, or a right guaranteed by federal law is involved does the Supreme Court have the authority to rule on a state court's decision. Appellate (appeals) courts' cases are reviewed only when they involve the national interest.

★ GED PRACTICE ★

Exercise 7: Interpreting Laws

Directions: Listed below are five landmark Supreme Court decisions made in the last thirty-five years. Read the decisions and answer the questions that follow.

Brown v. *Board of Education*, 1954, held that separate facilities for the races were not equal and therefore were unconstitutional.

New York Times Co. v. *Sullivan*, 1964, guaranteed that freedom of the press protected a newspaper from liability for defamation of a public official if it did not do so knowingly or recklessly.

Miranda v. *Arizona*, 1966, ruled that a person under arrest must be informed of his rights as an accused criminal, or any resulting confession would be invalid.

Roe v. *Wade*, 1973, stated that states could not prohibit abortion under certain conditions during the first six months of a pregnancy.

Rights of the University of California v. *Allan Bakke*, 1978, decided that reverse discrimination took place when a white man was refused entrance to medical school because of a minority quota system.

1. In each of the five landmark decisions described above, the Supreme Court assumed the role of

   (1) checking the powers of Congress.
   (2) checking the power of the president.
   (3) extending Congress's authority.
   (4) defending civil liberties.
   (5) limiting personal freedoms.

2. Which of the decisions listed above had the greatest impact on local law enforcement?

   (1) *Brown* v. *Board of Education*
   (2) *New York Times Co.* v. *Sullivan*
   (3) *Miranda* v. *Arizona*
   (4) *Roe* v. *Wade*
   (5) *Rights of the University of California* v. *Allan Bakke*

 ## Writing Activity 2

One example of a president's use of implied powers is the replacement of retiring Supreme Court justices with judges sympathetic to the appointing president's political views. For example, presidents Reagan and Bush, both conservatives, appointed conservative justices to the Supreme Court to fill vacancies. Do you think it is an abuse of presidential authority to appoint judges who agree with the president's political philosophy? Write two or three paragraphs defending your point of view.

★ **GED PRACTICE** ★

Exercise 8: Separation of Powers

Directions: The five actions of the federal government listed below apply to questions 1 and 2. Read the actions and answer the questions that follow.

Brown v. *the Board of Education* (1954)—Separate educational facilities declared inherently unequal by the Supreme Court

Central High School, Little Rock, Arkansas (1957)—Federal troops sent by the president to escort black students into a previously all-white school

U.S. Commission on Civil Rights (1957)—By authority of the president's office, allowed the U.S. attorney general to enforce voting rights in the states

Civil Rights Act (1964)—Outlawed racial discrimination in public accommodations and by employers, unions, and voting registrars

Voting Rights Acts (1965, 1970)—Stopped the use of literacy tests for voter qualification and gave greater power to the federal government to protect citizens' voting rights

1. Which of the following federal actions was primarily the work of the judicial branch?

   (1) *Brown* v. *the Board of Education* decision
   (2) the dispatch of federal troops to Little Rock High School
   (3) the enforcement of voting rights
   (4) the outlawing of racial discrimination in public accommodations
   (5) the prohibition of literacy tests to qualify people to vote

2. Which of the following federal actions *most directly affected* the voiding of a New York state law requiring voters to be able to write in English?

   (1) the *Brown* v. *the Board of Education* decision
   (2) the dispatch of federal troops to Central High School
   (3) the passage of the Civil Rights Act
   (4) the founding of the U.S. Commission on Civil Rights
   (5) the passage of the Voting Rights Acts

ANSWERS AND EXPLANATIONS START ON PAGE 298.

System of Checks and Balances

Key Words

checks and balances—the term that describes the balance of powers of the legislative, executive, and judicial branches of the U.S. government

veto—the authority of a chief executive to prevent enactment of a bill passed by the legislature

The Founding Fathers understood that the powers of the three branches had to be balanced so that no one center of power dominated the other two. To prevent this from happening, the U.S. Constitution allows the president to refuse approval of (veto) a bill sent to him by Congress.

Congress, however, could still pass the bill into law by a majority vote of its members. This procedure is called *overriding a veto*. Finally, if it is brought to the Supreme Court, the court can still declare the law unconstitutional if the justices feel the law contradicts the principles of the Constitution.

The diagram below shows how a bill is enacted into law.

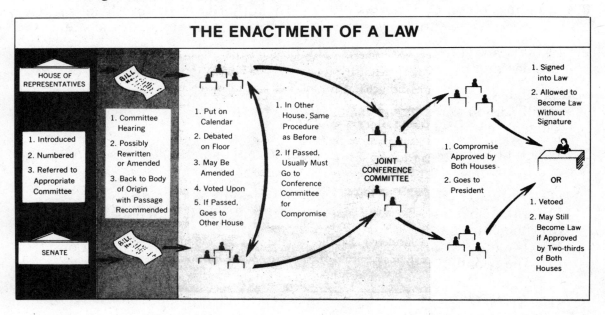

THE ENACTMENT OF A LAW

HOUSE OF REPRESENTATIVES

1. Introduced
2. Numbered
3. Referred to Appropriate Committee

1. Committee Hearing
2. Possibly Rewritten or Amended
3. Back to Body of Origin with Passage Recommended

1. Put on Calendar
2. Debated on Floor
3. May Be Amended
4. Voted Upon
5. If Passed, Goes to Other House

1. In Other House, Same Procedure as Before
2. If Passed, Usually Must Go to Conference Committee for Compromise

JOINT CONFERENCE COMMITTEE

1. Compromise Approved by Both Houses
2. Goes to President

1. Signed into Law
2. Allowed to Become Law Without Signature

OR

1. Vetoed
2. May Still Become Law if Approved by Two-thirds of Both Houses

SENATE

Exercise 9: The Enactment of a Law

Directions: Choose the best answer for the question below.

Which of the statements below is best supported by the chart on page 158?

(1) Bills justified by the elastic clause in the Constitution must be introduced directly by the president.
(2) Before being sent to the president, a bill must be approved in identical form by both houses of Congress.
(3) A filibuster on certain bills may not take place in either house.
(4) A bill introduced in the Senate may be changed by the House, but not the other way around.
(5) The president must sign all bills in order for them to become law.

Exercise 10: System of Checks and Balances

Directions: In column I below, write the branch of government that *exercises* the power described on the left. In column II, write the branch of government that is *checked* by the use of the power. The first one is done for you.

Power	I Who exercises power?	II Who is checked?
1. to appoint federal judges	(a) executive	(b) judicial
2. to impeach the president	(a) _____	(b) _____
3. to approve appointment of judges	(a) _____	(b) _____
4. to override a veto	(a) _____	(b) _____
5. to rule a law unconstitutional	(a) _____	(b) _____
6. to veto a bill	(a) _____	(b) _____

ANSWERS AND EXPLANATIONS START ON PAGE 298.

Amending the Constitution

As pointed out in the section on the judicial branch, the U.S. Constitution is often described as a "living" constitution because of its ability to adapt to changes in American society.

The means by which the Constitution adapts to changes is the amendment process. Article Five describes this two-step process:

1. An amendment first must be proposed by either two-thirds of both houses of Congress or by a national convention requested by the legislatures of two-thirds of the states.

2.   It must be ratified (approved) by three-fourths of the state legislatures.

There are only twenty-six amendments to the U.S. Constitution after more than two hundred years of changes in society. This is not only a credit to the Founding Fathers' farsightedness in writing the original document, but also a testimony to how difficult the amendment process is. The last proposed amendment to follow the procedure outlined above was the Equal Rights Amendment, which was defeated in 1982 because the required majority of state legislatures failed to ratify it.

The Bill of Rights

The first ten amendments to the constitution are called the *Bill of Rights*. The Founding Fathers added these guarantees of personal liberties after it became obvious that the states would not ratify the Constitution without them. The Bill of Rights allayed the fears of those who were afraid that the new government would threaten individual freedoms. The following amendments constitute the Bill of Rights:

1.   guarantees the freedom of religion, speech, the press, and assembly

2.   guarantees the right to belong to a state militia and keep weapons

3.   prohibits the government from housing soldiers in civilian homes without the owners' permission

4.   requires a warrant before property can be searched or seized

5.   guarantees the right to remain silent; establishes a grand jury to hand down indictments for a crime; also safeguards individuals from having to testify against themselves and forbids government seizure of property without compensation

6.   guarantees the right to a trial by jury after being informed of charges against oneself, the right to hear and see witnesses against oneself, and the right to a lawyer

7.   permits the privilege of a jury trial in most lawsuits

8.   forbids excessive bail or cruel and unusual punishment

9.   requires the government to increase the list of personal liberties if necessary

10.   gives the states and the people any rights not specifically denied them by the Constitution

---

★ **GED PRACTICE** ★

Exercise 11: The Bill of Rights

Directions: Choose the one best answer for each question or statement below.

1. When an arresting officer reads an accused man his "rights" and gives him a quarter to make one telephone call, the policeman is referring to which amendments?

   (1) The Seventh and Eighth Amendments
   (2) The First and Second Amendments
   (3) The Fourth and Fifth Amendments
   (4) The Fifth and Sixth Amendments
   (5) The Sixth and Seventh Amendments

2. "Your rights exist as long as they don't affect the well-being of others . . . in other words, you don't have the right to yell 'Fire!' in a packed theater." This quote refers to

   (1) the Tenth Amendment.
   (2) the Second Amendment.
   (3) the First Amendment.
   (4) the Sixth Amendment.
   (5) the Ninth Amendment.

 ## *Writing Activity 3*

In recent years, the First-Amendment right to freedom of the press has been a controversial issue at several universities and high schools across the U.S. Student newspapers have come under attack for printing items considered to be racist, sexist, or intolerant of religious differences. School administrators assert that these ideas contradict the open-minded tenets of their institutions.

   If school administrators take action against the publication of certain articles, are they violating the student journalists' right to freedom of the press? Write two to three paragraphs defending your position.

ANSWERS AND EXPLANATIONS START ON PAGE 299.

The U.S. Political System

Political Parties

Although it has existed for two hundred years, the political party system is not provided for in the U.S. Constitution. Political parties evolved out of necessity and have become an integral part of the American political process. The two major political parties in the United States are the Democrats and the Republicans.

Political parties are beneficial to the American system of government because they:

- help to determine which of a large number of possible candidates will run for office

- help pay for the burdensome costs of the candidates' campaigns

- present the issues and the party's stand on them

The differences between the major political parties have become blurred in recent years. However, over the years, each party has taken a definitive stand on certain issues. The issues often involve economic, social, and foreign policies and form the basis for party loyalty for most Americans.

Voters may change political parties if they feel that the party to which they belong no longer reflects their positions on a number of issues. Although party affiliation in the U.S. is to some extent influenced strongly by ethnic and family heritage, a growing number of voters classify themselves as independents. *Independents* do not follow strict party lines in voting, but consider the candidate's stand on the issues before casting their vote.

Party leaders are responsible for keeping the party platform in line with the thinking of the membership-at-large in order to maintain party loyalty.

Both parties maintain national party headquarters and staffs. A national convention is held every four years to nominate a presidential candidate. The convention participants are delegates from each of the fifty states. A testimony to the control of our political system by two major parties is that only the Democrats and the Republicans have controlled the presidency since 1900.

The chart below shows party control of the presidency from 1900 to 1988.

PARTY OF THE PRESIDENCY
1900–1989

Republican Party

Democratic Party

* 1901 '05 '09 '13 '17 '21 '25 '29 '33 '37 '41 '45 '49 '53 '57 '61 '65 '69 '73 '77 '81 '85 '89

■ In office   □ Out of office

*Dates indicate time from inauguration to expiration of term in office.

Exercise 12: Political Parties

Directions: Answer the following questions based on the chart shown on page 162.

(1) Which party controlled the presidency for the longest continuous stretch of

time? _____

(2) Which party controlled the presidency for the greatest number of terms over the eighty-eight years shown on the graph? (Remember that

presidential terms are four years long.) _____

(3) Which party is in control of the presidency at this time? _____

 ## Writing Activity 4

Do you think a third political party will ever gain control of the U.S. presidency? Write two to three paragraphs explaining why or why not.

ANSWERS AND EXPLANATIONS START ON PAGE 299.

Political Labels

Traditionally, the voting populace has been viewed as holding a range of political positions. These political positions are illustrated below as one of five segments of a continuum. The segments are generally referred to as political labels. The illustration below shows the range of political positions.

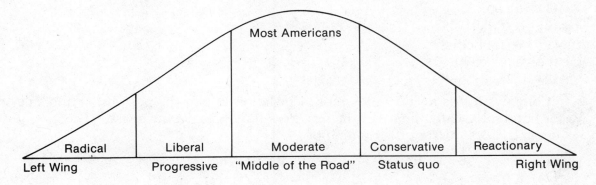

THE POLITICAL CONTINUUM

Most Americans

Radical	Liberal	Moderate	Conservative	Reactionary
Left Wing	Progressive	"Middle of the Road"	Status quo	Right Wing

In order to win an election, each political party must obtain the majority of votes cast. Since the majority of American voters occupy the middle of the continuum, both political parties must appeal to this group of voters to win an election. For this reason, you probably have heard candidates speak about representing "middle America," or you may have heard a candidate described as being a "middle of the roader."

Exercise 13: Political Labels

The five political labels shown in the diagram on page 163 are defined below:

radical: one who advocates sweeping changes in laws and methods of government with the least delay

liberal: one who advocates political change in the name of progress, especially social improvement through governmental action

moderate: one who believes in avoiding extreme changes and measures in laws and government

conservative: one who advocates maintaining the existing social order under a strict interpretation of the Constitution

reactionary: one who resists change and usually advocates a return to an earlier social order or policy

Directions: Read the paragraph below and answer the questions that follow.

A controversial issue that has dominated American life in recent years is gun control. Handguns seem to be increasingly accessible and are one of the leading causes of death in the United States. Americans have varying opinions about crime and handgun control. Read the quotes below and identify them with the correct label.

1. "Everybody should arm himself with a gun like people did in the Old West. Then you wouldn't have to worry about crime in the streets." The speaker is expressing the opinion of

   (1) a radical.
   (2) a liberal.
   (3) a moderate.
   (4) a conservative.
   (5) a reactionary.

2. "Congress needs to introduce more legislation to ban the possession and sale of handguns. Only then will the senseless handgun deaths cease." The speaker is expressing the opinion of

   (1) a radical.
   (2) a liberal.
   (3) a moderate.
   (4) a conservative.
   (5) a reactionary.

3. "The Second Amendment gives American citizens the right to bear arms. To deny this basic right is an infringement on our personal liberties. The law should remain the way it is."

The speaker is expressing the opinion of

(1) a radical.
(2) a liberal.
(3) a moderate.
(4) a conservative.
(5) a reactionary.

ANSWERS AND EXPLANATIONS START ON PAGE 299.

The Impact of the Media

Another significant force in the modern American political process is the media. Television, radio, newspapers, and magazines are all part of the media. But television, by far, has the greatest influence on the American voter. It is estimated that 97 percent of U.S. households own television sets.

Huge sums of campaign money are spent on television commercials each election year as politicians capitalize on the power of this medium.

Sometimes campaigns are won or lost on the basis of a candidate's media campaign. Political observers attribute John Kennedy's 1960 victory over Richard Nixon to the favorable image Kennedy projected on the television screen to voters.

The relationship between the government and the media often is adversarial, but the media serves as a necessary check in our society's system of checks and balances.

Pressure Groups

Key Words

pressure group—an independent organized group that seeks to influence public opinion, policies, and actions
lobbying—conducting activities to influence public officials

Along with the media, pressure groups influence government also. Pressure groups are organized groups, not associated with any political party, which actively seek to influence public opinion, policies, and actions. This attempt to influence legislation is called lobbying.

While members of pressure groups ordinarily do not seek political office they *do* support candidates sympathetic to their causes. Two types of lobbies are economic lobbies and social lobbies. Examples of economic lobbies are trade and professional associations, such as the American Bankers Association, the American Medical Association, and the AFL-CIO. Examples of social lobbies are the

National Education Association, the American Legion, and the National Welfare Rights Organization.

Through advertisements, meetings, mailings, and telephone calls, these pressure groups get their message out to the public and to the government.

Some political influencing is done more directly. For example, Political Action Committees (PACs) contribute to legislators' campaign funds in return for favorable votes on legislation important to the committees. Articles in law journals can also influence judicial decisions about cases. These tactics, however, are not without critics, who believe that such groups ultimately have a negative effect on the political process.

Public opinion is a third political force that affects politics in America. American citizens have unlimited sources of information upon which to form their opinions. These public opinions are the basis for surveys on a variety of topics. The results of these surveys are published in newspapers and magazines and are aired on television. Often, the media take polls, or surveys, of people's opinions on current events. Polls A and B below asked voters whom they would vote for in the election of 1948. The results of the 1948 election are also recorded below.

PUBLIC OPINION POLLS AND 1948 VOTE RESULTS

	Democrats (Truman)	Republicans (Dewey)	Others*
Poll A	44.5%	49.5%	6.0%
Poll B	37.5%	53.0%	9.5%
Actual Vote	49.5%	45.1%	5.4%

*Dixiecrat party and Progressive party candidates

The table above shows how two polls predicted the vote in the 1948 election and the final vote that elected President Truman.

Exercise 14: Public Opinion

Directions: Look at the chart above. Notice that there was a big difference between what the polls predicted and how the 1948 election turned out. Put an *H* in front of each statement that could be a reasonable hypothesis explaining this discrepancy. Since these are hypotheses, or possible explanations, more than one could be true.

_____ **(1)** Many voters changed their minds between the time of the surveys and the time of the election.

_____ **(2)** Dewey supporters were not as committed to him as pollsters were led to believe.

_____ **(3)** Poll A was conducted less scientifically than Poll B.

_____ **(4)** The people doing the surveys did not ask either enough people or the right people.

_____ **(5)** These public opinion polls were done by people in favor of Dewey.

★ **GED PRACTICE** ★

Exercise 15: Public Opinion Polls

Directions: This exercise is based on the passage below. Read the passage and answer the question that follows.

Some people say that public opinion polls should not be taken close to an election because the results might influence the voters. For example, during the 1980 election, the outcome was predicted by television networks before the polls closed. Informal surveys, **exit polls**, were being conducted outside the voting areas and vote percentages for each candidate were projected from them. These exit polls showed candidate Ronald Reagan with a substantial lead over incumbent Jimmy Carter. In fact, former President Carter lost the 1980 election to Ronald Reagan.

Which of the following *best* explains how the televised poll results could have affected the election's outcome?

(1) Carter's supporters who had not yet voted did not bother to when they saw the lopsided results.
(2) When it became known that Carter was trailing Reagan, more of Carter's supporters rushed out to vote than would have otherwise.
(3) Backers of Reagan who had not yet voted did not think it necessary to vote since he was far ahead.
(4) Happy about the obvious victory, Reagan supporters came out in even greater numbers to vote.
(5) Voters who were undecided before finally decided to join the winning team and vote for Reagan.

 ## Writing Activity 5

Do you agree with the television stations' practice of predicting the outcome of an election before all of the votes are cast? Write two to three paragraphs explaining why you agree or disagree with this practice.

ANSWERS AND EXPLANATIONS START ON PAGE 299.

State and Local Governments

State Governments

Unlike the Articles of Confederation, the U.S. Constitution did not provide for state sovereignty. In fact, it spelled out, in Section Ten of Article One, exactly what the states could *not* do. Other prohibitions are stated in amendments to the Constitution. The Constitution prohibits the states from:

- making treaties with other countries
- manufacturing paper money or coins
- giving out titles of nobility
- imposing taxes on imports or exports
- making agreements with other states without federal approval
- waging a war
- taking away privileges and rights of American citizens
- denying life, liberty, or property to anyone without due process
- depriving anyone of the right to vote because of race or sex

Since the Constitution was not specific about the powers of the states, the Supreme Court has played a major role in defining states' rights.

Some of the powers of the states include the establishing of most criminal codes, laws for contracts, and other regulations concerning the operation of business. Property and marriage and divorce laws also are the responsibility of the states, as is public education.

All fifty states have constitutions, and many are based on the U.S. model. Like the U.S. Constitution, they all have a system of checks and balances based on three branches of government: the legislative, executive, and judicial.

The Legislative Branch

Key Words

initiative—a procedure that enables the voters to propose a law and present it to the legislature and other voters for approval

referendum—a procedure that allows the voting public to approve or disapprove of a measure enacted or proposed by the legislature

recall—the procedure of removing a public official by popular vote

---

All but one state (Nebraska) have two-house legislatures. Most even call these legislatures by names similar to those used by the U.S. Congress. Most of their work is done by committee also.

Determining the distribution of state money is one of the most important functions of state legislatures, as this determines the state's spending priorities each year. Much of the revenue that the state takes in comes from taxes it imposes. Some money also is allocated to the states by the federal government.

Since the early citizens of the states feared powerful legislatures, they built into the state governments certain powers held by the voters. These powers serve as checks and balances at the state government level.

An initiative is a type of check in which the people can propose a law and sometimes even get it passed. Another type, a referendum, permits the voters to approve of or reject a law or proposal made by the legislature. In most states the voters can also recall, or remove, an official from office by vote.

The Executive Branch

Key Words

pardon—the excusing of a public offense
reprieve—a delay in punishment of a person convicted of a crime

The chief executive at the state level is the governor. Like the president, the governor has strong veto power. But limits on the governor's power have been carefully set, too.

In some states, either governors cannot succeed themselves or they serve very short terms. In others, the lieutenant governor (the equivalent of a vice president) can be from a different political party and can serve as the loyal opposition. This provides another opportunity to check the power of the executive officer.

The attorney general (the chief law enforcement officer in the state) is sometimes from a different party, too. The attorney general is not always elected by the people, however. Sometimes attorney generals are chosen by the legislature and are often given much power as legal guardians of the states' affairs. In six of the fifty states, this officer is appointed by the governor.

Like a strong president, a strong governor is a leader in proposing legislation, preparing budgets, and influencing public opinion. Governors usually have many departments and agencies under them through which much of the state's work gets done. The governor also commands the state militia (the National Guard), but he has less authority over other law enforcement agencies.

In most states, too, the governor can override a judicial decision by a pardon or a reprieve for a convicted criminal. A pardon is a full release from punishment, as if the crime were never committed. A reprieve is a delay in punishment, but it sometimes gives a lawyer for the accused enough time to gather evidence for a new trial. These powers often give the governor the final word in a state's criminal justice system.

Exercise 16: Powers of State Governments

Directions: Choose the one best answer for each of the following questions.

1. Which of the following would be an action not allowed a state by the Constitution?

   (1) establishing a state income tax
   (2) setting a residency requirement for a person to be allowed to vote
   (3) forbidding a news editor to criticize the governor
   (4) denying a convicted criminal the right to vote
   (5) depriving aliens the right to vote

2. What is the most likely reason that the writers of the U.S. Constitution found it necessary to forbid the states to grant a title of nobility?

   (1) Royal governors had used that power for their own benefit.
   (2) It would make the states more powerful than the federal government.
   (3) It contradicted the principle that "all men are created equal," a corner-stone of our democracy.
   (4) Clear standards had not been set for granting titles.
   (5) The states might become too powerful.

Exercise 17: State vs. Federal Powers

Directions: In the space provided, write *S* if the power belongs to the states, *F* if it belongs to the federal government, and *B* if it belongs to both.

_____ **1.** vetoing a bill by the chief executive

_____ **2.** passing laws that provide for the welfare of its citizens

_____ **3.** declaring war against a foreign country

_____ **4.** setting import quotas and duties

_____ **5.** establishing a legal age for marriage

_____ **6.** setting up guidelines for chartering a business

ANSWERS AND EXPLANATIONS START ON PAGE 300.

The Judicial Branch

The federal and state court systems have been kept separate, with the U.S. Supreme Court intervening only when a matter is clearly of national interest. The state courts use *magistrates* or *justices of the peace* for minor criminal and civil cases. Also at this level are lower courts—traffic courts and juvenile courts are examples. Most are conducted without trial or jury.

The next level includes circuit courts, county courts, district courts, and su-perior courts. They handle more serious criminal cases and civil cases that involve bigger fines, more punishment, and greater monetary rewards. Juries are available at this level, if desired.

Appellate courts review the decisions made by circuit, county, district, and superior courts. They are usually divided into two classes—intermediate and supreme. Supreme courts, like their federal counterparts, have the last say on the cases they hear. In appellate courts, judges decide the cases.

Judges are very powerful in state judicial systems. In most states they are elected by the people, but in some they are appointed by the governor or the legislature.

★ **GED PRACTICE** ★

Exercise 18: The Judicial Branch

Directions: Choose the one best answer for each of the following questions.

1. In which court is a case involving a personal injury suit likely to be heard first?

   (1) federal Supreme Court
   (2) federal district court
   (3) state circuit court
   (4) appellate court
   (5) state supreme court

2. An Ohio man is convicted of murder and is given the death penalty. After the trial, new evidence is uncovered that can prove the man's innocence. Which court will likely hear the case?

   (1) a state lower court
   (2) the federal Supreme Court
   (3) a circuit court
   (4) a state appellate court
   (5) a state district court

ANSWERS AND EXPLANATIONS START ON PAGE 300.

Local Governments

The level of government that most affects the daily lives of its citizens and the one that could be affected most by the actions of its citizens is the one usually given the least attention. Few Americans know who is taking care of local business—who are the mayor, the town council and the county board members, the sheriff, the highway commissioner, etc. Few even know how local government is structured.

The next level of government after the state system is the county (parish in Louisiana).

Counties

Counties were not defined or provided for in the U.S. Constitution. The county system of government began in Virginia and originally was established to govern sprawling, rural areas. Counties usually act as agents for the state, carrying out the powers of the state at a local level.

One important function is gathering revenue to provide services, usually through property taxes or through special taxes (on cigarettes or liquor, for example). The way the money is appropriated, or spent, depends on the needs of the population of the individual area.

The majority of counties in the fifty states have a system of government in which the administrative authority is shared by members of a board or commission. These members are elected by the voters of the county. This organizational plan is called the *plural-executive plan*.

This plural-executive plan has been criticized often for inefficiency and lack of individual accountability. For this reason, some counties have changed to a county-manager plan in which one person is hired to manage the county's day-to-day operations.

★ **GED PRACTICE** ★

Exercise 19: County Expenditures ▬▬▬▬▬

These pie charts show how two counties allocate the money they receive from taxes and other revenues.

Directions: Refer to the charts to answer the following questions.

COUNTY EXPENDITURES

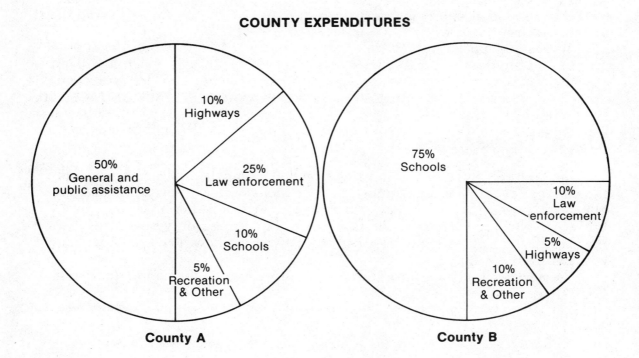

County A   County B

1. Which of the following can you infer about the makeup of Counties A and B?

   (1) County A has a greater concentration of children.
   (2) County A has more crime.
   (3) County A is smaller than County B.
   (4) County B has a greater concentration of children.
   (5) Counties A and B are both the same size.

2. Which hypothesis would best explain the difference between the two counties' expenditures for law enforcement?

   (1) It is more difficult to enforce the law in County B.
   (2) County A has a better law enforcement system.
   (3) Police officers are not needed in County B.
   (4) There is a greater need for law enforcement services in County A.
   (5) Too little money has been set aside for law enforcement in County B.

ANSWERS AND EXPLANATIONS START ON PAGE 300.

Townships and Municipalities

Key Words

incorporation—a legal process by which a town, city, or village sets up a plan under which it will operate

charter—a written instrument that establishes a city, village, or town

Below the county form of local government is the township and municipal level. The township, like the county, acts as an agent for the state and carries out many of the functions of the state at the local level.

Municipalities are established generally through incorporation, a legal process in which the town, city, or village sets up a charter under which it will operate. The charter provides a system for administering police and fire protection, libraries, paved streets, water, sewage disposal, etc.

Once incorporated, a community can raise its own money and share in state and county taxes. Without incorporation, a community is dependent upon the county government to provide necessary services.

The government of a village, town, or city can take a variety of forms: the mayor-council form, the commission form, and the council-manager form. The most commonly used form of city government in the U.S. today is the mayor-council plan. Under such a plan, either the mayor may wield the most power (strong mayor-council plan) or the council of aldermen may wield the most power (weak mayor-council plan). The least commonly used plan is the commission form in which members of a governing board share authority.

 Writing Activity 6

In a paragraph, describe the type of local government your town or city has.

ANSWER AND EXPLANATION STARTS ON PAGE 300.

Problems of the Cities

In recent decades, the cities, particularly in the Northeast and Midwest, have been experiencing such problems as the flight of the white, upper and middle classes to the suburbs, the rise in crime rates in the inner cities, the loss of tax bases as urban industries die off, and the drop in educational achievements in the older, city schools.

Despite their problems, the cities represent a crucial component of our economic and social life. One of the challenges facing America in the last part of the twentieth century is the revitalization of our large urban areas.

Exercise 20: The Plight of the Cities

Directions: Look at the cartoon below, which illustrates the plight of the cities, then fill in the blanks below with the appropriate words.

VICIOUS CIRCLE

Copyright 1969 by Herblock in *The Washington Post*

The man in the middle of the picture is labeled **(1)** _____ .

He is standing on an island surrounded by **(2)** _____ .

The fins are labeled **(3)** _____ ,

(4) _____ , **(5)** _____ ,

(6) _____ , **(7)** _____ ,

(8) _____ , and **(9)** _____ .

Exercise 21: Problems of the Cities

Directions: Choose the best answer for the question below.

What is the cartoonist implying about America's big cities?

(1) America's cities have seven major problems.
(2) The problems of American cities are so interconnected that it is hard to know where to start to correct them.
(3) The problems of city life have caused many people to move to the suburbs.
(4) American cities are experiencing a tremendous rebirth.
(5) Overcrowded schools and housing projects lead to crime.

ANSWERS AND EXPLANATIONS START ON PAGE 301.

7

BEHAVIORAL SCIENCES

To a biologist, a person is a living body of bones, muscles, tissues, and cells whose existence depends on the physical health of those parts. To an anthropologist, a person is a member of a unique culture. To a sociologist, a person is a member of a society who contributes to or detracts from the health of that society through interaction with others. And to a psychologist, a person is defined by his personality, intelligence, and behavior.

Biology is a natural science. All the others are ***behavioral sciences***, because they study the *behavior* of people rather than their physical makeup.

The Scientific Method

The behavioral sciences did not exist as separate fields of study before the 1800s. But of course, long before that, people wondered why human beings behaved as they did. In fact, the ancient Greek philosophers Plato and Aristotle knew the importance of understanding oneself and others. Both developed theories about the human mind and its relationship to the physical body. But these theories were highly speculative, were explained by "human nature," and thus were not based on the scientific method applied universally today.

The scientific method that both natural and social scientists use involve the following steps:

1. observing a problem

2. developing a theory (hypothesizing) about that problem

3. designing an experiment or carrying out research to prove or disprove the theory

4. carrying out the experiment and summarizing the findings

5. drawing conclusions from the findings and verifying the conclusions through more experiments

Only by following the steps described above can a scientist arrive at objective conclusions about how humans behave.

Exercise 1: Types of Scientists

Directions: Complete each of the sentences below by filling in the blank with the type of scientist the statement describes: *anthropologist, biologist, sociologist, or psychologist.*

1. The scientist who discovered that the brain produces a chemical that helps it defend itself when under attack was most probably a(n)

   _____ .

2. A scientist who studies the effects of presure on Israel's society while it is under constant threat of war would most likely be a(n)

   _____ .

3. A person who is tracing the development of India's culture from ancient times to this day would be called a(n)

   _____ .

4. A scientist who tries to discover the effects of stress on the personality and mental capabilities of individual children is a(n)

   _____ .

Exercise 2: The Scientific Method

Directions: Number the steps below (1–5) in the order of the scientific method. Refer to the scientific method on page 176.

_____ giving the questionnaire to students in high school and college classes and tabulating their answers

_____ hypothesizing that women can reverse sex roles more easily than men because men's roles have higher status and men are unwilling to give up the status associated with their roles

_____ finding that men are less willing to take the responsibility for housework and childcare than women; planning to survey adults by phone next

_____ observing that men cannot reverse sex roles as easily as women

_____ developing a questionnaire that asks men and women about their interest in reversing sex roles

ANSWERS AND EXPLANATIONS START ON PAGE 301.

What Is Anthropology?

Key Words

archaeology—the study of unearthed artifacts and skeletal remains of humans to determine their significance in the development of humans

culture—patterns of learned behavior shared by a group of people

cultural anthropology—the study of the unique characteristics of a culture, usually primitive or ancient

physical anthropology—the study of the origin and development of human physical characteristics

race—the concept by which man is classified by inherited physical characteristics

"May I have the pleasure of introducing you to yourself? Please meet *Homo sapiens,* meaning 'man of the the wise,' the most interesting creature on the face of the earth."

When writer Ashley Montagu began one of his books this way, he summed up the attitude of the professional anthropologist. The anthropologist is interested in many aspects of that fascinating creature, the human being. Anthropologists specialize in either cultural or physical anthropology.

Cultural Anthropology

Cultural anthropologists compare and contrast the different cultures of man today and of societies in the past. They study the art, religions, governments, and languages of a culture, as well as the customs or practices that make it unique.

The primary interest of cultural anthropologists is in primitive and ancient cultures, and many of their investigative techniques are used by sociologists in their study of modern peoples today.

Physical Anthropology

Physical anthropologists study the origin and development of human physical characteristics and how they vary from human to human, society to society, and race to race. Their job is as much related to biology as it is to the social sciences. They have categorized humans into races and have found similarities between man and the apes. Their work includes a range of activities from assembling bone fragments to reconstructing buildings from lost civilizations.

Anthropologists live with their subjects for long periods of time, read extensive writings by and about a culture, or dig up what is left of dead-and-gone societies. The diggers are called archaeologists and require specialized training to be able to recognize the cultural significance of such findings as broken pottery, bone fragments, primitive stone weapons, and parts of old tools.

Exercise 3: Physical and Cultural Anthropology

Directions: Fill in each blank below with the term that best fits the anthropologist described below.

1. Colin Turnbull lived among the Pygmies of the Congo, in Africa, to study every aspect of their unique life in the rain forest.

    Mr. Turnbull is a(n) _____ .
    cultural anthropologist   physical anthropologist

2. Louis and Mary Leakey have made many significant discoveries about ancient, primitive man through their analysis of skeletal remains dug up in Africa.

    The Leakeys are _____ .
    cultural anthropologists   physical anthropologists

ANSWERS AND EXPLANATIONS START ON PAGE 301.

The Evolution of Culture

Key Words

civilization—a classification of cultures by how they farm, domesticate animals, produce goods, and use oral and written language
clan—a group that believes its members are all biologically related
evolution—the gradual development of something into a more complex form
tribe—a social group whose members share a distinct culture and language

Physical anthropologists have found much evidence that man is a close relative of the ape. Man and apes share the characteristics of a complex brain; efficient vision; relatively flat face; flexible hands, feet, and forearms; and even internal biological makeup, including reproductive capabilities. Their young are cared for by adults for longer periods of time than is the case with other animals.

Many scientists believe that the process of evolution has gradually distinguished the apes from other animals and has distinguished humans from the apes. Moreover, most anthropologists believe that man's culture has evolved from a simpler to a more complex form as human beings themselves became more complex. The passage below illustrates how civilizations changed from a simple to a more complex form.

Exercise 4: Evolution of Culture

Directions: Read the passage below, then number each event in the order in which it occurs in the passage.

> After thousands of years, humans abandoned hunting of big game as their primary means of obtaining food and clothing, and they turned to farming and domesticating of animals to meet their survival needs.
> This change led to the establishment of clans and tribes and the organization of work and responsibilities. This organization created the need for rules for people to live by.
> As people prospered and focused less on basic survival, they had more time for leisure. Out of this leisure, they crafted items of handiwork, art, and other trappings that reflected their unique culture.
> These goods created a demand that contributed to the development of villages and towns around trading centers. Increasing trade demanded the efficiency of a written language for the purposes of communication. Through this evolutionary process, what anthropologists call "civilization" emerged.

_____ Farming and domestication of animals is learned.

_____ Arts and crafts become a part of society.

_____ Big game is hunted as a source of food and clothing.

_____ Clans and tribes are established.

_____ Written language is created.

_____ Towns grow out of trading centers.

_____ Organized rules are set for society.

★ **GED PRACTICE** ★

Exercise 5: Emerging Civilizations

Directions: Choose the one best answer for each statement or question below.

1. According to the information in the passage above, art was created primarily because

   (1) a wealthy class emerged to support artists.
   (2) the people desired some form of beauty in their harsh environment.
   (3) artists from other advanced communities exposed primitive people to it.
   (4) the people had the leisure time in which to create art.
   (5) the rulers established a class of artists.

2. Based on the passage above, which of the following led directly to the creation of written language?

   (1) the abandonment of hunting in favor of farming and domestication of animals
   (2) the establishment of clans and tribes
   (3) material prosperity, which led to more time for leisure

(4) the development of trade between villages

(5) the emergence of civilization

3. Of the following statements, which is supported by the passage above?

(1) Society developed rules and laws to encourage the domestication of animals.

(2) The growth of leisure time led to disorder and chaos.

(3) Tribes and clans preferred hunting to domesticating animals.

(4) Tribes and clans developed written language so that they could write down their laws.

(5) The production of goods led directly to the establishment of villages as trading centers.

ANSWERS AND EXPLANATIONS START ON PAGE 301.

Race and Culture

Most anthropologists agree that population groups exist whose members are linked by geographic location, certain physical characteristics, and a cultural heritage.

In general, anthropologists divide mankind into three racial categories: **caucasoid**, **mongoloid**, and **negroid**. The races and their characteristics are outlined in the chart below.

RACIAL CLASSIFICATIONS AND THEIR PHYSICAL CHARACTERISTICS

Classification	Physical Characteristics
caucasoid	• skin color ranging from reddish-white to dark brown • hair color ranging from blond to dark brown • build ranging from medium to tall • nose shape tends to be high and narrow
mongoloid	• skin color ranging from pale yellow to reddish-brown • hair color ranging from brown to brown-black • build ranging from medium short to medium tall • eyes characterized by a fold of skin at the corners
negroid	• skin color ranging from light brown to brown-black • hair color ranging from dark brown to brown-black • build ranging from very short to very tall • hair that may be described as curly or woolly • noses and lips that tend to be broad and thick

Geographic location is often the most important cause of the differences among certain population groups. For example, members of the population inhabiting what is now Asia did not mate with humans living in ancient Africa because they were separated by an expanse of land and ocean. So the physical characteristics of the two populations are quite distinct. Also, groups living in areas of intense heat have developed dark skin that protects them from harmful ultraviolet rays; in contrast, groups living in colder areas characteristically have light skin.

But what effect have these varying physical characteristics had on culture? Anthropologists say there is no scientific evidence that cultural differences are due to racial differences. Differences among cultures do exist, but they probably are due more to an accident of geography and history than to race.

Anthropologists have demonstrated that cultures in various geographic areas have advanced far beyond their contemporaries, only to fall behind several generations later. The Aztec culture of Mexico is a good example. During the fourteenth century, the Aztecs produced astronomers, artists, roads, and magnificent buildings that rivaled those in Europe. By the end of the sixteenth century, however, they had been conquered by the better-armed Spanish soldiers and today are part of the poverty-stricken peasant population of Mexico.

Exercise 6: Race and Culture

Directions: Place a check before the situation or situations below that support the statement in the passage, "Differences among cultures *do* exist, but they probably are due more to an accident of geography and history than to race."

_____ **(1)** Eskimos have been shown to have a larger brain size, on the average, than people of European descent.

_____ **(2)** Mexican youth are described as dishonest by some Americans because they do not maintain eye contact with their elders when talking, even though this action is a sign of respect for elders in Mexican culture.

_____ **(3)** Definite differences in learning styles among races have been found as a result of educational research.

_____ **(4)** Unlike Africans in urban areas, members of African tribes wear only loin cloths in their native lands.

_____ **(5)** Japanese-Americans are perceived as clannish by other Americans because their society believes it important to maintain close family contact.

 ## Writing Activity 1

What differences in culture have you observed among Americans of ethnic groups other than yours? Choose one group with which you are familiar and write two paragraphs describing a cultural difference in the area of dress, family relationships, child rearing, or any other aspect with which you are familiar.

ANSWERS AND EXPLANATIONS START ON PAGE 302.

Religion and Culture

Key Words

creed—a formal set of beliefs proclaimed as true that may or may not be based on a religion
folklore—tales, sayings, or customs preserved by members of a culture
ritual—in religion, the established form for a ceremony
shaman—a leader in a primitive religion who uses magic

Religion is a system of beliefs within a culture that guides the members' actions. Most religions are based on the belief in one supreme being, but some primitive religions embrace more than one god. This supreme being is supernatural; that is, it does not exist in a material sense—one cannot see or touch it.

Many religions are supported by a creed, which is a formal set of beliefs on which the faith is founded. This creed often serves as a guide to help the members of the culture distinguish between right and wrong behavior.

Certain principles on which a religion is based cannot be violated. The breaking of these sacred principles is tabu; in doing so, it is believed, the violator risks punishment by the supreme being. In most cases, however, those who break a society's sacred laws are punished by the larger society. Punishment may be death or ostracism—extreme isolation from other members of the society.

Most religions acknowledge the existence of a soul or spirit that survives the human body after death. This belief was held by primitive cultures long ago. Some cultures believe that animals and even some plants have souls.

Some primitive religions are based on the belief that certain of their members can control the supernatural. Magic plays a significant role in the rituals of these religions. Leaders in primitive religions who use magic are called shamans by anthropologists.

Magic is ever present in the religious traditions of the Melanesians of the Pacific islands, the Plains Indians of North America, and certain tribes in Africa.

A culture transmits its ways of life and explains its customs through its folklore. Folklore includes myths and legends, tales from the past that are not provable but that explain a people's customs, beliefs, and world view.

Exercise 7: Religion and Culture

Directions: Complete each sentence in the passage with the appropriate word listed below:

supernatural   folklore   ritual   shaman   tabu

According to tales in primitive religious **(1)** _____ , there is one High God who is a **(2)** _____ being. Only the **(3)** _____ can communicate with the High God but usually does not even try. Instead, if a favor is needed, a specific **(4)** _____ is established through which a lower god or spirit is contacted and convinced to react favorably. Not following the right procedure with the High God or lower gods, however, risks their becoming angry over the disregard of a sacred **(5)** _____ .

ANSWERS AND EXPLANATIONS START ON PAGE 302.

Ethnocentrism and Cultural Relativity

Key Words

cultural relativity—judging another culture objectively
ethnocentrism—using one's culture as the standard by which to judge another culture

Often, we assume that our culture is the "right" one and is superior to others in the world. We might describe other cultures as being heathen, backward, savage, and barbarian. Such attitudes show our ethnocentrism. Ethnocentrism is the act of judging another culture on the basis of one's own cultural values.

To avoid being ethnocentric, anthropologists strive to be objective in their assessments of the cultures they observe. By practicing cultural relativity, anthropologists are able to appreciate and understand the customs of the diverse cultures of the world.

★ GED PRACTICE ★

Exercise 8: Understanding Ethnocentrism

Directions: Choose the one best answer for each question below.

1. Which of the following situations illustrates the concept of ethnocentrism?

   (1) the Filipinos forcing into exile Ferdinand Marcos, whom they believed abused his power
   (2) the criticism of the U.S.S.R. by Russian dissident Andre Sakharov
   (3) the refusal of devout Catholics to eat meat on Fridays during the season of Lent
   (4) a nonsmoker agreeing to smoke a peace pipe during an Indian ritual
   (5) an American woman's describing European women who refuse to shave their legs as "masculine"

2. In India, Hindus dispose of their dead's remains by building a funeral pyre and cremating the body during a public ceremony. At the late Indian prime minister Indira Gandhi's cremation, her oldest son Rajiv applied the torch. Which of the following attitudes of an American tourist reflects the concept of cultural relativity?

   (1) Cremation is a barbaric way to dispose of a person's remains.
   (2) The human body is sacred and therefore should not be burned.
   (3) The Hindu rite of cremation is a moving, religious experience.
   (4) Burial is the only Christian way to dispose of a person's remains.
   (5) Cremation is better than burial because it is cheaper, efficient, and conserves land.

ANSWERS AND EXPLANATIONS START ON PAGE 302.

Cultural Diffusion

Key Word

cultural diffusion—the spreading of cultural elements to different societies

The saying, "It's a small world" is probably truer today than in any other period in human history. Many conveniences of the modern world such as air travel and telecommunications have bridged the distances between people. The result is that there is hardly any corner of the world that has not been explored by man.

Wherever humans travel, they bring their culture with them. For example, even in the remotest regions of the world, an American can obtain a Coke or a McDonald's hamburger and thus feel right at home. When one culture adopts cultural elements from another, the process is called cultural diffusion. According to anthropologists, cultural diffusion has both advantages and disadvantages to the culture that accepts the changes.

The passage below illustrates the process of cultural diffusion as it applies to the Pygmies in central Africa.

★ **GED PRACTICE** ★

Exercise 9: Cultural Diffusion ━━━━━━━━━━━━━━━━━

Directions: Read the passage and answer the questions that follow.

The Pygmies of central Africa were most probably an isolated tribe thousands of years ago. Pygmies rely very much on hunting and gathering for their basic needs, and such techniques are considered the most primitive for a human society. Although they still live in the thick, sunless rain forest, today they do much business with the Bantu, an African tribe that is more "civilized" in its culture.

In Pygmy society, as in other "primitive" societies, many rituals and religions are tied closely to food-gathering. However, many of these institutions have begun to change. Since rituals and religions reinforce group solidarity and dependence on one another, the group is weakened when the rules begin to bend or are ignored.

Food-gathering techniques, rituals, and religions are not the only aspects of the culture that are changing, however. The use of environmental materials in traditional house building is being replaced by the use of prefabricated materials such as tin roofs and cement blocks.

Crude stone and wooden tools are becoming scarce as ready-made hammers and screwdrivers are becoming available to the previously secluded natives. Handicrafts are produced less for use by home and society than for sale to tourists.

Once "primitives" come into contact with the outside world, an innocence and unquestioning contentment is lost. A visible example of this can be seen in the way they dress. For Pygmies and other African tribes who live in warm areas, modesty is not innate. Most wear few articles of clothing, if any, until they learn to feel ashamed by tourists from more "advanced" cultures.

Anthropologists understand that the disappearance of "primitive" peoples from this earth would mean a loss to human culture in general, since we have much to learn from them.

1. Based on the above passage, which of the examples listed below illustrates the process of cultural diffusion?

    (1) the Pygmies' policy of trading with the Bantu
    (2) the Pygmies' use of prefabricated materials to build their houses
    (3) the Pygmies' reliance on hunting and gathering to meet their basic needs
    (4) the weakening of tribal bonds among the Pygmies
    (5) the Pygmies' production of handicrafts for use by home and society

2. The author of the passage apparently feels that the effect of cultural diffusion in central Africa

    (1) has had a good effect on the Pygmy society.

(2) has had no observable impact on Pygmy society.
(3) has had a negative impact on Pygmy society.
(4) did not really take place in Pygmy society.
(5) had a greater effect on Bantu society than Pygmy society.

3. The words *civilized*, *advanced*, and *primitive* are in quotations in the passage. In emphasizing these words, the author is

(1) being ethnocentric—judging Pygmy society according to his own values.
(2) emphasizing how cultural diffusion works in some societies.
(3) suggesting that the Bantu tribe is more advanced and civilized than any other African tribe.
(4) implying that the descriptions *civilized*, *advanced*, and *primitive* should never be used.
(5) suggesting that those cultures described as *civilized*, *advanced*, and *primitive* may not be what we think they are.

Exercise 10: The Pygmies

Directions: Study the map of the Ituri Forest below. Then place an *X* next to the statement(s) that can be concluded from the information on the map.

_____ **(1)** The Pygmy camps are smaller than plantations.

_____ **(2)** Apa must mean "camp" or "tribe" in Pygmy language.

_____ **(3)** The Ituri Forest is a rain forest in central Africa.

_____ **(4)** The villages are located inside plantations.

_____ **(5)** Most Pygmy camps range from east to west in the Ituri Forest.

ANSWERS AND EXPLANATIONS START ON PAGE 302.

What Is Sociology?

Key Words

group—two or more people who interact because of certain shared characteristics or interests

primary group—a group in which the members share highly personal relationships

secondary group—a group in which the members work together for a common purpose but do not share close personal relationships

Sociologists attempt to understand today's society and its organization by observing people's behavior in groups and by studying the rules that govern group behavior.

According to sociologists, a group is two or more people who interact with each other. A load of passengers on an airplane is not a group unless the members have something in common; for instance, they are professional football players on their way to a game with a rival team, or senior citizens on a charter flight to a distant city, or even a group of businessmen and tourists suddenly bonded together by the fate of a hijacking.

Basically, sociologists study two types of groups: primary and secondary. Primary groups include your family and personal friends with whom you share close relationships. Secondary groups include your work team, classmates, church members, or any group in which your relationship with the members is more impersonal than with a primary group.

Society today is placing more emphasis on secondary groups than ever before in history. Frequently, this is because of the widening geographic distance between families, a growing feature of modern American life. For example, when a young single parent has to work these days, she may have to seek a professional daycare center (a secondary group relationship) instead of relying on her mother or other relatives (a primary group relationship).

Some sociologists believe that this distancing of families may be beneficial to society at large. As a widely diverse society, we are getting to know people who differ from us in many ways. As a result, sociologists feel Americans are becoming more tolerant of differences among people than before.

Exercise 11: Primary and Secondary Groups

Directions: Indicate whether the examples below represent primary or secondary groups by writing *P* in the space for a primary group and *S* for a secondary group. Remember that primary group members share close personal relationships while secondary group members work together for a common purpose.

_____   **1.**   members of a Bruce Springsteen fan club

_____   **2.**   all the members of a large fraternity

_____   **3.** members of the Democratic Party

_____   **4.** your child's closest playmates

_____   **5.** players on the Chicago Bears football team

_____   **6.** employees of the Acme Screw Company

_____   **7.** members of the Brotherhood of Electrical Workers

_____   **8.** your grandparents and great grandparents

_____   **9.** senior citizens on a charter flight to Hawaii

_____   **10.** members of a household

 Writing Activity 2

Write a paragraph describing the primary and secondary groups to which you belong. What makes these groups primary and secondary in your life?

ANSWERS AND EXPLANATIONS START ON PAGE 302.

Social Institutions

An *institution* is a system organized by society to provide for its members' important needs. The function of many institutions is to teach citizens a society's appropriate customs and behaviors.

In complex societies like the United States, five major institutions exist: **family, religious, political, economic,** and **educational**. The most important of these, however, is the **family**.

The Family

Key Words

nuclear family—a family group consisting of a mother, father, and children who live in the same household

extended family—a family group composed of members beyond the immediate members of mother, father, and children, all of whom live in the same household

monogamy—a form of marriage wherein a person has only one spouse

polygamy—a form of marriage wherein a person is permitted to have more than one spouse

To most Americans, a family consists of a husband, a wife, and their children, if they have any. There is close interaction among the members of this family. Sociologists call this the nuclear family.

In other countries, and in some cultures within the United States, however, the family is said to be extended because it contains not only the husband, wife, and children, but also other blood relatives among whom there is close interaction. An extended family might include the nuclear unit plus the husband's or wife's mother and father, brothers and sisters, and the husbands, wives, and children of those brothers and sisters.

The establishment of a new family or a new branch of a family begins in most cultures with a marriage. Every society sets its own norms or accepted practices for such a union. For example, in the U.S. a husband may have only one wife and vice versa. Therefore, marriage in the U.S. is described as monogamous. Other cultures, however, permit its members to have more than one spouse. Marriage in these cultures is described as polygamous.

Other cultures may differ according to who selects the mate and where the couple will live. In the U.S., the individuals themselves usually choose the person whom they want to marry. In other cultures, the parents may choose the mate for their son or daughter. The matter of where to live is left up to the married couple in the U.S.; in some other societies the newlyweds don't have such freedom of choice. Sometimes they are required to live near the family of either the husband or the wife.

Exercise 12: Nuclear and Extended Families

Directions: Write *N* in the space if the situation below describes a nuclear family, and write *E* if it describes an extended family.

_____ **1.** An engaged couple heed the advice of friends who warn them that, if they want to be happy, they should move far away from their in-laws after marriage.

_____ **2.** A tribal law requires a husband and wife to maintain a home in the same compound as his relatives.

_____ **3.** A woman depends on her brothers for help in raising her children, while her husband takes care of his sister's children.

_____ **4.** In Japan, a married couple with children is still responsible for housing and supporting their elderly parents.

_____ **5.** The typical family in the United States is changing. This is causing an increase in single-parent households with mothers raising children alone.

★ **GED PRACTICE** ★

Exercise 13: The Family

Directions: Read the passage below and answer the questions that follow.

"The Seminole are organized into matrilineal clans. Inheritance and descent are through the mother's side of the family. The mother is head of the household. When a man marries he lives with his wife's family. In clan functions, a boy receives instruction from his mother's brother, who is in his clan, rather than from his father. Marriage inside one's clan once was forbidden, but this rule is no longer observed strictly."

From *Vanishing Tribes* by Roy Pinney

1. In the Seminole tribe, the mother's brother rather than her husband may be more of a father figure to her sons because

    (1) the uncle lives with them, and the father does not.
    (2) the uncle is part of the mother's blood family, and the father is not.
    (3) the brother is the true biological father, not the husband.
    (4) the father of the son is more important to the clan than is the uncle.
    (5) the uncle is the head of the mother's clan.

2. Which of the following would be a likely hypothesis about Seminole matrilineal clans, based on the information in the paragraph?

    (1) Women are not the central figures in their own nuclear families, but are the central figures in the extended family.
    (2) Women are central figures in both the nuclear and extended families.
    (3) Women are not the central figures in either nuclear or extended families.
    (4) Women are more concerned with the care of children than men are.
    (5) Women are less concerned with the care of children than men are.

 Writing Activity 3

Write a paragraph describing your family structure—its members, the amount and degree of interaction, its living arrangements. Can your family be described as nuclear or extended?

ANSWERS AND EXPLANATIONS START ON PAGE 303.

Changing Families

Families always and everywhere have been charged with the responsibility of raising children, providing love and affection to one another, and protecting members from physical and economic harm.

But families are changing. In the U.S. especially, the birth rate is decreasing, and families, therefore, are getting smaller. The traditional role of the mother in the American family has undergone change as more and more mothers find it necessary to work in order to help meet the family's economic needs.

Also, divorce has become more accepted and frequent than ever before. One result of divorce—broken families—has contributed to problems of delinquency among youth.

Exercise 14: Changing Families

Directions: Study the table about juvenile delinquency below and answer the questions that follow.

SELF-REPORTED DELINQUENCY BY MEN LIVING AT HOME, BY RACE
(in percent)

| | Question: "Do any of these men live at your home now?"* | | | | | |
| | White | | | Black | | |
Self-Reported Acts	Real Father	Step Father	None	Real Father	Step Father	None
None	58	50	59	54	45	53
One	25	21	25	25	23	27
Two or more	17	29	17	20	32	20
Totals	100	100	101	99	100	100

*Possiblities excluded from the table were "foster father" and "guardian," which together account for very few students in the sample.

1. Which of the following is best supported by the data provided in the chart above?

   (1) Delinquent boys are most often being raised in homes with no father figure present.
   (2) Boys with a stepfather present in the home report more acts of delinquency than those with no father present.
   (3) Boys become delinquent most often because of a difficulty in living with their natural fathers.
   (4) White males are more likely than black males to become delinquents because of their experiences in broken homes.
   (5) Boys with no father figure have fewer acts of delinquency than boys with a poor father.

2. Which of the following hypotheses best explains why the number of reported acts of delinquency is higher when boys live with stepfathers than is the case when they live with their real fathers?

   (1) Stepfathers rarely stay home to spend time with their stepsons.
   (2) Stepfathers place unreasonable demands on their stepsons.
   (3) Stepfathers never accept the sons of their new wives as their own.
   (4) Poor relationships between stepsons and stepfathers cause the boys to transfer their hostilities.
   (5) Whether they live with their real fathers or stepfathers, boys are harder to raise than girls.

3. Based on the table, into which of the following categories would you place the majority of black males reared by their natural fathers?

   (1) nondelinquent
   (2) delinquent; committed more than two acts
   (3) delinquent; committed one act
   (4) delinquent; committed two acts
   (5) delinquent previously, but not any longer

ANSWERS AND EXPLANATIONS START ON PAGE 303.

Roles and Status

> ## Key Words
> *role*—the behavior that goes with one's position
> *ascribed status*—the position in society one inherits through birth or attains with time
> *achieved status*—the position one attains through individual effort

Your role in society is the behavior that is expected of you because you occupy a certain position. For example, the role of a parent requires a different pattern of behavior from one of an employee. Closely related to role is *status*. Status is the position you hold in society.

In Japan, a common expression is translated to mean "nothing is as unimportant as a Japanese woman." This expression communicates clearly the traditional status of the female in that culture. And, in fact, the Japanese woman's traditional role as a meek, obedient wife supports the statement.

In recent years, however, in Japan as in many Westernized nations, women are beginning to adopt roles that have been considered traditionally male. This phenomenon is called *role reversal*.

Role reversal has been encouraged for females in the United States. Examples include girls being allowed to participate in traditionally male sports and women taking on such jobs as telephone installers and engineers. Role reversal is generally not encouraged for males. Sociologists theorize that females are positively rewarded for role reversal and males are not because the male role is one of higher status in U.S. culture.

Roles based on gender are not the only ones dictated by our society. Within our jobs we play certain roles. Our marital status also determines how we behave in certain settings, as do our economic status and our ethnic background.

Because we are born into one sex or the other, sociologists say the status that comes with the role is ascribed. That is, society assigns a particular status to being male or female, regardless of individual qualities. Also, age gives one a unique status in many societies. For example, the elderly often are respected because of their age, and teenagers looked down on because of theirs.

On the other hand, when we attain a certain status through our own effort, be it through educational or professional training, the status is achieved.

In countries like the U.S., where more opportunities for occupational choices exist, an individual has more chances to gain an achieved status. However, in any society, your position is affected by ascribed status, as you can never completely escape the category society places you into at birth.

Exercise 15: Role Reversal

Directions: Male and female roles have been changing rapidly during the twentieth century. Indicate role reversal in each of the situations below by writing the correct name in the spaces.

1. Debra and Claude are married and have two preschool-age children.

    Presently, both parents work, but _____ has decided to quit soon to stay home with the kids during the day because of the lack of good day care facilities.

2. Dr. Scott has been working for three years with Nurse Davis, whom many consider to be the most warm and caring R.N. in the hospital. Their mutual respect has not been affected by the fact that

    _____ is a woman and _____ is a man.

3. Betty Sue and Jimmy are given the opportunity to choose an elective class

    their senior year of high school, so _____ chooses home economics and _____ chooses auto mechanics.

Exercise 16: Roles and Status

Directions: Identify each of the following as *ascribed* (given by birth or attained by age) or *achieved* (earned) status.

_____ **1.** being a member of the mongoloid race

_____ **2.** becoming a policeman

_____ **3.** retiring from the work force at age sixty-five

_____ **4.** obtaining a GED certificate

_____ **5.** inheriting a royal title

ANSWERS AND EXPLANATIONS START ON PAGE 303.

Social Classes

> ## Key Words
>
> *social class*—a ranked level of social status in a society
> *stratification*—the categorizing of people into different social classes

Closely related to status is social class. Your social class is where you stand in relation to other members of the larger society. The importance of social class was shown humorously in an episode of the popular sitcom, "Kate and Allie." Kate, a single, working mother, is given a mink coat under an improbable set of circumstances. She finds that when she wears the mink she is treated differently by strangers than she otherwise would have been.

At a French restaurant, she does not have to wait for service, she is treated formally and politely, and it is assumed that she has a wealthy background and a high position at her job. In other words, she is taken to be a member of the upper class. The mink coat indicated that she had money. And, while money may not be the only determination of class position in our society, it is the most important one.

Social class indicates an attitude and a way of life. It takes a lot of money to be considered a member of the upper class, but is an unemployed factory worker automatically considered to be a member of the upper class after winning several million dollars in a lottery? Sociologists tell us, "No!" The lottery winner's children or grandchildren *may* achieve upper class status *after* the money has been in the family for a couple of generations. However, the "newly rich" generally do not possess and exhibit the appropriate lifestyle of the upper class. Nor do the "nouveau riche" understand the customs that set the upper class apart from the lower class.

Obviously, money is not the only criterion that determines status in our society. College professors, for example, are accorded high social status and rank by most people but earn less money per year than skilled tradesmen, who have much less prestige in a community. This contradiction may be explained by the fact that the degree of formal education also contributes to social status in America.

Social classes are neither unique to the U.S. nor to Western society. They develop out of the division of labor. The more jobs and divisions that exist in a society, the more flexible the structure of the job market, and the greater the **social mobility** or movement between classes.

In the U.S., there is much social mobility, especially for members of the middle class. The ease of movement between classes in the U.S. compared to other societies is part of the reason that one cannot distinguish easily between members of one class and another.

★ GED PRACTICE ★

Exercise 17: Social Status

Directions: Choose the one best answer for each question below.

1. Of the statements below, which is supported by the information above?

    (1) Money is the sole criterion for determining status in the U.S.
    (2) When you have money, you are automatically accepted by members of the upper class.
    (3) A combination of money and amount of formal education contributes to social status in the U.S.
    (4) The poor have no status in the U.S.
    (5) It is impossible to improve your status in the U.S.

2. Based on the criteria above, which of the following might be considered to have the highest status in American society today?

   (1) a newspaper journalist
   (2) a professional basketball player
   (3) a brain surgeon
   (4) a university professor
   (5) a television actress

Exercise 18: Social Classes

Directions: Read the passage below. Place an *X* before each conclusion that logically can be drawn from the passage.

> "The school was small, the families mostly Jewish and Catholic, and were well up in the middle economic class, happy with their simple escape from the troubles of the city.
>
> "Now, in the short time of six years, the population of the suburb has doubled. The original settlers who could afford it have moved on down the road, onto newly excavated, paved, and wired hillsides. The city moved out to replace them. Their replacements were more often working class, spoke more Spanish, were darker, more occasionally black, had more children, fewer dads, collected more welfare, and took achievement tests less well."
>
> from *The Way It Spozed to Be*, by James Herndon

_____ **(1)** There are more Hispanics and blacks in the working class than in the middle class.

_____ **(2)** The working class lives primarily in the city and has little hope of escaping.

_____ **(3)** The social mobility of the classes can be proven by their ability to move from one location to another.

_____ **(4)** Children of working-class parents do not do as well in school, on the average, as middle-class children.

_____ **(5)** Receiving welfare from the state is more common among the working class than the middle class.

_____ **(6)** When the working class moves to the suburbs, its attitudes and lifestyles become more like the middle class.

 ## Writing Activity 4

There is a lot of controversy about exactly how much social mobility there is in American society. The "American Dream" is that anyone who works hard can succeed economically in this country. Is the American Dream being realized? If not, why not? Write two to three paragraphs defending your position on this question. Be sure to include specific examples to support your position.

ANSWERS AND EXPLANATIONS START ON PAGE 303.

Social Deviation

" 'I don't enjoy hurting people unless they mess with me. Then I enjoy it. If you mess with me, I'm going to try to kill you. I don't fight by the rules. I go for all. And I don't shake hands when it's done.'

" 'Ruby Calhoun is an antisocial person,' an early report warned; 'if something is not done soon, he will become a dangerous man.' "

from *The Devil's Stocking*, by Nelson Algren

Why is Ruby Calhoun antisocial? Ruby is what sociologists would consider a social deviate—someone who fails to conform to the norms and values of society. Why isn't he conforming to the norms and values of American society?

Several factors must be considered to answer this question. However, sociologists theorize that social deviates are formed in homes in which role models have been nonexistent or inconsistent. When role models are lacking in the home, they often are sought elsewhere, sometimes in street gangs. In the gang culture, not only is there primary group pressure to obey unique, often antisocial rules, but also there exists a "mob mentality" that makes people do things they would never do as individuals.

It is possible that Ruby Calhoun came from a good family, had all the advantages society had to offer, and still became antisocial. If this is the case, a psychologist would need to examine Ruby Calhoun's personality to determine the individual motivation for his antisocial behavior.

The case of Ruby Calhoun illustrates one man's deviation from norms that are vital to the welfare of society. However, when a law does not reflect the values of a significant percentage of a society's members, it is difficult to enforce. For example, the Eighteenth Amendment forbade the sale of liquor in the U.S. It was violated widely because millions of Americans did not agree that drinking an intoxicating beverage was immoral or harmful.

Exercise 19: Social Deviation

Directions: In the space provided below, indicate with a check those laws that are violated and are difficult to enforce because many people do not believe the laws are vital to the welfare of society.

_____ **(1)** Laws against littering in public areas

_____ **(2)** Laws against jaywalking, or crossing the street in an illegal manner

_____ **(3)** Laws against shoplifting in a department store

_____ **(4)** Laws against riding in a car without a seat belt fastened

_____ **(5)** Laws against exceeding the fifty-five-mile-per-hour speed limit

_____ **(6)** Laws against kidnapping

ANSWERS AND EXPLANATIONS START ON PAGE 304.

What Is Psychology?

Psychological Theories

> ### Key Words
>
> *behaviorism*—a field of psychology that focuses mainly on the treatment and study of behavior
>
> *psychoanalysis*—a method of treating emotional disorders that emphasizes early childhood experiences
>
> *psychiatry*—a branch of medicine that specializes in the diagnosis and treatment of mental illness

A psychologist is a scientist whose aim is to explain, predict, and control the behavior of individuals. Psychology is related to psychiatry; however, psychiatry is not a behavioral science. It is a branch of medicine that specializes in the diagnosis and treatment of mental illness. Although many theories of psychology have been developed, two that probably have had the greatest impact on the field are psychoanalysis and behaviorism. Behaviorists and psychoanalysts have very different approaches to correcting behavioral disorders.

Psychoanalysis

> ### Key Words
>
> *id*—the part of the personality that is unconscious and represents instinctual needs and drives
>
> *ego*—the part of the personality responsible for conscious decision-making
>
> *superego*—the part of the personality that represents socially accepted values; the conscience

Sigmund Freud (pronounced "Froyd"), an Austrian, developed the theory of psychoanalysis. According to psychoanalytic theory, much of human behavior is motivated by unconscious instinctual drives. We are unaware of these drives because they are hidden from us. Many of these drives are linked to childhood experiences, so psychoanalysts probe this area of a patient's life.

Freud believed that the sex drive also has great influence on human motivation, and his pioneering work in this area of the unconscious made him unpopular with some of his contemporaries.

According to psychoanalytic theory, the human subconscious may be divided into three parts: the id, the ego, and the superego.

The id consists of all the basic drives and instincts that we are born with. According to Freud, the id provides our life force—the energy that keeps us going. The id is basically pleasure-seeking and can cause trouble for us in its drive to satisfy the needs for food, water, sex, and self-protection.

The ego acts as a check on the id's never-ending search for pleasure. It is the ego that keeps us from having "too much of a good thing." The ego is the center of thought, reasoning, and common sense.

The superego acts as the conscience. It determines the difference between morally right and wrong behavior and stops us from doing things that may satisfy the id but hurt society.

People who are considered to be emotionally healthy and behaviorally normal have an id, an ego, and a superego that work in cooperation. When one or another of these three components has gone out of control, a person may go to a psychologist or therapist to restore the balance. People with problems, of course, do not usually recognize this imbalance. It is when their behavior constantly causes problems for themselves or others that they seek professional help.

Exercise 20: Psychoanalysis

Directions: Read the situation below and answer the questions that follow.

> Lenny loves cookies. One day, he is hungry and can't wait for dinner. He robs the cookie jar and takes five cookies. Although there are still many cookies left in the jar, he takes only five to avoid getting sick from eating too many. After he has eaten the cookies, he feels guilty because he knows he is not supposed to eat sweets before a meal.

1. What drive represents the id in this case? _____
   _____

2. What action represents the functioning ego? _____
   _____

3. What represents the superego for Lenny? _____
   _____

ANSWERS AND EXPLANATIONS START ON PAGE 304.

Behaviorism

Key Words

conditioning—the means by which an animal or human learns a pattern of behavior

positive reinforcement—in the conditioning process, the act of rewarding an individual for a correct response

negative reinforcement—in the conditioning process, the act of punishing an individual for an incorrect response

Methods for changing human behavior are studied and applied by a group of psychologists called *behaviorists*. The process of changing human behavior is called *behavior modification*.

B. F. Skinner and many other American psychologists have done much experimentation to learn methods of changing behavior. One such method is termed conditioning.

Conditioning involves the use of positive or negative reinforcement to encourage or discourage a certain behavior. In positive reinforcement, the subject is given a *reward* for demonstrating an appropriate behavioral response. In negative reinforcement, a subject is *punished* for exhibiting inappropriate behavior. After repeated rewards or punishments, the subject is conditioned to exhibit an appropriate behavior.

Russian physiologist Ivan Pavlov was the first to experiment with such conditioning. In Pavlov's experiments, he first observed that when dogs saw meat they automatically salivated. By presenting meat simultaneously with the ring of a bell, he found that the dogs produced saliva when they heard the bell and saw no meat. Thus, the dogs were conditioned to respond to the sound of the bell.

Conditioning of human behavior often happens by chance. Many young parents have discovered how easy it is to condition a baby to expect to be picked up, cuddled, diapered, or fed whenever it cries! While opinions may differ as to whether this reinforcement by the parents produces a spoiled child or a secure one, almost everyone agrees that reinforcement has encouraged more of the same behavior.

★ GED PRACTICE ★

Exercise 21: Behaviorism

Directions: Read the short passage below and answer the question that follows.

1. In business, a well-known philosophy for managing employees is called the "carrot and stick" approach. According to this belief, people really are not motivated to work; they have to be supervised closely, threatened with some kind of punishment, or rewarded before they will perform. The psychological basis for this management attitude lies in

   (1) human nature.
   (2) psychoanalytic theory.
   (3) conditioning.
   (4) negative reinforcement.
   (5) positive reinforcement.

2. A parent is trying to encourage a child to do better in school. Which of the following is an example of the use of positive reinforcement?

   (1) grounding the child until his grades improve
   (2) suspending his allowance until the grades improve
   (3) having periodic discussions about study habits
   (4) buying the child a desired gift if grades improve
   (5) meeting with the school guidance counselor to get the child placed in easier classes

Exercise 22: Behaviorism and Psychoanalysis

Directions: In each of the cases below, write *B* in the blank if behaviorist theory is illustrated and *P* if psychoanalytic theory is shown.

_____ **1.** Kevin exhibits very stubborn behavior as an adult. His therapist suggests that it may be because he was over three years old when he finally was toilet-trained.

_____ **2.** David hates to go to bed at night and will not get up when called in the morning. His mother bought him an alarm clock that rings loudly. Now that he is forced to awaken by the alarm clock, David goes to bed and rises on time without the clock's going off.

_____ **3.** Lillie is overweight because of her compulsive eating. She has tried every type of diet. Finally, she joins Weight Watchers and is losing steadily now that each weight loss is applauded by other members each week.

_____ **4.** Al has been trying to quit smoking but without success. Even when he is without cigarettes, he finds himself chewing on pens or pencils. His therapist suggests that Al didn't have enough oral stimulation as a baby.

_____ **5.** Johnny is learning to use the computer in math class. Each time he correctly completes a problem on the computer, a "smiley face" appears on the screen and a new problem appears for him to solve.

 ## Writing Activity 5

Based on your experience, which is likely to be the most effective—positive reinforcement (rewarding desired behavior) or negative reinforcement (punishing undesired behavior)? Write two to three paragraphs explaining your position. Be sure to provide examples to support your point of view.

ANSWERS AND EXPLANATIONS START ON PAGE 304.

Frustration and Conflict

Key Words

approach-approach conflict—a conflict in which a person is attracted to two different, desirable goals

avoidance-avoidance conflict—a conflict in which a person is caught between two undesirable choices

approach-avoidance conflict—a conflict in which a person is both attracted to and repelled by the same goal

According to psychologists, *frustration* is the response that occurs when a goal is not reached or a need is unfulfilled. Most commonly, however, frustration develops over conflicts between goals and desires. Psychologists have identified three basic types of conflicts that people encounter in life. They are approach-approach conflicts, avoidance-avoidance conflicts, and approach-avoidance conflicts. An example of each is illustrated below.

Approach-approach conflicts

Brenda and Cliff were recently married. Brenda wants to work in order to help pay bills and to fulfill her desire to have a career. However, she also wants desperately to have a child. Brenda's situation illustrates an approach-approach conflict because both of her alternatives are attractive to her and she experiences some degree of frustration in trying to satisfy both of them. In order to resolve the conflict, Brenda has to either satisfy one goal first or give up one goal for the other.

Avoidance-avoidance conflicts

Brenda decides to accept a full-time bank job that she grows to dislike. She can't quit because Cliff depends on her income to help pay the bills they have accumulated, some of which he incurred before they were married. Although she dislikes her job, Brenda can't quit because the job market is tight and she knows she'll have trouble landing another job.

Brenda's situation now reflects an avoidance-avoidance conflict. She faces the undesirable choices of staying on a job she dislikes and losing her income if she quits. Whatever choice she makes, she has to suffer the consequences of it. Avoidance-avoidance conflicts are common in everyday life.

Approach-avoidance conflicts

Brenda grows to resent the fact that she has to work when she wants to start a family. This resentment has begun to affect her marriage. Linc, the bank president's son, is interested in Brenda, and she likes him. They go out to lunch frequently. Brenda realizes that, if she left Cliff and married Linc, she would no longer have to work and could start the family she's been wanting. But hers would be the first divorce in her family and would cause a scandal once her parents learned the facts.

Now Brenda is experiencing an approach-avoidance conflict. She is attracted to Linc, but the possibility of divorce repels her. There is no way out of this situation unless Brenda changes basic values that were instilled in her as a child. For this reason, approach-avoidance conflicts often are the most difficult to solve.

Exercise 23: Frustration and Conflict

Directions: In each case below, identify the conflict as approach-approach, avoidance-avoidance, or approach-avoidance.

1. José has a sore tooth and does not want to go to the dentist, but he knows he must, or the tooth will just get worse.

   _____

2. Keisha is asked by popular, handsome Lionel to go out Saturday night, but she has already promised her best friend she would help her celebrate her birthday that night.

   _____

3. Hal needs to buy a new car but does not want to go further into debt to do so.

 Writing Activity 6

We all have frustration and conflicts in our lives. Think of a conflict you had recently. Was it an approach-approach, avoidance-avoidance, or approach-avoidance conflict? Write a paragraph or two describing the conflict and identifying which kind of conflict it was. Also, explain how you resolved the conflict.

Exercise 24: Recognizing Conflicts

Directions: Some conflicts are summed up in everyday common sayings. Match the conflict on the right with the correct saying shown on the left. Some of the terms on the right may be used more than once.

_____ **1.** between the devil and the deep blue sea   **(a)** approach-approach

_____ **2.** honey's sweet, but the bee stings   **(b)** avoidance-avoidance

_____ **3.** caught between a rock and a hard place   **(c)** approach-avoidance

_____ **4.** no rose without a thorn

_____ **5.** having your cake and eating it too

ANSWERS AND EXPLANATIONS START ON PAGE 305.

Defense Mechanisms

In each of the three situations Brenda found herself in, she had to make some adjustment, or cope. She could cope directly by changing either herself or the situation. Human beings use many methods to deal with their frustrations. ***Defense mechanisms*** are ways in which people reduce frustration.

The use of defense mechanisms can be healthy for an individual. Sometimes they are the only methods by which an individual can deal with an unbearable situation. We all use them. In fact, those people who are diagnosed as mentally disturbed often have not learned to use defense mechanisms to their benefit. As a result, the stress of everyday life becomes too much for them to bear. Listed below are five common defense mechanisms illustrated by an example.

rationalization—disguising the reason for one's failure to reach a goal

> **Example:** Julian cuts classes to play cards in the student lounge. When he flunks all of his classes, he complains that they were boring anyway.

repression—keeping unpleasant thoughts that cause anxiety hidden in one's subconscious; temporarily "forgetting"

Example: Fred "forgets" to pay his rent because paying it will leave him flat broke.

projection—assigning a bad trait or problem of one's own to another person

Example: Gertrude, a single woman who is filled with yearning, refuses to leave her house for fear that the man across the street is waiting to attack her.

displacement—transferring one's frustrations to the person or object that did not cause them

Example: Susie has a baby brother who is now the center of her parents' attention. She is jealous and wants to hurt the baby but knows that it would be wrong. Instead, she takes her frustration out on her doll and succeeds in completely destroying it.

reaction-formation—behaving in a way opposite to one's beliefs and feelings

Example: Deep down, Walt hates cats, but whenever he visits his grandmother he lets her Siamese sit in his lap and strokes the cat lovingly.

★ **GED PRACTICE** ★

Exercise 25: Defense Mechanisms

Directions: The exercise below is based on the five defense mechanisms listed above. Reread the definitions and choose the best answer below.

1. A dishonest politician accuses her opponent of not being truthful with the voters. The defense mechanism used is

   (1) rationalization
   (2) repression
   (3) projection
   (4) displacement
   (5) reaction-formation

2. A man, who, deep down, enjoys watching X-rated films, joins a campaign to have them banned from the local theater. The defense mechanism used is

   (1) rationalization
   (2) repression
   (3) projection
   (4) displacement
   (5) reaction-formation

Study the cartoon below and answer the question that follows.

3. The defense mechanism the bowler is using is

   (1) rationalization
   (2) repression
   (3) projection
   (4) displacement
   (5) reaction-formation

(Roir, Ben Roth Agency)

 Writing Activity 7

Choose one of the defense mechanisms described above and write a paragraph describing a situation in which you or someone you know well used it.

ANSWERS AND EXPLANATIONS START ON PAGE 305.

Neuroses

Key Words

anxiety—uneasiness of mind or fearful concern
neurosis—a personality disorder in which a person is unusually anxious or miserable in his or her work or relations with others
phobia—an irrational fear

Have you ever been so depressed you couldn't work? So restless you couldn't sleep? So afraid you couldn't breathe? If so, you have had a glimpse of the world of the emotionally disturbed.

Psychologists like to classify the mentally ill by type of disorder and by degree of illness. Generally, the less severe disorders come under the heading neurosis. Neurotics usually function well on a day-to-day basis. But every now and then they experience anxiety that makes it difficult to perform tasks or to relate to others. The six case studies below describe a variety of neuroses. Read each case and be prepared to answer the questions at the end of this section.

Phobic Phil

Phil has a phobia. He has such a paralyzing fear of small, closed-in places (claustrophobia) that he does not ride airplanes, use elevators, or go very far in automobiles. He is successful in avoiding those situations, so most of his co-workers and acquaintances do not know of his problem.

Most psychologists believe that such phobias are linked to a biological trait developed in humans during evolution but triggered by an unpleasant experience. Phil may have been frightened by something when he was in his small crib as an infant, or he may have been left there for long periods of time.

Other such phobias that psychologists believe have a biological base are acrophobia (fear of high places), nyctophobia (fear of the dark), and ophidiophobia (fear of reptiles).

It is easy for us to understand such fears, but few of us go to the extremes a neurotic does to avoid them.

Complaining Claude

Claude has a different problem. He is normal in almost every regard, but he constantly complains and worries about being physically ill. His physician has decided that Claude is a *hypochondriac*. In other words, Claude feels sick but has no real symptoms beyond his voiced complaints.

Sometimes hypochondriacs, and otherwise healthy people, do develop real biological problems after long periods of anxiety and its resultant stress. Ulcers, migraine headaches, asthma, high blood pressure, and heart conditions have all been found to be the results of psychological disorders for some people. Such diseases are called *psychosomatic* (they are caused by the mind) and are considered to be a conversion-reaction to an emotional problem. That is, the emotional problem is converted into a physical symptom.

Immaculate Isabel

Isabel likes her home to be neat, clean, and orderly. In fact, Isabel is obsessed with cleanliness. She does nothing much all day every day except scrub, polish, dust, vacuum, pick up, put away, and rearrange. She compulsively follows her family around, cleaning up after them.

Isabel has a disorder described by psychologists as obsessive-compulsive. Many psychologists would theorize that some childhood experience involving the need for approval triggered Isabel's neurosis.

Down-in-the-Dumps Dollie

Dollie responds to her failures and disappointments more severely than most people. When she fails a test, loses a job, or gives a boring party, she gets extremely depressed. She cannot sleep, eat, or do much of anything. She is sad and apathetic, blames herself entirely, and feels worthless—for days, weeks, or months at a time. Psychologists say she is experiencing a neurotic depression or depressive reaction.

Anxious Anna

At least Dollie knows why she is depressed. Anna, on the other hand, feels anxious much of the time but cannot figure out why. She cannot relax for days at a time. She is uneasy, restless, and apprehensive, and she does not know why.

Psychologists often can help people like Anna with their anxiety neuroses by connecting their anxiety to a source (repressed feelings of anger or sexual desires, for example).

Wandering Wayne

Wayne's case is even more dramatic. He works two jobs to support his wife and four children. He has left home a couple of times and been found many miles away some time later, leading a less stressful, less responsible kind of life. He does not remember leaving home, starting a new life, and making the decisions he made. Psychologists call Wayne's disturbance a fugue state for Wayne cannot control his impulses and cannot face his awesome responsibilities and decisions. He does not really have a multiple personality because he keeps the same basic personality traits when he goes into his fugue states.

Exercise 26: Theory and Neuroses —————

Directions: In the blanks below, write *behaviorist* if the case describes the behaviorist theory of psychology and *psychoanalytical* if the case describes the psychoanalytical theory.

1. The cases of Phobic Phil and Immaculate Isabel are similar in that the

   causes can be linked to childhood experiences. The _____ theory of psychology best explains Phil's and Isabel's actions.

2. If Complaining Claude needs attention and receives it only when he complains about being ill, his behavior is said to be conditioned. In this

   case, the _____ theory of psychology would best explain his actions.

★ **GED PRACTICE** ★

Exercise 27: Neuroses —————————

Directions: You play psychologist. Diagnose each of the following patients. The neuroses are redefined below:

phobia—a crippling fear

conversion-reaction—an emotional problem converted into a physical symptom

obsessive-compulsive—a reaction characterized by an obsession (a preoccupation with an idea) and a compulsion (an irresistible impulse to perform an act)

depressive reaction—a reaction characterized by mental depression

fugue state—a reaction in which a person consciously performs an act but upon recovery does not remember it

1. George cannot function without excessive order in his life. Even his record albums must be kept in special groupings on the shelf or he becomes upset. George's neurosis may be described as

    (1) a phobia.
    (2) conversion-reaction.
    (3) obsessive-compulsive.
    (4) depressive reaction.
    (5) fugue state.

2. After Sylvia had been missing for six months, she was found living on the streets like a "bag lady," though she had a husband, children, a nice home, and an important job with a great deal of responsibility. When found, Sylvia did not remember ever having left her home and family. Sylvia's neurosis may be described as

    (1) a phobia.
    (2) conversion-reaction.
    (3) obsessive-compulsive.
    (4) depressive reaction.
    (5) fugue state.

3. Lavonna's husband is very good to her, but she realizes she doesn't love him anymore. She had an affair with a friend of her husband's not too long ago and now is experiencing severe stomach cramps that no doctor can find a physical cause for. Lavonna's neurosis may be described as

    (1) a phobia.
    (2) conversion-reaction.
    (3) obsessive-compulsive.
    (4) depressive reaction.
    (5) fugue state.

4. Bill has had a fear of water since he was a youngster. In fact, he quit the Boy Scouts when they insisted he learn to swim. When his company chartered a yacht for a party, Bill declined to attend even though he would have had access to a life preserver. Bill's neurosis is

    (1) a phobia.
    (2) conversion-reaction.
    (3) obsessive compulsion.
    (4) depressive reaction.
    (5) fugue state.

 Writing Activity 8

Do you know someone whose behavior might be considered neurotic? Write a two-paragraph paper describing this person and his or her neurosis.

ANSWERS AND EXPLANATIONS START ON PAGE 305.

Psychoses

<table>
<tr><td>

Key Word

psychosis—a mental or personality disorder, more severe than a neurosis and often requiring institutionalized treatment

</td></tr>
</table>

A psychosis is a more serious personality disorder than a neurosis. Psychotics cannot think, feel, or behave in a manner appropriate to reality.

Some forms of psychosis are displayed by extremely inappropriate moods and emotions. Katherine, for example, acts severely depressed and apathetic one day and uncontrollably excited, talkative, outgoing, and confident the next. She is a *manic-depressive*, and neither of her moods is ordinarily triggered by anything in particular in the real world.

Schizophrenia is probably the most publicized form of psychosis. People suffering from this type of disorder fantasize and hallucinate and often retreat into their own worlds.

Psychiatrists generally handle these personality disorders. In addition to psychotherapy, they may use a variety of methods ranging from electric shock therapy to medication in treating these severe behavioral problems.

★ GED PRACTICE ★

Exercise 28: Psychoses

Directions: Schizophrenia is believed to have some biological basis. "For every twisted thought there is a twisted molecule" is how some psychologists put it. Which of the statements below best supports this theory?

(1) Both members of a set of identical twins will not necessarily develop schizophrenia.

(2) Cases of both identical twins being schizophrenic are much more common among sets that have been raised together in the same environment.

(3) Both members of a set of identical twins are much more likely to be schizophrenic than two non-twin brothers or sisters.

(4) A member of a set of fraternal twins (nonidentical) is likely to be schizophrenic if the other twin is.

(5) Families that produce schizophrenics often display patterns of individual isolation or excessive closeness to one another.

ANSWER AND EXPLANATION START ON PAGE 308.

8
GEOGRAPHY

Where do you live? To begin, you live within the *universe*, in which lies a huge *galaxy* of stars, the Milky Way. To be more specific, you live within the *solar system*, within which the planet *Earth* moves.

To narrow the focus more, the earth is comprised of the oceans, seas, and seven *continents*. You live on the continent of _____ .

The continents are further divided into *nations*. The nation to which you belong is _____ .

The nation you live in is divided into *regions*—the North, South, East, and West. These regions are further divided into the Northeast, Northwest, Southeast, Southwest, and Midwest. The region of the country you live in is _____
_____ .

These broad regions are composed of the fifty *states*. The state you live in is _____ .

The next largest division within a state is the *county* (*parish* in Louisiana). The county in which you live is _____ .

Counties are divided further into *townships*. Your township if you have one is _____ .

Townships are divided into *towns*, *villages*, *boroughs*, and *cities*. Your town, village, borough, or city is _____ .

Residents of large cities live in neighborhood *communities*. If you live in a large city, your neighborhood community is called _____ .

Your *neighborhood* is made up of a *street* that may run north and south or east and west. Your *house number* and street determine your *address*, which finally pinpoints your location—unless you are studying for the GED tests away from home!

In this explanation, you could see your relationship to the world, from the broad perspective of a terrestrial being living on the planet Earth to the specific perspective of a member of a neighborhood community.

What Is Geography?

The *geographer* is interested in the places where human beings live and their relationships with the part of the world they live in. The location of people is important because so much of their culture is affected by it.

What we eat is determined by the climate and soil conditions. The kind of clothing we wear and the types of homes we build are dictated by the climate. Location even determines what kind of recreation is available.

The geographer studies locations by visiting and reading about them. Herodotus, a Greek who lived during the fifth century B.C., is sometimes credited with being the first geographer. He traveled to places like Italy, North Africa, and Persia and recorded in detail what he observed. Though the people of his time learned much from his writings, they were still limited by the points of view held by Herodotus and society in general. Most people believed that the earth was flat, that the Mediterranean and Black Seas were at the center of this world, and that a mysterious, unnamed ocean totally surrounded the lands and seas. Christopher Columbus later proved them wrong, of course, but not before many centuries worth of misinformation had been passed along.

Though very little of the earth's surface remains unexplored, geographers are still noting natural and man-made changes in the earth's composition, striving for accuracy in mapmaking, and recording population shifts.

THE WORLD ACCORDING TO HERODOTUS

The questions below are based on the map on page 211. Study the map and answer the questions that follow.

According to the map of the world, as Herodotus and his contemporaries saw it,

did the country of your birth exist? _____

How many continents did the ancient Greeks think there were? _____

What were their names? _____

_____

If you are a native American, the country of your birth could not have existed according to the map of the world as Herodotus saw it. The continents on the map of the world are written in all capital letters; therefore, the ancient Greeks thought there were three continents—*Europe, Asia,* and *Libya.*

★ **GED PRACTICE** ★

Exercise 1: The World According to Herodotus———

Directions: Refer to the map above to answer the following questions.

1. During Herodotus's day, explorers believed that the center of the world existed where they lived. If this was the case, you could infer that Herodotus was a citizen of

    (1) Thebes.
    (2) Sardes.
    (3) Caucasus.
    (4) Babylon.
    (5) Euphrates.

2. Which of the concepts studied in the "Anthropology" section most closely describes the above viewpoint held by Herodotus and others like him?

    (1) cultural diffusion
    (2) cultural relativity
    (3) ethnocentrism
    (4) primitivism
    (5) racism

ANSWERS AND EXPLANATIONS START ON PAGE 306.

The Tools of the Geographer

Key Words

map—a flat representation of the surface of a region
globe—a spherical representation of the surface of the earth
projection—the way in which the round earth is represented on a flat surface
scale—the proportion used to show distance on a map
legend or *key*—the explanatory description of how to read a map or chart

We have known for almost five hundred years that the earth is not flat; rather, it is round—shaped like a sphere. So we use globes in classrooms and libraries and in some homes when we want to locate a particular place. It is difficult to carry a globe with us when we take a trip by car, however; so we still use flat maps.

But when we use a *flat* map to show the *round* world, we get a distorted picture in which natural relationships are misrepresented. For example, some countries may appear smaller or larger than their true size, some land masses may appear to be shaped differently than they actually are, or some distances between regions may appear to be greater or smaller than they really are. Therefore, the type of projection mapmakers choose depends on what information is most important for them to highlight.

Types of Projection

Two types of projections mapmakers generally use are **Mollweide** and **Mercator** projections. The differences between the two can be seen in the illustration below.

MOLLWEIDE PROJECTION

MERCATOR PROJECTION

Notice the apparent difference in size between the Mollweide and Mercator projections of Greenland (located northeast of North America) and Antarctica. The Mollweide shows a relatively accurate depiction of land sizes, but the Mercator does not; yet the Mercator is used more often. This is because the Mercator does not distort the shape of the more populated areas far from the North and South Poles (top and bottom of the earth), and it represents true and constant directions on a compass used by navigators to travel the vast oceans.

On which map is the area of the oceans likely to be shown most accurately?

_____

Because the Mollweide projection shows land sizes more accurately, it must also show the sizes of the oceans more accurately than the Mercator projection.

Showing Distance on a Map

Distance is another important factor to someone planning a journey by using a map. Naturally, great distances have to be shown smaller on a map, but they still must be proportional. As you read on page 33 of the "Reading Skills" section of this book, the legend, or key, on a map often contains a scale that shows that proportion.

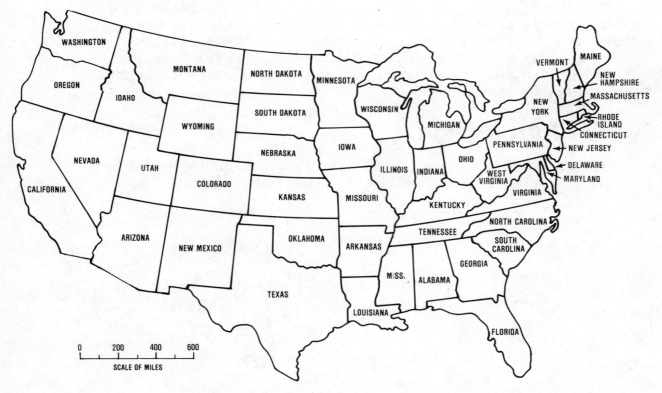

On this map, one inch represents about five hundred miles. You can measure with a ruler or with your finger to approximate any number of distances shown by the scale. You should be able to see that the United States covers about three thousand miles from coast to coast.

Latitude and Longitude

Key Words

Equator—the imaginary line that circles the earth, dividing it into the Northern and Southern Hemispheres

hemisphere—a half of the earth, east or west, north or south

latitude—a system of parallel lines measuring distance north or south of the equator

longitude—a system of parallel lines measuring distance east or west of the prime meridian

prime meridian—the imaginary line that divides the world into the Eastern and Western Hemispheres

grid—the pattern on a globe or map formed by the intersecting lines of latitude and longitude·

The Equator touches such exotic places as Cayambe in Ecuador, South America; Pontianak in Indonesian Borneo; and Entebbe in Uganda, Africa. These places are located on a line that divides the world into two hemispheres, north and south. Distance from the Equator is measured on a map by degrees of latitude. Latitude is a system of parallel lines measuring distance north or south of the Equator. The equator is at 0 degrees latitude, and the poles are at 90 degrees north and 90 degrees south.

Most of the continental United States, including Alaska, lies between 25 and 50 degrees north latitude. Lines of latitude are shown in the diagram below.

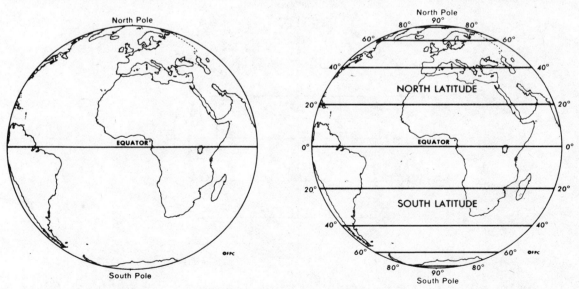

The U.S., in addition to other countries north of the Equator, lies within the Northern Hemisphere. All places south of the equator are said to lie in the Southern Hemisphere.

Longitudinal lines run north and south and measure distances east and west of the prime meridian. The Greenwich meridian, or prime meridian, is another name for the 0 degree line of longitude. There are 180 degrees east of the prime meridian and 180 degrees west of it, for a total of 360 degrees around the circular earth. Most of the continental U.S., including Alaska and Hawaii, lies between 65 and 125 degrees west longitude. Lines of longitude are illustrated in the diagram below.

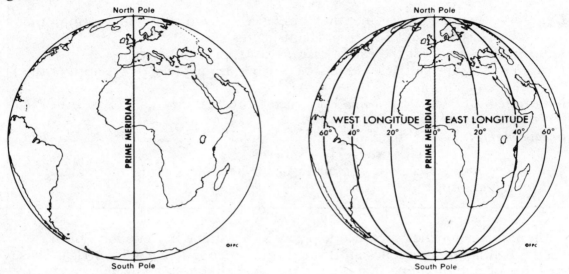

The lines of latitude and longitude cross each other to form a **grid**. To locate a particular place on a globe or map, find the point where these two lines intersect.

In the diagram below, eastern Spain is located at approximately 40 degrees north latitude and 0 degrees longitude. A grid is shown in the diagram below.

Based on the above grid, what continent is found at 20 degrees south and 60 degrees west? _____

You should have answered *South America*. The point where the 20-degree south line of latitude meets the 60-degree west line of longitude is the large continent of South America.

★ GED PRACTICE ★

Exercise 2: Latitude and Longitude

Directions: The following questions are based on the grid shown on page 216.

1. Which of the following is the location of 20 degrees north, 20 degrees east?

    (1)   The north Atlantic Ocean
    (2)   The south Atlantic Ocean
    (3)   North Africa
    (4)   South Africa
    (5)   Northern Europe

2. If you traveled westward 50 degrees from the above location (20 degrees north, 20 degrees east) where would you be?

    (1)   the North Atlantic Ocean
    (2)   the South Atlantic Ocean
    (3)   North Africa
    (4)   South Africa
    (5)   Northern Europe

3. Which of the following countries is located nearest 40 degrees north latitude and 60 degrees west longitude?

    (1)   Nigeria
    (2)   the United States
    (3)   Chile
    (4)   Argentina
    (5)   Greenland

ANSWERS AND EXPLANATIONS START ON PAGE 306.

The International Date Line

Key Word

international date line—the longitudinal line that indicates where a new day begins

The 180-degree longitude line runs through the middle of the Pacific Ocean and is directly opposite the prime meridian. It marks the approximate location of the international date line. The map on the next page illustrates the international date line.

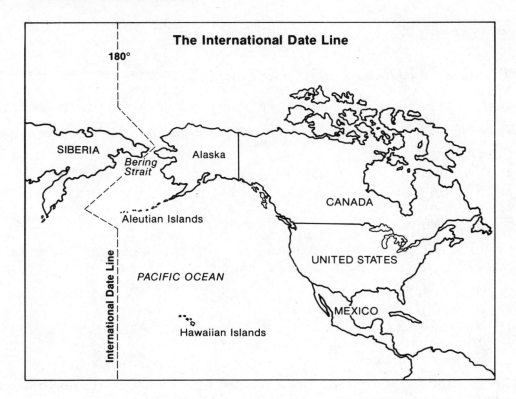

The International Date Line

Notice how the international date line zigzags from the 180-degree mark. The line zigzags so that there are not two different dates in one country.

As travelers proceed westward across the date line, they move into the next day. For example, if people on a westward cruise across the Pacific Ocean reached the line at 3:00 P.M. Tuesday, the day and time would change to 3:00 P.M. Wednesday when they crossed the date line. They would have "lost a day," as we say. Travelers going eastward would "gain a day." For example, they would go back to 3:00 P.M. Monday if they crossed the line at 3:00 P.M. Tuesday.

Time Zones

Key Word

time zone—an area within imaginary boundaries that uses one uniform clock time across its whole region

There are 24 hours in a day. By dividing the earth (which totals 360 degrees) into 24 one-hour-long sections, 15 degrees are equivalent to each hour of the day. So, as people travel west they move into an earlier time zone for every 15 degrees that they travel. For example, someone completing his journey west through the Eastern Time zone in the U.S. at 5:00 P.M. would have to move his watch to 4:00 P.M. as he crossed over into the next time zone, Central Time.

TIME ZONES ACROSS NORTH AMERICA

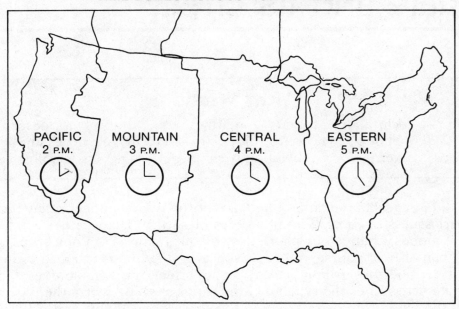

Based on the map above, in what time zone is the city in which you live? _____

★ **GED PRACTICE** ★

Exercise 3: Time Zones

Directions: Choose the one best answer for each question below.

1. According to the Time Zones map, what time is it in San Francisco when it is midnight in Chicago?

   (1) 9:00 A.M.
   (2) 10:00 P.M.
   (3) 11:00 P.M.
   (4) 1:00 A.M.
   (5) 2:00 A.M.

2. What time is it in New York when it is midnight in Salt Lake City?

   (1) 5:00 A.M.
   (2) 10:00 P.M.
   (3) 2:00 A.M.
   (4) 1:00 A.M.
   (5) 9:00 P.M.

ANSWERS AND EXPLANATIONS START ON PAGE 306.

Climate and Its Effect

Key Words

weather—a local and temporary condition in the atmosphere; described by how hot or cold, wet or dry, calm or stormy, clear or cloudy it is
climate—an average or a prevailing weather pattern at a particular place

The old adage, "Man can only *talk* about the weather" accurately indicates our powerlessness in controlling the forces of nature. The weather can affect our emotional moods, change our plans, destroy our homes, ruin our crops, and even kill us. It can also, of course, raise our spirits and help our crops to grow. One day's weather does not usually have a lasting effect, but climate does.

Climate determines the type and amount of clothing worn, the type of housing built, the kind of crops raised, and the species of animals and plant life that can survive. Climate is affected by five factors:

1. The relationship of the earth's axis to the sun

2. The topography of the earth

3. The relationship of the earth's land to bodies of water

4. The distribution of moisture in the air

5. The distribution of air pressures and winds

The Earth's Axis and the Sun

Key Words

axis—the imaginary line through the poles of the earth that tilts at an angle (23½ degrees) in relation to the sun
seasons—the divisions of the year by climate, determined by the earth's relationship to the sun

Of all the elements important to climate, temperature is probably the most significant, for in order for life to exist, the temperature of the environment must be able to support it. Since nearly all the earth's heat comes from the sun, the position of a region with reference to the sun greatly affects its climate.

The earth, tilted on its axis, spins around the sun. Therefore, the relationship of regions of the earth to the sun changes continually. The seasons of the year are determined by the earth's degree of tilt toward the sun.

On the first day of spring and fall, the sun's rays extend from the North Pole to the South Pole, and day and night are of equal length over the entire earth.

On that day, the sun's rays strike the Equator to form a right angle. When the Northern Hemisphere experiences spring, the Southern Hemisphere experiences fall and vice versa.

On the first day of summer and winter, the sun's rays strike the earth's surface unequally. In summer, one half of the earth gets more sunshine (and has longer days) than the opposite half. The hemisphere that receives the most sunshine experiences summer; the hemisphere that receives the least experiences winter.

The areas near the Equator always receive plenty of direct sunshine. These areas are given the names the Tropic of Cancer (23½ degrees north of the Equator) and the Tropic of Capricorn (23½ degrees south of the Equator). The Tropics are hot all year round. The illustration below shows the earth's climate zones.

THE EARTH'S CLIMATE ZONES

The Tropics of Cancer and Capricorn are "mirror images" of each other in climate. This means that when one experiences a particular season, the other experiences its opposite. The same effect continues into the next climate areas, called the *temperate zones.*

Almost the entire United States lies within the North Temperate Zone. Seasonal changes are much more characteristic of the temperate zones than of the Tropics.

At the extremes on either end of the earth are the arctic zones, sometimes called the *polar regions.* Both areas are known for their frigid temperatures. Because of a lack of sunshine, these areas cannot support very much plant and animal life.

Exercise 4: Climate and Its Effect

Directions: Choose the one best answer to each question or statement below.

1. The line of latitude that *most* affects the changing seasons of the earth is

    (1) the Arctic Circle.
    (2) the Tropic of Cancer.
    (3) the Equator.
    (4) the Tropic of Capricorn.
    (5) the Antarctic Circle.

2. Based on the illustration above, which region of the world is in a climate zone that is a mirror image of most of the U.S.?

    (1) Central America
    (2) the northern area of South America
    (3) the middle section of South America
    (4) the southern area of South America
    (5) the southern tip of Greenland

ANSWERS AND EXPLANATIONS START ON PAGE 306.

The Topography of the Earth

Key Words

elevation—altitude; height above sea level
relief—the measure of difference of elevation in related land surfaces
mountains—elevations of over 1,000 feet from the base and with inclined sides and pointed or rounded tops
topography—a method in mapmaking in which the terrain of specific places on earth is shown
contour line—a line representing the outline of an irregular shape such as a mountain or hill; used on topographical maps

Humans are first, last, and always creatures of the land. Our activity in the oceans and in the air is guided by what we want and need to do as land creatures. Geographers basically divide the land into *flatlands* (or plains) and *highlands* (or mountains, hills, and plateaus).

Mountains are elevations over 1,000 feet, usually with steep rocky inclines on all sides and a pointed or rounded top. *Hills* are lower in elevation, with sides sloping up to rounded or flat tops. *Plateaus* rank third in terms of height, rising sharply above the level of neighboring areas. They have elevations of lower than 500 feet and broad flat tops. *Trenches* running through them produce steep-sided valleys and marked relief in the immediate area. *Plains* have fairly uniform low relief and flat or gently sloping land.

Topography is the method in mapmaking of illustrating the terrain of specific places on the earth. Mapmakers illustrate the varying heights of land masses by using contour lines that show elevations in numbers of feet or meters. The closer together the contour lines, the steeper the degree of incline. The illustration below shows contour lines as used in mapmaking.

Mountains often act as boundaries between different climate regions. The lower slopes of the mountains usually share the climate of the surrounding area, but the higher up one goes, the colder the air gets. This is because the atmosphere is "thinner" in higher elevations and less able to hold heat. Also, the mountains tend to get wetter as the altitude rises because cooler air can hold less moisture.

The climate of plateaus, too, is affected by the climate of the regions in which they are located. Those that are in areas of high elevation are cold, windy, and hostile to humans. Those located in tropical regions are often a pleasant contrast to the hot areas they rise above, however. Hills and plateaus that rise from the plains share the same climate characteristic of the plains near which they are located.

★ **GED PRACTICE** ★

Exercise 5: The Topography of the Earth ——————

Directions: The questions below are based on the illustration below.

1. The terrain shown in the contour map would be classified as

    (1) mountains.
    (2) plateaus.
    (3) hills.
    (4) trenches.
    (5) valleys.

2. It is most likely that the area labeled "Buckhorn School" has a climate much like

(1) most of the rest of the area shown on the map.
(2) the lowlands of the area on this map, but not the highlands.
(3) the highest elevation of any mountain area.
(4) The plains near any ocean anywhere.
(5) the hills of any area in any zone.

3. Which of the following is supported by the map?

(1) The area is a desert.
(2) The area is unpopulated.
(3) The area is populated.
(4) The climate is cold and dry.
(5) The climate is humid.

 Writing Activity 1

In one or two paragraphs, describe the topography of the area in which you live. Do you live near mountains, hills, plains, or plateaus? Describe how the topography of your region affects the work that people do.

ANSWERS AND EXPLANATIONS START ON PAGE 306.

Water's Effect on Climate

The relationship of the earth's land to bodies of water is another important factor that affects climates. Part of the variation in climate is caused by the differing location of regions with respect to large bodies of water.

The climate of the arctic tundra plains, for example, is affected by the Arctic Ocean. The movement of water on the surface of the ocean helps to keep the tundra warmer than the rest of the Arctic Zone. Therefore, changes of seasons and temperature ranges are not as extreme near the Arctic Ocean as they are farther inland.

The effects of the ocean are seen in other parts of the world as well, and in areas other than the plains. The Pacific Ocean's many warm currents moderate the climate from the western edge of Alaska, down the Canadian and American coasts, into the Pacific islands, and up through the eastern edge of Asia.

The Atlantic Ocean keeps much of the southeastern seaboard warm in the winter and relatively cool in the summer, especially along the coast. Even gulfs, like the Gulf of Mexico, and lakes, like the Great Lakes, have streams and currents that help temper the climate of regions near the body of water itself.

★ GED PRACTICE ★

Exercise 6: Water's Effect on Climate ——————

The graph below shows how the Arctic Ocean affects the climate in two places located in the same latitude.

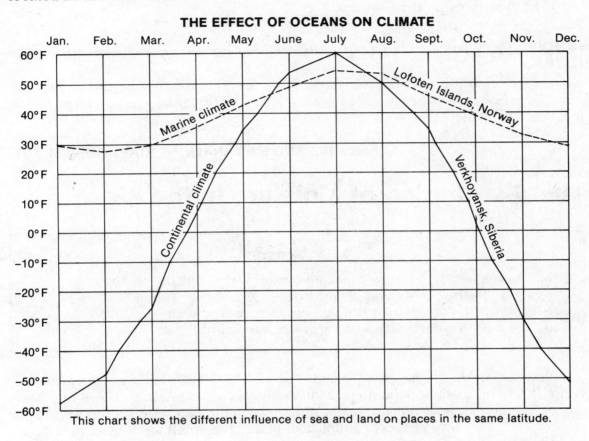

THE EFFECT OF OCEANS ON CLIMATE

This chart shows the different influence of sea and land on places in the same latitude.

Directions: Based on the graph and the passage above, choose the one best answer for each question below.

1. Which of the following conclusions may be drawn from the information in the above graph?

   (1) The Lofoten Islands have a more severe climate than Verkhoyansk, Siberia.
   (2) Verkhoyansk, Siberia, experiences more extremes in temperature than the Lofoten Islands.
   (3) Coastal temperatures have a greater range than inland ones.
   (4) Coastal temperatures are generally higher than inland ones.
   (5) Inland temperatures do not show the seasonal changes that coastal ones do.

2. Based on the information in the passage above, it is reasonable to conclude
that during the winter season in the U.S., it is likely to be colder in

   (1) Michigan than in Ohio.
   (2) South Dakota than in the state of Washington.
   (3) North Carolina than in South Carolina.
   (4) Arizona than in Nevada.
   (5) Pennsylvania than in New York.

 Writing Activity 2

Do you live near a large body of water? If so, describe in a paragraph or two
how the weather in your area is affected, during both summer and winter, by its
location near water.

ANSWERS AND EXPLANATIONS START ON PAGE 307.

The Distribution of Moisture in the Air

Key Words

precipitation—rain or snow that falls to the surface of the earth
evaporation—the conversion of moisture or liquid into vapor
arid—very dry; containing little or no moisture in the air
humid—moist or damp; containing water vapor in the air

    Nowhere in the frigid Arctic is snowfall heavy. As surprising as this may
seem, this is because precipitation results only when warm air is cooled and becomes less able to hold moisture. Not much warm air ever reaches the Arctic;
therefore, this cooling process cannot take place. The small amount of precipitation that does fall in the Arctic hits the coastal areas more frequently and more
heavily than the inland regions. The large amount of ice and snow that can be
found in that region is preserved there by the freezing temperatures and little
evaporation.
    There is more rain in the tropics than in other regions of the earth because
the rays of the sun hit the earth directly there, intensely heating the air at the
surface. As this very hot air rises, it cools and releases its moisture in the form of
rain. The farther away one gets from the Equator, the more seasonal and the less
consistent the rainfall gets. In fact, there are sections where little rain falls at all.
Geographers say that these areas are arid.
    Precipitation in parts of the temperate zones is frequent and heavy, espe-
cially in the summer. This is because of the frequent change of temperature that
results from varying topography and wind patterns in those areas. Cold air often
meets warm air, and the moisture held by the warm air falls to the earth in the
form of rain or snow. Areas that receive large amounts of precipitation and relatively little evaporation are said to be humid.

★ GED PRACTICE ★

Exercise 7: The Distribution of Moisture in the Air

Directions: Choose the one best answer for each statement or question below.

1. It can be inferred from this passage that snow falls more frequently and heavily on the coasts of the Arctic than inland because

    (1) the coasts' temperatures are warmer than inland temperatures.
    (2) it is colder near the ocean when the warm air hits it from inland.
    (3) there is less moisture in the air near the coast.
    (4) there is no moisture in the air near the coast.
    (5) little evaporation of moisture takes place near the coast.

2. Based on its location in the United States, which state is likely to have the most humidity during the summer?

    (1) Arizona
    (2) California
    (3) Louisiana
    (4) Mississippi
    (5) Florida

 ## Writing Activity 3

Describe in one to two paragraphs the amount of precipitation the area in which you live receives during both the summer and the winter. What accounts for the abundance or lack of precipitation in your area?

ANSWERS AND EXPLANATIONS START ON PAGE 307.

The Distribution of Air Pressures and Winds

Key Word
prevailing winds—winds that have the greatest effect on the weather of a region

The area around the Equator is always warm; warm air is lighter in weight than cold air. An area in which warm air is rising has little pressure on it, so geographers call it a *low-pressure belt*. The equatorial area is a low pressure area. The arctic region is always cold. A region in which heavy cold air sinks toward the ground is a *high-pressure belt*. The polar regions are high-pressure areas.

Patches of highs or lows can move out from the main pressure belts around the world and affect the weather. Cold air that moves away from high-pressure belts brings relatively clear, calm, and cool weather with it. Weather created by a low-pressure condition, on the other hand, is usually stormy, cloudy, and warm.

Winds result from the movement of air from high-pressure belts to low-pressure belts. Winds that have the greatest effect on weather are called the prevailing winds. If the earth were standing still, the prevailing winds would flow exactly north and south. But, of course, the earth does not stand still, so the prevailing winds are turned by its rotation.

The prevailing winds of the North American continent originate primarily in the West, which explains why the West Coast of the U.S. experiences a milder climate than the interior and northern East Coast of the country.

The moderating effect of the Pacific Ocean is contained along a narrow strip on the West Coast of the U.S. because of the mountain ranges that run north and south of the coast. The diagram below illustrates the prevailing wind patterns of the earth.

PREVAILING WIND PATTERNS

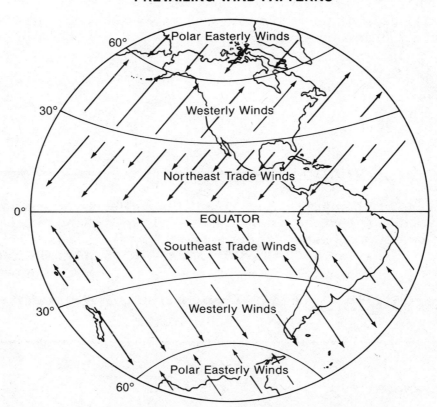

Exercise 8: Air Pressure and Winds

Directions: Place a check before each conclusion about westerly winds that can be drawn from the map above.

_____ **(1)** Westerly winds are found only in the Northern Hemisphere.

_____ **(2)** Westerly winds usually occur between the 30- and 60-degree latitudes.

_____ **(3)** Westerlies generally blow from east to west.

_____ **(4)** Westerlies generally blow from west to east.

★ **GED PRACTICE** ★

Exercise 9: Prevailing Wind Patterns

Directions: Choose the one best answer for each question below.

1. Which of the following statements is best supported by the information in the diagram of Prevailing Wind Patterns?

    (1) The tilt of the earth's axis causes all the prevailing winds to turn in the same direction.
    (2) The patterns of prevailing winds are mirror images of each other on either side of the equator.
    (3) The West Coast of any continent has a more moderate climate than its East Coast.
    (4) The horse latitudes are low-pressure belts that mark the start of the westerlies.
    (5) The trade winds are more influential on climate than the westerlies or the easterlies.

 ## Writing Activity 4

Does the wind play a major role in the region in which you live? In one to two paragraphs, describe the role of the wind—whether your area experiences much of it or not—in determining the climate where you live.

ANSWERS AND EXPLANATIONS START ON PAGE 307.

Population Distribution and Migration

Key Words

population demographics—the statistical study of the numbers and locations of people in a region

migrate—to move from one region in order to settle in another

rural—having to do with small towns and country living, especially near agricultural areas

urban—having to do with large cities

suburban—having to do with the outlying, residential towns around a city

Sunbelt—the southern part of the U.S. from Virginia to California, known for its relatively warm weather

The study of where people live and how they are distributed or spread out in a region is called population demographics by geographers. Climate and topography clearly affect where people live and why they migrate. The U.S. would not have achieved the position it has in the world were it not for its temperate climate and predominance of plains. But what other factors have such effects? And what else causes people to move, or migrate, from one location to another?

The location of work can and often does affect population distribution. For example, when agriculture was a major source of employment, our country's population was concentrated in outlying rural areas. As you read in the "History" section of this book, when industries developed and expanded, the cities that grew up around them attracted large numbers of residents.

Today, this trend seems to apply to the suburbs, especially in the U.S. Suburbs have become more desirable places than big cities in which to live and to build businesses. This is largely because of their relative safety from crime as compared to the big cities, their newness and cleanliness, their wider spaces, and their better educational systems.

Another trend that is present in American life today is the decline of heavy manufacturing jobs in the U.S. economy and a rapid growth in the service industries. As a result, the midwestern and eastern cities are no longer the industrial centers they once were.

Fast-growing industries such as computer technology and financial planning depend less on the availability of natural resources than they do on the availability of human labor and skills.

States like Georgia, California, and Arizona, described as Sunbelt areas, have especially benefited from the relocation of "high-tech" industries there.

Exercise 10: Population Distribution and Migration

Directions: Exercise 10 is based on the map of Iowa, the information provided below, and what you may already know about geographic regions of the U.S.

POPULATION DISTRIBUTION OF IOWA

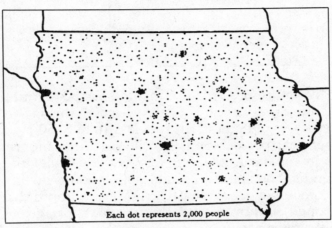

Each dot represents 2,000 people

U.S. Bureau of the Census

1. Iowa is one of the flattest states in the U.S. Based on the information in the map above, which of the following inferences can be made about population distribution in Iowa?

   (1) Farming is still a major industry and influence in the state of Iowa.
   (2) Lowlands allow for an even distribution of population.
   (3) Iowa is being drained of its population by the Sunbelt.
   (4) Iowa is one of the most heavily populated states.
   (5) There are few big cities on the plains of the U.S.

2. Which of the following states would be most unlike Iowa in terms of population distribution?

   (1) Kansas
   (2) Nebraska
   (3) West Virginia
   (4) Ohio
   (5) Indiana

 ## Writing Activity 5

Describe in two to three paragraphs the population distribution in your state. Is it densely or sparsely populated? Why? Is your state gaining or losing residents? Why?

ANSWERS AND EXPLANATIONS START ON PAGE 307.

Standards of Living Around the World

Key Words

standard of living—measurement of quality of life based on certain indicators
demographics—statistics that describe a population
average life expectancy—the length of time, on the average, a baby born in a
    certain place can be expected to live
infant mortality rates—the frequency of deaths among babies of a region
population growth—the rate at which the population of an area is increasing
    or decreasing

Standards of living are most tied to income per person in the country. In highly developed countries like the U.S. and Sweden, this is over $4,000 a year per adult. In underdeveloped countries, it is less than $750 a year per adult.

The income per year per person is just one of the demographics that describe differences in standards of living across the world. Others include average life expectancy, infant mortality rates, and population growth.

Average life expectancy in developed countries is more than seventy years of age; in underdeveloped countries it is only fifty years of age.

Infant mortality rates account for some of that difference. The rate of children dying in infancy is less than 25 deaths for every 1,000 children in most developed countries; it is over 250 deaths for every 1,000 children in many underdeveloped ones. Population growth in developed countries is less than 1 percent per year; in underdeveloped countries it is more than 2.5 percent per year.

The growth rate in a country is significant because overcrowding often contributes to a poor standard of living. Natural resources, jobs, and money have been spread thin in some countries like India that have large populations and large growth rates.

There are examples like Japan, of course, that are densely populated but are not underdeveloped. Such countries have overcome the handicap of large people-to-land ratios through a wise use of natural resources and human ingenuity. A traditional emphasis on education and technological manufacturing have helped in that regard.

Japan and other developed countries as densely populated have also made a concentrated effort to keep their birth rate down. Through family-planning programs, such countries have managed to keep families, and therefore the growth rate low.

Whether standards of living can be raised significantly and quickly by organized family planning in underdeveloped countries is a theory still being tested. But one thing that is certain is that the people of those countries are becoming increasingly aware of how their standard of living compares to that in developed countries. Being more aware has made them more desirous of material goods and their benefits. Natural resources have not been distributed evenly throughout the world, however, and that fact alone may keep some countries underdeveloped for generations to come.

Exercise 11: World Population

Exercise 11 is based on the graph below.

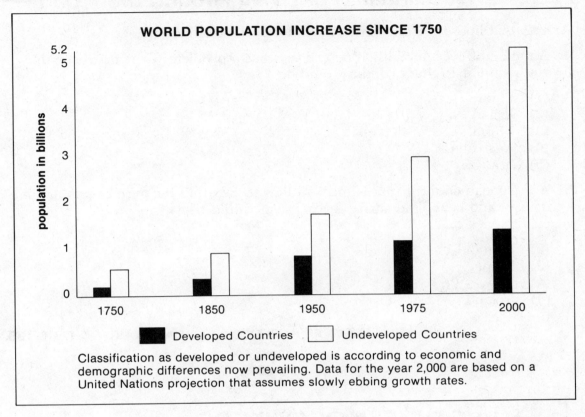

WORLD POPULATION INCREASE SINCE 1750

population in billions

Developed Countries   Undeveloped Countries

Classification as developed or undeveloped is according to economic and demographic differences now prevailing. Data for the year 2,000 are based on a United Nations projection that assumes slowly ebbing growth rates.

Directions: In the space provided, write *YES* next to each of the following statements that can be supported by information on the graph and *NO* next to those that cannot.

_____ **1.** The populations of developed countries far exceeds that of undeveloped countries.

_____ **2.** Populations of undeveloped countries are growing at a faster rate than developed ones.

_____ **3.** By the year 2000, the world's population will be over five times the population of 1750.

_____ **4.** The population of developed countries has represented a minority of the world's population since at least 1750.

★ **GED PRACTICE** ★

Exercise 12: Standards of Living Around the World——

Directions: Choose the one best answer for each statement below.

1. A nation of over one billion people that has a problem with large growth rates similar to that of India would be

   (1) Canada.
   (2) Brazil.
   (3) China.
   (4) Australia.
   (5) France.

2. A European country that is most similar to Japan in the area of population density and heavy industrial development would be

   (1) Spain.
   (2) England.
   (3) France.
   (4) Italy.
   (5) Ireland.

ANSWERS AND EXPLANATIONS START ON PAGE 308.

The World's Resources

Since its discovery, North America has offered great opportunities to people wanting to improve their standard of living. The fertile lands and temperate climate were a major attraction in the first two centuries of exploration and settlement. When the Industrial Revolution began, the continent contributed to America's success because of its rich supply of resources such as coal, natural gas, and water. As the nation developed, Americans became dependent on petroleum as a source of energy.

Coal

Key Words

environmentalists—people concerned about pollution of the environment and the careless use of natural resources

pollutants—poisons or contaminants

Coal remains an important resource because of its importance in producing electricity. But reliance on coal also causes safety and environmental problems that threaten our quality of life.

Underground mines are vulnerable to cave-ins, explosions, and gas leaks. Strip, or surface, mines create large areas of gaping, exposed holes from which rains wash pollution into the lakes and streams. Besides these problems, coal is also criticized by environmentalists as a dirty fuel because it emits pollutants into the air when burned.

Petroleum

Petroleum is a source of fuel that is becoming increasingly vital to industrial and personal use. In its natural state, it is used to produce heat and light; in its refined state, it is used to make gasoline and other products.

Petroleum is another "dirty" fuel that pollutes the environment when it is burned or spilled into the oceans. Fires on offshore oil rigs also pose dangers. However, the importance of petroleum as a fuel is growing rather than diminishing. Petroleum-poor nations, like the U.S., use huge quantities of petroleum and must depend on oil-rich Middle Eastern countries for their supply. In 1960, the Organization of Petroleum Exporting Countries (OPEC) was founded to counteract falling petroleum prices. Skyrocketing oil prices in the 1970s have established many of these countries as oil-rich.

Natural Gas

Natural gas is found together with or separate from oil deposits. The vapor or dry gas that we use as fuel for heat and cooking in our homes is taken from natural gas after liquid fuels like butane, propane, and gasoline are removed. Besides its use as a fuel in homes and business, gas is used in the manufacture of important products such as plastics, drugs, and dyes.

Water

Although all of the world's natural resources are of limited and decreasing supply, the resource of most critical scarcity is water. It is absolutely necessary to the survival of humanity, each person on earth requiring at least two or three quarts per day.

In the U.S., the standard of living demands 50 gallons a day for every man, woman, and child. Water is not as easily transported over long distances as are other commodities like coal and natural gas.

The supply of ocean water is large but presently of limited use. Fresh water is distributed unevenly around the world. To correct this problem, icebergs have been towed from the polar regions and water has been piped from mountain ranges, but at great trouble and expense. In addition, pollution of the lakes, rivers, and streams has decreased the exisiting supply of fresh water.

★ GED PRACTICE ★

Exercise 13: Regional Water Shortages

Directions: Choose the one best answer for each question below.

The graph below predicts the water shortage that will occur in the U.S. in future decades. In the graph, the artist compares what might happen if families continue to have an average of two children with what might happen if families average three children.

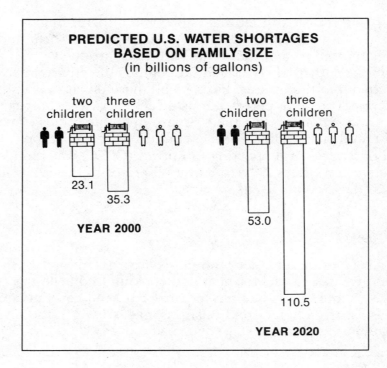

PREDICTED U.S. WATER SHORTAGES
BASED ON FAMILY SIZE
(in billions of gallons)

two children   three children   two children   three children

23.1

35.3

YEAR 2000

53.0

110.5

YEAR 2020

1.   The artist has failed to consider which of the following?

   (1)   Three-child families use more water than two-child families.
   (2)   Water shortages will continue to increase with either two-child or three-child families.
   (3)   The faster the increase in population, the greater the degree of water shortage.
   (4)   No new technologies for finding, processing, or transporting fresh water supplies will be found by 2020.
   (5)   Technologies that will help find, process, and transport fresh water supplies will help lessen the shortages by 2020.

2. What would likely be the outcome if the population growth pattern projection through the year 2020 was reduced from two-child to one-child families?

   (1) The amount of water available to the general population would triple.
   (2) The amount of water available to the general population would hold steady.
   (3) The amount of water available to the general population would decrease.
   (4) The water shortage for the general population would be reduced.
   (5) There would be enough water for all Americans, in all regions of the country.

3. Based on what you know about the geography and climate regions of the U.S., which region would you infer to have the most limited supply of water?

   (1) the Northeast
   (2) the Middle West
   (3) the Northwest
   (4) the Southeast
   (5) the Southwest

ANSWERS AND EXPLANATIONS START ON PAGE 308.

Nuclear and Solar Energy

Key Words

nuclear energy—energy released through atomic reactions
solar energy—energy from the sun's rays

Because of the environmental hazards of burning coal and petroleum, alternative sources of energy are being explored and applied. The most important and most controversial of these is nuclear energy.

Problems associated with atomic power include the disposal of radioactive wastes and the accidental release of radioactive particles into the atmosphere. Both the 1979 accident at Three Mile Island in the U.S. and the 1986 incident at Chernobyl in the Soviet Union dramatized the potential dangers of nuclear energy.

Solar energy is a clean, safe alternative source of power. Solar "batteries" have been invented that capture the sunlight and store it for long term use.

The following exercise is based on the map below:

NUCLEAR POWER REACTORS IN THE U.S.

Number of Operational
Nuclear Power Reactors
as of 1981

- 8
- 5 to 6
- 3 to 4
- 1 to 2
- 0

Exercise 14: Nuclear and Solar Energy

Directions: Study the map, then choose the one best answer for each question or statement below.

1. According to the map, which of the following states has the greatest number of nuclear power plants?

   (1) Illinois
   (2) California
   (3) New York
   (4) Florida
   (5) Texas

2. Which statement may you infer about the states that have the greatest number of nuclear energy plants?

   (1) They have few coal reserves.
   (2) They are all located in the East.
   (3) Most have large populations and are high energy users.
   (4) They have no other alternatives for energy.
   (5) Most have expanses of land far from human habitation.

3. Some states have not had to turn to nuclear energy production because they are not industrialized states and, therefore, do not require as much electrical power. Which of the following states is most likely in that category?

   (1) Montana
   (2) Nebraska
   (3) Texas
   (4) Maryland
   (5) Illinois

4. This map lends support to the argument that one of the greatest dangers of accidents at nuclear energy plants is that

   (1) they are located too far away from city rescue services.
   (2) they are often in densely populated states.
   (3) they are not used cooperatively among the states.
   (4) they have not been regulated adequately by the government.
   (5) there are more of them in existence than is necessary.

 Writing Activity 6

Is our dependence on nuclear energy plants to produce electrical power worth the risk they pose to human life? Write a three-paragraph essay defending your point of view on this issue. Be sure to include facts to support your position.

ANSWERS AND EXPLANATIONS START ON PAGE 308.

World Trade

Key Words

import—to bring goods into a country for the purpose of selling them
export—to sell goods to another country
world trade—the international exchange or sale of goods
cartel—an agreement among countries that possess a resource to control the price of that resource on the world trade market

---

The U.S. has a wealth of natural resources, but it does not have all it needs to support its standard of living. It must import many goods like rubber, tin, chrome, sugar, coffee, and petroleum.

In turn, the U.S. exports many manufactured goods such as cars, canned foods, computers, and plastics. Importing and exporting goods among nations is called world trade, and without it, nations such as Japan that are poorly endowed with natural resources would not have been able to develop into major industrial powers.

Without world trade, an oil-glutted nation like Saudi Arabia would be stuck with an oversupply of crude petroleum that could not feed its people or provide clothing or shelter.

Generally, the poorest countries of the world are not involved in the world trade market. Developing nations are involved in exporting raw materials and importing manufactured goods and services. The most highly developed nations import more raw materials than manufactured goods and export large numbers and varieties of man-made products and services.

Developing countries may improve their standard of living by using their own natural resources to produce goods and services within their own borders. They could, therefore, avoid the high cost of some imports and possibly produce enough to export for profit.

Another opportunity for improvement might be gained by charging higher prices for their raw materials in the world trade market. Many countries have been able to raise prices by forming cartels; OPEC, formed during the 1970s, is an example of a cartel. Member nations of OPEC agreed to set prices for exported petroleum to oil-dependent countries like the U.S. To some extent, the prices we pay at the gas pump are a direct result of this price-setting policy.

Exercise 15: World Trade

Directions: In the spaces provided below, write the name of the country—*the U.S., Japan,* or *Saudi Arabia*—that correctly completes the statements below.

1. Great Britain's rise to power in the world trade market most resembled

   _____'s in that it had few natural resources but imported what it needed to manufacture goods to sell for high prices elsewhere.

2. South Africa must import many goods necessary for its population but can afford such an imbalance in trade since it has accumulated wealth from the international sale of its large supply of gold. In this regard,

   South Africa is much like the country of _____ .

3. The former Soviet Union had an abundance of mineral resources that helped develop its manufacturing capabilities and resultant position as a

   world power. Thus, the Soviet Union was like _____ in this respect.

ANSWERS AND EXPLANATIONS START ON PAGE 309.

9 ECONOMICS

The Green Thumb is a small company that produces indoor and outdoor plants that it distributes through home parties. Its sales personnel visit people's homes to show them the plants, explain how to grow and care for them, and convince the people to be buyers, or consumers, of the plants.

The plants are **goods**; the selling of them is a **service**. The people who took the risk to establish the business are **entrepreneurs**. They are attempting to fill a need in society. If they succeed, their activity will pay off, or return a profit for the money they invested in the business.

In the production of the plants, raw materials, called **natural resources**, are used. **Human resources**, or labor, are the gardeners, the salespeople, and the office workers of The Green Thumb. **Capital**, which includes the greenhouse, gardening tools, grow lights, and money, is also invested in the effort.

The study of the process of producing and distributing these plants and how it relates to buying, selling, and making a profit in a society is the interest of the economist.

Additionally, economists explore the role of the government in regulating such business activity and examine how the government gathers money for its own needs.

Exercise 1: The Basics of Economics

Directions: Based on the reading on page 241, match the terms on the left with the descriptions on the right by writing the correct letter in the space provided.

_____ **1.** producers   **(a)** interior designers and homemakers who buy Green Thumb plants

_____ **2.** distributors   **(b)** the different varieties of plants Green Thumb sells

_____ **3.** consumers   **(c)** the trucks that deliver the nursery-grown plants to Green Thumb outlets

_____ **4.** goods   **(d)** what the Green Thumb's salespeople give potential buyers

_____ **5.** service   **(e)** Green Thumb and other companies like it

ANSWERS AND EXPLANATIONS START ON PAGE 309.

Economic Systems

Key Words

capitalism—an economic system that is based on the private ownership of property and the resources of production

communism—an economic and social system in which private ownership of property is not permitted

socialism—an economic system under which a country's major industries and services are owned publicly and cooperatively

free enterprise—an economic system based on private ownership and operation of businesses with little or no government control

As much as people try to distinguish politics from economics, it is difficult to separate them totally. A nation's political system often determines the type of economic system that the nation operates under.

The world's three major types of economic systems are **capitalism, socialism**, and **communism**. How each operates is illustrated below.

Capitalism

The Happy House Painters, Inc., is a small company run by individual investors for their own private profit and is allowed to operate with few government restraints. The company is located in a capitalist country. Capitalism is an economic system that works on the theory that, under free enterprise, resources and income are most fairly distributed. Free enterprise means little or no government involvement in business practices.

Under capitalism, investment decisions are made mainly by the individual rather than by the government. The production, distribution, and prices of goods and services are determined by competition in a free market. The government intervenes only when necessary to protect the public interest. The economy of the United States is based on the economic principle of capitalism.

Over time, the U.S. economic system has evolved to permit more government control than is the ideal of free enterprise. The degree of government involvement in the economy changes with each political administration although, generally, the Democratic Party favors more involvement and the Republican Party favors less.

Socialism

A socialist does not attempt to separate politics from economics. For example, in a country whose economic system is based on socialism, the Happy House Painters would have to answer to the government on many issues. The government might be the sole owner of the oils out of which the paint is made. Or it might run the transportation system that distributes the paint to its final destination or the electric company that provides the lights and power to accomplish the work. The number of hours that employees work or the amount of wages they earn might be regulated by the government. Most certainly, health and welfare benefits would be provided for the workers by the state, which would get much of the money for such efforts by taxing companies.

Socialists believe that the entire country benefits from such government ownership and control, that there is more efficiency in industrial output, and that wealth is distributed more equally and fairly. Elements of socialism exist today in democracies such as Great Britain, Sweden, and West Germany.

Communism

Under communism, all property is owned by the people and regulated by the state. The state is run by one political party that controls more than just the economy.

In a communist country, even the name of the company might be regulated by the state. The Happy House Painters might be the State Decorating Company—or perhaps a name would not be designated at all, since under communism there is no competition among companies. In fact, if the state determined that painting houses was no longer necessary, the company would not exist at all. The People's Republic of China and Cuba are two countries that operate under communist economies today.

Mixed Economics

None of the three economic systems described above exists in pure form in any country. That is, no *completely* capitalist, socialist, or communist economy exists in the modern world. In its operation, each of the economic systems incorporates some aspect of the other. Each economic system is modified to meet the needs of the nation it serves.

For example, though the U.S. has a capitalist economy, government agencies regulate, to some extent, the practices of certain businesses. The Federal Trade Commission's responsibility is to eliminate false advertising and to prevent the formation of monopolies. The Food and Drug Administration can remove from the market any food, drug, or cosmetic it deems to be dangerous to the public. The Department of Agriculture inspects and grades meats, dairy products, and produce bought and sold across state lines.

Exercise 2: Economic Systems

Directions: Fill in each description below with the appropriate word: *capitalist, socialist,* or *communist.*

1. Vladimir Lenin carried the beliefs of Karl Marx to an extreme that many believe Marx himself would not have agreed with. Lenin led the Russian Revolution against a system wherein the peasants had been exploited by a few aristocrats. He replaced that system with one in which the state owned and controlled all enterprises. Lenin may be described

   as a _____ .

2. Adam Smith wrote a book called *The Wealth of Nations* in which he introduced the theory of a free market that could prosper without government interference. Adam Smith is thought of as the first

   _____ theorist.

3. Eugene Debs ran for the presidency in the United States in 1912 and included in his platform the economic ideas that wealth should be distributed more evenly throughout the population and that the government should have more say so in accomplishing that. Debs may be

   described as a _____ .

 ## Writing Activity 1

Thoreau, in paraphrasing Emerson, is quoted as saying, "The government that governs least, governs best." However, others point out that, without governmental involvement, unscrupulous individuals or companies would take advantage of people.

Each of the questions below asks whether government should involve itself in a certain activity. Choose *one* and write one to two paragraphs to support your view.

1. Should cigarette manufacturers be permitted to advertise?
2. Should pornographic magazines be sold?
3. Should the government require inflatable airbags on all new cars?

ANSWERS AND EXPLANATIONS START ON PAGE 309.

Supply and Demand

Key Words

demand—the desire and ability of consumers to buy a product or service
supply—the quantity of goods and services available for sale at all possible prices
surplus—a situation in which the supply of a product far exceeds the demand for it
equilibrium—the price at which supply equals demand

The American free enterprise system is based on the interplay between supply and demand. Supply is the quantity of goods and services available for sale at all possible prices. Demand is the desire to buy a product or service and the ability to pay for it. Producers or suppliers provide a supply of goods and services. Consumers who are willing and able to buy these goods and services create a demand.

The amount of production of an item and the price for it depend on the cost of production and the demand in the marketplace. If there is a great enough demand for a product, a high price can be charged for it, the cost of production can be covered, and a profit can be made.

For example, the owners of the Happy House Painters, Inc., went into business when they discovered that no company existed that painted houses within a ten-mile radius of their location, and yet there were many busy families seeking such a service. The entrepreneurs who founded Happy House Painters, Inc., also learned that paint could be bought at low cost, workers could be hired at low hourly wages, high prices could be charged, and a good profit could be made.

The Dynamics of Supply and Price

In general, the higher the price, the greater the number of competing companies that supply the product or service. This is because a high-priced item or service that yields a good profit for a business will attract many producers who will compete with each other for a share of the market. As a result, the Happy House Painters soon found themselves in competition with four other similar companies within their ten-mile working radius.

When too many producers compete for business, the supply of a product or service becomes so great that supply exceeds demand. A **surplus** results when the supply of a product far exceeds the demand for it. Under such a condition, the price is driven down. Often, competing businesses cannot make a profit and therefore are forced out of business. The graph below illustrates the supply curve. (In the graphs below and on pages 247 and 248, the lines appear straight because the numbers were simplified for clarity. The actual figures would appear as a curve.)

THE SUPPLY CURVE

In the graph, as the rate (price) per square foot for house painting goes up, the number (supply) of house-painting companies increases. In this graph, at a rate of $.20 per square foot, only one house-painting company exists. As the rate rises to $.80 per square foot, four companies compete for the business.

According to this graph, what would happen to the number of house-painting companies if the price reached $1.00 per square foot?

_____

By locating $1.00 per square foot on the graph, you can see that there will now be five house-painting companies competing for business.

The Dynamics of Demand and Price

Just as the price of a product or service affects supply, price also affects demand. In general, when prices go down, demand goes up; conversely, as prices go up, demand goes down. For example, if the homeowners in the area felt that the Happy House Painters, Inc. and their competitors charged too much to paint houses, the homeowners might paint their houses themselves or put off painting their homes. As a result, the number of house-painting companies would decrease, since the demand for the service would fall off. The graph below illustrates the demand curve.

THE DEMAND CURVE

In the graph above, as the rate for house painting goes down, the number of house painting companies goes up (the demand for the service increases). At $1.00 per square foot, only one company is needed to satisfy demand. If the rate were lowered to $.40 per square foot, four companies would be needed to satisfy the increased demand. According to the graph, if the price were lowered to $.20 per square foot, would demand (and the number of companies needed to satisfy demand) increase or decrease? By how many?

According to the graph, if the price were lowered to $.20 per square foot, demand would increase to five companies.

Does this seem confusing? Does it seem like two contradictory things are occurring here? Acutally, the supply and demand curves are based on economists' theories. In real life, supply, demand, *and* price are all interrelated. To understand how these components work together, we have to understand what economists call equilibrium.

Supply, Demand, and Equilibrium

In order to service exactly the number of customers who need their homes painted, producers must determine at what point supply equals demand. Economists call this point the equilibrium. Equilibrium occurs when the supply of a product or service equals the demand for it. This establishes the market price for a product or service. When the price is greater than the equilibrium point, demand falls, and there is more of a product or service than people need. This is called a *surplus*. When the price falls below the equilibrium point, demand increases, and a shortage in the product or service exists.

★ **GED PRACTICE** ★

Exercise 3: Supply, Demand, and Equilibrium———

Directions: The following questions are based on the graph shown below:

1. According to the graph, the market price for painting houses would be approximately

   (1) $1.00 per sq. ft.
   (2) .80 per sq. ft.
   (3) .70 per sq. ft.
   (4) .60 per sq. ft.
   (5) .20 per sq. ft.

2. If companies lowered their rates for painting houses, what would likely be the result?

   (1) Demand would decrease.
   (2) All of the house-painting companies would lose money and go out of business.
   (3) Demand would increase.
   (4) House-painting companies would expand their market area.
   (5) All of the house-painting companies in the area would enjoy record profits.

Exercise 4: Diminishing Returns

Directions: The following questions are based on the information and the chart provided below.

When the business of the Happy House Painters, Inc., began to increase, the company had to hire more workers. At a certain point, the company should have stopped hiring painters and, instead, should have accepted fewer jobs because it was no longer cost efficient to take on more jobs. Thus, the company had not heeded the law of diminishing returns, and it began losing money. The chart below illustrates the productivity of the Happy House Painters, Inc.

Number of Painters	Number of Houses That Can Be Painted Each Day
2	1
4	3
6	5
8	5
10	6
12	7

1. At a certain point, adding more workers did not result in a substantial increase in the number of houses painted. According to the chart, at what point did this occur?

    (1) 4 painters for 3 houses
    (2) 12 painters for 7 houses
    (3) 10 painters for 6 houses
    (4) 8 painters for 5 houses
    (5) 6 painters for 5 houses

2. In the situation described above, the company failed to heed the law of diminishing returns. Which explanation below *best* defines the law of diminishing returns described above?

    The law of diminishing returns is the point at which

    (1) the amount of money invested is less than the return on the investment.
    (2) the amount of money invested on equipment diminishes and the investment in labor increases.
    (3) the return on investment fails to increase in relation to the additional investment in labor.
    (4) profit far exceeds the additional labor costs.
    (5) profit and the labor costs are exactly equal.

Writing Activity 2

During the summer of 1986 the members of OPEC voted to reduce the amount of oil drilled in order to boost the price of petroleum exported to other nations. The U.S. imports one-third of the petroleum it uses. Write one paragraph from the oil-producing nations' point of view. Why do they think they should be able to raise prices? Write another paragraph from the consumer's point of view. How might this action affect the supply and price of oil and gasoline to the consumer?

ANSWER AND EXPLANATION STARTS ON PAGE 309.

Money and Monetary Policy

Money is a medium of exchange accepted by a society in payment for goods and services. Before money appeared, many methods of exchange were used, including barter. **Barter** is an item-for-item trade that is still used in some societies. Under the barter system, for example, you could exchange the extra tomatoes you had grown in your garden for some of your neighbor's spare lettuce.

In most purchases today, however, we use money as the medium of exchange because money works more efficiently than barter. Money has a standard value that both buyers and sellers recognize and readily accept. How many tomatoes are a fair exhange for a head of lettuce—and what about the varying sizes of each? Fifty cents a pound or seventy cents a head are much clearer values to all parties concerned.

Financial Institutions

The establishment of financial institutions was a natural outgrowth of a monetary system of exchange. People needed a safe place to secure their paper and coin currency.

Financial institutions attract deposits and make money by lending their savers' deposits for a fee, called **interest**. These institutions keep, as income, part of the interest received from loans and pay part of it to the depositor. The most common financial institutions in the U.S. are banks, savings and loan associations, and credit unions.

Commercial banks are the most numerous of all financial institutions in the U.S. They make their money by lending to businesses. The interest rate they charge to their best customers is known as the **prime rate**.

Establishment of the Federal Reserve System

Key Words

Federal Reserve System—the nation's central banking system which regulates banks and influences the flow of money and credit

monetary policy—the regulation of the nation's supply of money and credit by the Federal Reserve Board

reserve ratio—the percentage of nonlendable deposits that financial institutions must set aside

discount rate—the interest rate that the Federal Reserve charges banks that borrow from it

The need for the establishment of a national bank in the United States was recognized early in the country's history, and in recognition of this need the Bank of the United States was founded in 1791. The constitutionality of the Bank of the United States was questioned, however. It failed, as did a second national bank that was founded in 1816 but was opposed by President Andrew Jackson.

It was not until 1913 that the permanent Federal Reserve System was set up. The main purpose of the system is to regulate the nation's money supply and to provide a source of credit (serve as the central bank) for the nation's banks. Most of the nation's banks are required to be members of the Federal Reserve System. Without a central banking system, the supply of money fluctuates (goes up and down) too easily, and the entire economy becomes unstable.

The Federal Reserve stabilizes the economy by regulating the supply of money and credit. This process is known as establishing monetary policy. One method by which the Fed regulates the money supply is by setting the reserve ratio for banks. Banks are required to set aside a certain amount of money that is deposited in them. This amount cannot be loaned out. The Federal Reserve sets the percentage that cannot be loaned out. This is the reserve ratio. The diagram below shows the effect on the economy of raising and lowering the reserve ratio.

HIGH RESERVE RATIO   LOW RESERVE RATIO

By raising the percentage, the Fed is able to decrease the amount of funds banks are able to lend. By lowering it, the Fed is able to increase the amount of money in circulation.

Another method by which the Fed controls the money supply is by regulating the discount rate. The ***discount rate*** is the interest rate it charges banks that borrow money from it. When the discount rate is raised, banks can borrow less money, charge higher interest rates to their customers, and make fewer loans. This is a described as *tight money policy*. When the discount rate is lowered, banks can borrow more money, charge lower interest rates to their customers, and make more loans. This is described as a *loose money policy*. The diagram below illustrates the impact on the economy of raising or lowering the discount rate.

TIGHT MONEY POLICY

LOOSE MONEY POLICY

Another service of the Federal Reserve System is to act as a clearinghouse for most checks written on checking accounts from most banks across the country.

Exercise 5: The Federal Reserve System

Directions: Circle *T* if the statement below is true based on the reading above, or *F* if it is false.

T F **1.** The chief role of the Fed is to lend the U.S. government money when it needs it.

T F **2.** The Fed's lowering the discount rate for banks results in more money in circulation.

T F **3.** The interest rate the Fed charges member banks to borrow from it is called the *prime rate*.

T F **4.** Two ways by which the Federal Reserve influences the money supply are coining money and setting the prime rate.

T F **5.** When the Federal Reserve System lowers the reserve ratio, consumers can borrow more money.

★ **GED PRACTICE** ★

Exercise 6: Money and Monetary Policy

Directions: Based on the passage, choose the one best answer for each question below.

1. In a situation in which there is too much money in circulation and there are too few goods to satisfy demand, the dollar loses its value. To correct this condition, the Fed would likely

   (1) lower the discount rate for banks.
   (2) increase the reserve ratio for banks.
   (3) increase the discount rate for banks.
   (4) both (1) and (3)
   (5) both (2) and (3)

2. In a situation in which there is too little money in circulation and there are too many goods to satisfy weak demand, the dollar gains in value. To correct this condition, the Fed would likely

   (1) lower the reserve ratio for banks.
   (2) lower the discount rates for banks.
   (3) increase the reserve ratio for banks.
   (4) both (1) and (2)
   (5) both (2) and (3)

3. Will Rogers was an American humorist who once said, "There have been three great discoveries in the history of man: fire, the wheel, and central banking." Which of the following statements expresses an opinion that Rogers would support?

   (1) The Federal Reserve System presents a foolproof way to avoid an economic depression.
   (2) Central banking in the U.S. has been the source of preventing economic disaster since colonial times.
   (3) A national banking system gives the federal government a means to keep the economy steady during shaky times.
   (4) The federal banking system has been a success since the beginning of human civilization.
   (5) A central banking system has not been very successful in preventing economic catastrophe.

ANSWERS AND EXPLANATIONS START ON PAGE 310.

Government and Fiscal Policy

Key Words

fiscal policy—governmental use of its taxing and spending powers to influence the nation's economy

deficit spending—an economic condition in which the government spends more money than it collects in taxes

---

"In this world nothing is certain but death and taxes," said Benjamin Franklin. We still recognize that taxes are unavoidable, for there is no other way to pay public officials, to build roads, to provide for defense, or to care for the poor and homeless among the population. However, there will probably always be debate over who should pay taxes, how much they should pay, and how the money should be collected.

Like the Federal Reserve Board, the national government exerts some influence on the nation's economy; however, the government's influence is more indirect than the Federal Reserve's. The federal government affects the nation's economic condition through its fiscal policy. Fiscal policy involves the government's taxing and spending measures.

In establishing fiscal policy, the president proposes an annual budget to Congress. As Congress determines which programs are needed, it must consider how these programs are to be funded. Levying taxes is the answer. By increasing government spending, money is taken out of the hands of consumers. By decreasing spending, taxpayers' purchasing power is increased. Thus, the government indirectly influences the nation's supply of money and credit.

When the government spends less than it receives in taxes, a **budget surplus** is the result. Conversely, when the government spends more than it takes in, the condition is described as deficit spending. A **balanced budget** results when the income from taxes equals the money spent on programs.

In 1985, the U.S. Congress passed the Gramm-Rudman-Hollings Act, which required that the federal government have a balanced budget by 1991. Despite this law, the federal budget continued to reflect a deficit—$200 trillion in 1990 alone. The struggle to balance the budget revolves around these issues:

1. Should the federal government cut its programs or raise our taxes?

2. If programs are cut, where should the emphasis be? Military spending? Government waste? Social programs for the poor and needy? Maintenance of federal highway, water, and environmental programs?

These questions continue to be at the center of the nation's political debate.

Exercise 7: Government and Fiscal Policy

Directions: Study the cartoon below and answer the question that follows.

PINOCCHIO

CONGRESS

SPENDING CUT PLEDGES

DON HESSE
Courtesy St. Louis Globe-Democrat

1. In the cartoon, the artist shows Congress to be

   (1) overwhelmed by the task to cut federal spending.
   (2) tangled up in its own web of excessive spending.
   (3) led by the nose by the American public.
   (4) insincere in its promise to cut government spending.
   (5) unaware of the true extent of excessive government spending.

2. Read the passage below and answer the question that follows.

The nation's budget deficit created a controversy that demanded much newspaper coverage and television air time during the 1980s and 1990s. Many politicians and voters expressed the opinion that either more taxes should be collected or government spending should be cut to reduce the national debt. Many others felt, however, that the debt was unavoidable in complex times like ours and that, indeed, national security and economic stability depend on just such a debt.

Which of the following statements supports the opinion described in the last sentence of the passage above, that "the debt was unavoidable in complex times like ours and that, indeed, national security and economic stability depend on just such a debt"?

(1) The Department of Defense's budget demands, needed to carry out the modernization of its programs, were a major cause of the growing national debt of the 1980s.
(2) The Department of Defense could provide for national security on much less than the sum of money it received during the 1980s.
(3) Though the Department of Defense spent huge sums of money during the 1980s, national security suffered rather than improved.
(4) The Federal Reserve Board was able to bring down inflation during the 1980s despite its relatively small outlay of funds.
(5) The Federal Reserve Board was unable to control inflation during the early 1980s despite the great expenses it laid out to try.

 Writing Activity 3

Some critics of the congressional legislation to cut the budget deficit complain that the budget is being balanced "on the backs of the poor." This means that federal programs implemented to help the needy are being cut in order to reduce government spending. Do you believe that the poor are carrying an unfair burden in the government's budget reduction efforts? State your position in one or two sentences and write two to three paragraphs defending your point of view.

ANSWERS AND EXPLANATIONS START ON PAGE 310.

Measures of Economic Activity

Key Words

gross national product (GNP)—the amount of all goods and services a nation produces in one year

inflation—an increase in the supply of money and credit, accompanied by an increased demand for fewer goods resulting in reduced purchasing power

business cycles—regular economic trends in businesses

depression—a severe decline in economic activity accompanied by falling prices and increased unemployment

recession—a period of reduced economic activity characterized by rising unemployment

When you buy a new car, or clothing, or a ticket for a seat on an airline, you are contributing to the gross national product (GNP) of the country. When a business invests in some new machinery or in a new warehouse, it too is contributing to the GNP. The GNP is one of the most important measurements of economic growth. It represents the total amount of all goods and services produced by a nation in one year.

Many economists believe that to truly understand the GNP one must understand the effects of inflation. Inflation occurs when the prices of goods rise faster than the dollar's purchasing power. As a result, the dollar loses value.

Even after adjustment for inflation, the GNP figure is to be interpreted as a general guideline with far from perfect accuracy. Nonetheless, it is a guide to how well the economy is doing, in general, throughout the country. It is computed four times a year and reflects trends, or business cycles, of the nation as a whole.

A falling GNP indicates a slowdown in business activity. When the slowdown results in unemployment, the economy experiences a recession. The U.S. economy experienced severe recessions in the mid-1970s and in the early 1990s, when unemployment rates climbed and business growth and investment fell. If a recession is prolonged and extreme, a depression results such as the U.S. experienced during the late 1920s and early 1930s.

Depressions and recessions are characterized by high unemployment and falling prices that develop into patterns difficult to change, even through the nation's fiscal or monetary policies. In the mid-1980s economists were faced with a new problem—high unemployment combined with inflation, which resulted in the coining of a new word, *stagflation*.

The Consumer Price Index

In the U.S., the rate of inflation is measured by the ***Consumer Price Index*** (CPI). The CPI is the measure of change in prices of a group of goods or services that a typical consumer would purchase.

Using 1967 as a base year (100%), the CPI figures other years' prices as percentages in comparison to it. For example, in 1980 items that cost you $244.40 would have cost you only $100.00 in 1967. Based on those dollar figures, the CPI for 1980 was 244.4

★ **GED PRACTICE** ★

Exercise 8: Measures of Economic Activity——

The questions below are based on the following table:

	CONSUMER PRICE INDEX, 1960–1981	
Year	Consumer Price Index in dollars 1967 = 100	Percent Change Over Previous Year
1960	88.7	—
1961	89.6	+1.0
1962	90.6	+1.1
1963	91.7	+1.2
1964	92.9	+1.3
1965	94.5	+1.7
1966	97.2	+2.9
1967	100.0	+2.9
1968	104.2	+4.2
1969	109.8	+5.4
1970	116.3	+5.9
1971	121.3	+4.3
1972	125.3	+3.3
1973	133.1	+6.2
1974	147.7	+10.9
1975	161.2	+9.1
1976	170.5	+5.8
1977	181.5	+6.4
1978	195.4	+7.7
1979	217.4	+11.3
1980	244.4	+12.4
1981	266.2	+8.9

Directions: Read the table and answer the following questions.

1. Based on the data in the CPI, what was the effect of the 1974 rise in oil prices?

   (1) a marked increase in prices throughout the economy
   (2) a gradual inflationary rise in prices over several years
   (3) a sudden recession throughout the country that year
   (4) a gradual drop during the year into a recession
   (5) a cycle of inflation/recession during that year

2. What has been the general trend of consumer prices in dollars since 1960?

    (1) up and down cycles of unpredictability
    (2) predictable up and down cycles
    (3) a general rise in prices
    (4) a constant fall in prices
    (5) a steady evenness in prices

Question 3 is based on the cartoon below.

Directions: Study the cartoon and answer the question.

EUGENE PAYNE
Courtesy WSOC-TV, Charlotte

Inflation hasn't slowed travel

3. Based on the information in the cartoon, the artist would likely agree with which of the following statements?

    (1) Americans' spending is greater than it's ever been.
    (2) Americans' spending has fallen off because of inflation.
    (3) Americans' spending is supported more and more by credit.
    (4) Americans' spending far exceeds the spending of foreign consumers.
    (5) Americans' spending habits are going to drive the economy into a tailspin.

ANSWERS AND EXPLANATIONS START ON PAGE 311.

Unemployment and Economic Activity

Key Words

unemployment—the lack of jobs for all those who want to and are able to work

cyclical unemployment—unemployment caused by recession or other unstable economic times

dislocated (or displaced) workers—workers who have lost their jobs due to the relocation of an industry

structural unemployment—unemployment caused by a rapid change in the character of the economy

The nation's unemployment rate is another important measurement of economic activity. Unemployment may be described as a lack of jobs for all of those who want to and are able to work. The unemployment rate is released during the first week of each month, and economists and government officials await its release to spot trends in the economy. Government economists believe that an unemployment rate of less than 4 percent is acceptable for a healthy economy.

Different categories of unemployment are observable in an economy as illustrated in the passage below.

During the decade of the 1960s, many businesses, including the Pleasure Boat Corporation, were enjoying healthy economic times. Unemployment rates were low, people had plenty of extra money to spend, and pleasure boats sold well all over the country.

During the mid-1970s, however, various events caused the economy to take a turn for the worse. The one that affected the Pleasure Boat Corporation the most was the OPEC oil embargo. It resulted in increased prices on many fuel-dependent items, including cars, planes, buses, and boats. Fewer people took long trips in cars or short excursions in boats. As a result, fewer boats were manufactured, and many people at the Pleasure Boat Corporation lost their jobs.

Soon the country entered a recession, with widespread unemployment. The Federal Reserve System can fight such cyclical unemployment by adopting a monetary policy of lowering reserve ratios for its member banks and lowering interest rates. The federal government itself can adopt a recession-fighting fiscal policy of increased spending, or it can decrease taxes to increase consumer spending. But each of these methods takes a long time to change an economic trend. Thus, the 1970s closed without a significant improvement in the nation's economic condition.

The 1980s saw a gradual improvement in the economy, but by then the Pleasure Boat Corporation had been bought out by a larger corporation that had made the decision to relocate south, where it was found that lower wages could be paid to a much less union-dependent population.

The employees who were left behind in the Midwest were labeled dislocated (or displaced) workers and were offered the chance to be retrained by the federal government for a different or more technologically advanced field. Unemployment caused by rapid change in the character of the economy is called structural unemployment by economists, and it, too, is difficult and slow to change.

Given the rapid rate of economic and technological change, it may be that massive unemployment is here to stay. Only creative, long-range solutions can help the economy and our people cope with this problem.

★ GED PRACTICE ★

Exercise 9: Unemployment

Directions: The following definitions apply to questions 1–3.

cyclical unemployment—unemployment caused by recession or other unstable economic times

structural unemployment—unemployment caused by a rapid change in the character of the economy

frictional unemployment—unemployment caused by workers quitting jobs for reasons of dissatisfaction

seasonal unemployment—unemployment caused by a change from one season or time period to another

normal unemployment—the level of unemployment that is considered acceptable for a healthy economy (usually less than 4 percent)

1. Construction workers are often out of work for long periods of time during the winter in the North and Midwest of the U.S. Theirs is said to be

    (1) cyclical unemployment.
    (2) structural unemployment.
    (3) frictional unemployment.
    (4) seasonal unemployment.
    (5) normal unemployment.

2. The increasing importance of computers in various business and industry settings has most likely caused

    (1) cyclical unemployment.
    (2) structural unemployment.
    (3) frictional unemployment.
    (4) seasonal unemployment.
    (5) normal unemployment.

3. The number of new housing starts is an important indicator of the health of the nation's economy. Under a slow economy, the number of housing starts decreases and construction workers are laid off. When the economy picks up again, these workers are rehired. This type of unemployment is

   (1) cyclical unemployment.
   (2) structural unemployment.
   (3) frictional unemployment.
   (4) seasonal unemployment.
   (5) normal unemployment.

★ **GED PRACTICE** ★

Exercise 10: Displacement of Workers——

Questions 1, 2, and 3 are based on the bar graph below.

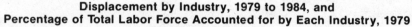

**Displacement by Industry, 1979 to 1984, and
Percentage of Total Labor Force Accounted for by Each Industry, 1979**

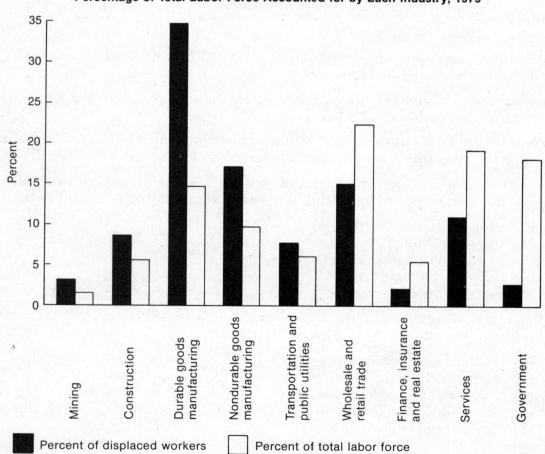

Directions: Study the bar graph and then answer the following questions.

1. Based on the information shown in the bar graph above, which industry experienced the greatest displacement of workers during the period 1979–1984?

    (1) wholesale and retail trade
    (2) nondurable goods and manufacturing
    (3) services
    (4) durable goods manufacturing
    (5) construction

2. According to the graph, which industry has the highest number of total employees?

    (1) durable goods manufacturing
    (2) nondurable goods manufacturing
    (3) wholesale and retail trade
    (4) services
    (5) government

3. Which of the following statements is supported by the graph above?

    (1) The finance, insurance, and real estate industries are the smallest of all the industries in the U.S.
    (2) The manufacturing industries were hardest hit by the recessions of the late 1970s and early 1980s.
    (3) In 1979, 35 percent of all workers were engaged in durable goods manufacturing.
    (4) There were more workers unemployed than employed in the mining industry.
    (5) Service industries are on the decline.

 Writing Activity 4

Do you accept or reject the belief that a certain level of unemployment in the U.S. is acceptable? State your position in two to three sentences and then write two to three paragraphs to support your position.

ANSWERS AND EXPLANATIONS START ON PAGE 311.

SOCIAL STUDIES POSTTEST

Directions: This social studies posttest will give you the opportunity to evaluate your readiness for the actual GED Social Studies Test.

This test contains 64 questions. Some of the questions are based on short reading passages, and some of them require you to interpret a chart, map, graph, or political cartoon.

You should take approximately 85 minutes to complete this test. At the end of 85 minutes, stop and mark your place. Then finish the test. This will give you an idea of whether or not you can finish the real GED test in the time allotted. Try to answer as many questions as you can. A blank will count as a wrong answer, so make a reasonable guess for questions you are not sure of.

When you are finished with the test, turn to the evaluation and scoring charts on page 282. Use the charts to evaluate whether or not you are ready to take the actual GED test, and if not, what areas need more work.

Posttest Answer Grid

1 ① ② ③ ④ ⑤	17 ① ② ③ ④ ⑤	33 ① ② ③ ④ ⑤	49 ① ② ③ ④ ⑤
2 ① ② ③ ④ ⑤	18 ① ② ③ ④ ⑤	34 ① ② ③ ④ ⑤	50 ① ② ③ ④ ⑤
3 ① ② ③ ④ ⑤	19 ① ② ③ ④ ⑤	35 ① ② ③ ④ ⑤	51 ① ② ③ ④ ⑤
4 ① ② ③ ④ ⑤	20 ① ② ③ ④ ⑤	36 ① ② ③ ④ ⑤	52 ① ② ③ ④ ⑤
5 ① ② ③ ④ ⑤	21 ① ② ③ ④ ⑤	37 ① ② ③ ④ ⑤	53 ① ② ③ ④ ⑤
6 ① ② ③ ④ ⑤	22 ① ② ③ ④ ⑤	38 ① ② ③ ④ ⑤	54 ① ② ③ ④ ⑤
7 ① ② ③ ④ ⑤	23 ① ② ③ ④ ⑤	39 ① ② ③ ④ ⑤	55 ① ② ③ ④ ⑤
8 ① ② ③ ④ ⑤	24 ① ② ③ ④ ⑤	40 ① ② ③ ④ ⑤	56 ① ② ③ ④ ⑤
9 ① ② ③ ④ ⑤	25 ① ② ③ ④ ⑤	41 ① ② ③ ④ ⑤	57 ① ② ③ ④ ⑤
10 ① ② ③ ④ ⑤	26 ① ② ③ ④ ⑤	42 ① ② ③ ④ ⑤	58 ① ② ③ ④ ⑤
11 ① ② ③ ④ ⑤	27 ① ② ③ ④ ⑤	43 ① ② ③ ④ ⑤	59 ① ② ③ ④ ⑤
12 ① ② ③ ④ ⑤	28 ① ② ③ ④ ⑤	44 ① ② ③ ④ ⑤	60 ① ② ③ ④ ⑤
13 ① ② ③ ④ ⑤	29 ① ② ③ ④ ⑤	45 ① ② ③ ④ ⑤	61 ① ② ③ ④ ⑤
14 ① ② ③ ④ ⑤	30 ① ② ③ ④ ⑤	46 ① ② ③ ④ ⑤	62 ① ② ③ ④ ⑤
15 ① ② ③ ④ ⑤	31 ① ② ③ ④ ⑤	47 ① ② ③ ④ ⑤	63 ① ② ③ ④ ⑤
16 ① ② ③ ④ ⑤	32 ① ② ③ ④ ⑤	48 ① ② ③ ④ ⑤	64 ① ② ③ ④ ⑤

Questions 1–4 are based on the information below.

The following terms describe five climate regions found throughout the world.

tundra—land frozen solid most of each year with very short periods of thawing

rain forest—area of heavy vegetation and almost continual rain and heat

Mediterranean—region of little rain or temperature change, except during the rainy part of the winter

desert—territory of little rain along with quick evaporation and much heat

continental—region of extreme seasonal changes and much moisture year-round

1. Southern California has hot, dry summers and mild, wet winters. In which climate region is it located?

   (1) tundra
   (2) rain forest
   (3) Mediterranean
   (4) desert
   (5) continental

2. The central Corn Belt has warm, wet summers and cold, damp winters. In which climate region is it located?

   (1) tundra
   (2) rain forest
   (3) Mediterranean
   (4) desert
   (5) continental

3. The Amazon River region is hot and rainy all year and contains an abundance of plants and trees as a result. In which type climate region is it located?

   (1) tundra
   (2) rain forest
   (3) Mediterranean
   (4) desert
   (5) continental

4. Death Valley is an arid region of southeast California. It is scorching hot during the day and extremely cold at night. In which climate region is it located?

   (1) tundra
   (2) rain forest
   (3) Mediterranean
   (4) desert
   (5) continental

Questions 5 and 6 are based on the following cartoon.

"All right, deep down it's a cry for psychiatric help—but at one level it's a stick-up."

© *Punch*/Rothco

5. Based on the robber's response, you can tell that the man who is being robbed

   (1) has been robbed many times before.
   (2) is trying to analyze his attacker.
   (3) does not have any money with him.
   (4) does not realize he is being robbed.
   (5) has refused to cooperate with his attacker.

6. This cartoonist is saying that psychiatrists

   (1) blame criminals' social misbehavior on a need for attention.
   (2) believe that criminals cause their own problems.
   (3) do not really understand the motivation of criminals.
   (4) are just as socially maladjusted as criminals.
   (5) are not a very intelligent professional group.

Questions 7 and 8 are based on the following chart.

PREDICTED CHANGES IN POPULATION
1980–89
(Ranked from highest to lowest predicted population percentage
growth during decade)

Rank	Area	1980–89
1	Las Vegas, NV	31.3
2	Austin, TX	28.4
3	Tucson, AZ	25.5
4	Houston, TX	24.1
5	Phoenix, AZ	23.7
6	San Diego, CA	22.6
7	Tulsa, OK	21.8
8	Salt Lake City, UT	21.5
9	Portland, OR	20.7
10	Seattle, WA	20.1

7. According to the chart, what general trend is occurring in U.S. population?

   (1) a move to the Midwest and Northeast

   (2) a move to the North and East

   (3) a move to the South and West

   (4) a move away from the North and West

   (5) a move away from the Southeast and East

8. Based on this trend, which of the following cities would you not expect to be on a list of places ranked 11 through 20 in predicted population growth?

   (1) New York City, NY

   (2) El Paso, TX

   (3) Tampa, FL

   (4) Baton Rouge, LA

   (5) Oklahoma City, OK

9. From the end of the Civil War until the Spanish American War in 1898, most Americans would have identified themselves as isolationists. What was most likely the cause of such widespread desire for withdrawal from international affairs?

   (1) the lack of information about events taking place in foreign lands

   (2) the desire to expand the U.S. boundaries farther across the continent into Canada and Mexico

   (3) the disillusionment with foreign allies who had refused to take sides during the Civil War

   (4) the preoccupation with reconstruction and industrialization after the Civil War

   (5) the resentment toward the new immigrants flooding this country

10. The passing of the Federal Reserve Act in 1913 was one of the most significant contributions of the Wilson administration. The law remedied almost all the ills of American banking and currency of the time. Without this act, the country would not have been able to adjust to the financial strains of World War I.

What implication has the author made about the significance of the Federal Reserve Act for the World War I years?

   (1) It helped keep the U.S. out of involvement in World War I.

   (2) It helped absorb the shock of the expense of World War I.

   (3) It helped keep down our expenses during World War I.

   (4) It helped prevent individuals from going bankrupt during World War I.

   (5) It helped keep bankers honest during World War I.

Questions 11 and 12 are based on the following passage.

When Cesar Chavez began the United Farm Workers in 1963 with his famous grape boycott, he and his fellow workers were receiving 90 cents an hour. By 1985, they earned up to $5.00 an hour.

In July 1984, another grape boycott was called for by Chavez. However, it was less successful than the first. In fact, membership in the UFW had decreased from almost 100,000 in the late 1960s and early 1970s to about 25,000 by 1984.

11. Which of the following is the most likely explanation for the dramatic rise in wages for the members of the UFW?

 (1) The federal government forced the growers to pay the workers more money.
 (2) The growers were pressured to raise wages because they had lost sales.
 (3) Inflation over the two decades caused everyone's wages to increase that much.
 (4) The farm workers accepted more responsibilities in turn for more money.
 (5) The pressure tactics of the UFW backfired on them.

12. What hypothesis would *best* explain the drop in membership in the UFW?

 (1) The members of the UFW were not happy with the slow progress made for them since the 1960s.
 (2) There were far fewer farm workers during the 1980s than there were during the 1960s and 1970s.
 (3) Boycotts by buyers do not work on the same kind of product more than once.
 (4) The farm workers were not motivated to join the UFW once they began receiving fairer wages.
 (5) The people of the 1980s were much more conservative than people of the 1960s and 1970s.

Questions 13 and 14 are based on the following passage.

Progressivism thrived during the early years of the twentieth century, and the inspiration for much of its spirit and purpose was President Theodore Roosevelt. He was only forty-two when he became president, and, as the youngest chief executive in American history, he brought joy and excitement to the office. *Intelligent, energetic, ambitious,* and *adventurous* are words often used to describe "Teddy," but his success in office was due as much to his political savvy and sense of fairness as it was to his more colorful attributes. He was known as a trust-buster and champion of labor, yet he supported growth of industry as natural and beneficial, and he insisted on the open shop for government workers and optional union membership for private industry.

13. In the passage, Teddy Roosevelt is described as a trust-buster. *Trust* in this sense refers to

 (1) faith in the character and ability of others.
 (2) property held by one person for the benefit of another.
 (3) a bank that administers funds or property.
 (4) a combination of corporations that control a single market.
 (5) an office or position of responsibility.

14. Which of the following opinions of Theodore Roosevelt would the author of the above passage support?

 (1) Roosevelt was an unpopular president because of his reputation as a bully.
 (2) Roosevelt did not handle the labor issue well despite his skill in other areas.
 (3) Progressivism contributed little to the nation's growth and development as an industrial nation.
 (4) Roosevelt was successful because he did not cater to either workers or big corporations.
 (5) Roosevelt's popularity may be attributed more to his young age and personality than to his actions.

Questions 15 and 16 are based on the paragraph and map below.

"The world must be made safe for democracy." On April 2, 1917, Woodrow Wilson spoke these words to a special session of Congress called by him to ask that they declare war on Germany. Congress did so on April 6, 1917.

THE EUROPEAN POWERS AT WAR

15. By declaring war on Germany, the U.S. was also declaring war on

    (1) Norway, Sweden, and Spain
    (2) Russia, France, and Italy
    (3) Austria-Hungary, Bulgaria, and Turkey
    (4) Italy, Greece, and Turkey
    (5) Africa, France, and Russia

16. By declaring war on Germany, the U.S. was also aligning itself with

    (1) Norway, Sweden, and Switzerland
    (2) Great Britain, Italy, and Russia
    (3) Austria-Hungary, Bulgaria, and Turkey
    (4) Italy, Greece, and Turkey
    (5) Great Britain, Norway, and Sweden

Questions 17–22 are based on the passage below.

Public assistance, or welfare as we know it, has been a much-used system for helping needy citizens since the Great Depression in the U.S.

Most of the help has been in the form of direct payments, but during the 1960s the welfare programs were expanded to include job training, preschool programs, hot lunches, and many more diverse programs.

Great Britain, however, has a much more extensive cradle-to-grave welfare system than the U.S. In 1948, the British established a system that provides such support as extra money when a child is born and help when the dead must be buried. It also provides good medical coverage, free meals and clothing for some, vitamins, college grants, utilities, and payment for property taxes. Furthermore, it guarantees a pension for retirees. It is this latter provision, however, that many feel is bankrupting the system.

17. Which of the following American groups would be most likely to oppose introducing the British welfare system to the U.S.?

  (1) communists
  (2) progressive Democrats
  (3) conservative Republicans
  (4) socialists
  (5) the poor and the elderly

18. According to many Britons, the British welfare system is being bankrupted by

  (1) college grants
  (2) medical coverage
  (3) property taxes
  (4) retirement pensions
  (5) burial allotments

19. Which of the following is most likely to be true of the British economy, based on its generous welfare system?

  (1) Taxes in Britain are likely to be higher than in other industrial nations.
  (2) More Britons are out of work than in any other industrial nation.
  (3) The British government always operates at a deficit.
  (4) Taxes in Britain are likely to be lower than in other industrial nations.
  (5) The British economy experiences periods of inflation more often than other industrialized nations.

20. Which of the following consequences could be a direct result of Great Britain's welfare and economic policies?

  (1) The British pound is at its lowest level ever.
  (2) Britons have no faith in their prime minister.
  (3) Great Britain is one of the world's worst places in which to live.
  (4) Great Britain is the world's most expensive place in which to live.
  (5) Britain's wealthy entertainers are leaving the country and choosing to live in America where taxes are lower.

21. Which of the countries listed below has the most generous welfare program?

  (1) Mexico
  (2) Japan
  (3) Sweden
  (4) France
  (5) India

22. The British welfare system is representative of certain values that the British place above others. What priorities does the British welfare system represent?

  (1) lives over property
  (2) full employment over government interference in the economy
  (3) concern for the welfare of its citizens over concern about government spending
  (4) balancing the nation's budget over caring for its nation's poor
  (5) sensitivity to world opinion over excessive government spending

Questions 23–26 are based on the following passage.

The Great Wall of China is reputed to be the only man-made feature visible from the moon. Although it was once thought to have been built entirely during the Ch'in Dynasty between 221 and 206 B.C., it is now believed to have been started earlier.

The 15-foot-high, 25-foot-wide, 1500-mile-long structure was undoubtedly erected to keep out invading barbarians. To the common people of the empire, who had been forced to build the wall, it was not worth it, however. The wall, and other public works accomplished by the Ch'in Dynasty, had taken a great toll on the wealth and human life of the country. As a result, an indignant population rose up in rebellion against the Ch'in Dynasty, and in 207 B.C. the Han Dynasty began.

Because of its rich history and magnificent appearance, the Great Wall attracts tourists, scientists, and historians to this day and will continue to do so for generations.

23. According to the author of this passage, the Han Dynasty was able to come into power because

(1) barbarians were not effectively prevented from invading the empire.
(2) it had started the work on the wall and really controlled it all along.
(3) the common people rebelled against the empire that had forced them to work on the Great Wall.
(4) the Ch'in emperor lost all his personal wealth in the creation of the Great Wall.
(5) the Great Wall had become famous and attracted many tourists.

24. The main idea of this passage is that

(1) the emperor of the Ch'in Dynasty was a slave driver.
(2) invading barbarians were a problem in ancient China.
(3) the common people of ancient China were very poor.
(4) modern man has overestimated the importance of the Great Wall.
(5) the human achievement of the Great Wall is widely appreciated.

25. With which of the following opinions would this author most likely agree?

(1) The building of the pyramids of Egypt was not worth the human sacrifice it involved.
(2) The pyramids of Egypt are also intriguing to modern man because of the human effort they represent.
(3) The pyramids of Egypt would probably be visible to a human standing on the moon.
(4) The human significance of the pyramids of Egypt is greater than that of the Great Wall.
(5) The human significance of the pyramids of Egypt is not as great as that of the Great Wall.

26. The writer has not directly stated, but would support, the opinion that

(1) astronauts have taken a personal interest in the history of the Great Wall of China.
(2) the common people of the Ch'in Dynasty were the ones who provided the labor in constructing the Great Wall.
(3) work on the Great Wall was started before the Ch'in Dynasty came into existence.
(4) the Great Wall of China is a great human achievement and was probably worth the effort it took.
(5) the common people of today's China still resent the use of forced labor to build the Great Wall.

Questions 27 and 28 are based on the following graph.

PRODUCTIVITY OF FARM WORKERS

27. The change in agricultural productivity most closely resembles which of the following advances in the U.S.?

    (1) the movement of the population to the Sunbelt
    (2) the loss in population of the northeast industrial cities
    (3) the change in the character of the economy from a manufacturing emphasis to a service emphasis
    (4) the decline in the profitability of the U.S. family farm
    (5) the increased efficiency of operations brought about by the widespread use of computers

28. According to the information in the graph, advanced technology has caused agricultural productivity since World War II to

    (1) slow down gradually.
    (2) decline rapidly.
    (3) increase slowly.
    (4) increase sharply.
    (5) decrease significantly.

Questions 29 and 30 are based on the following graph

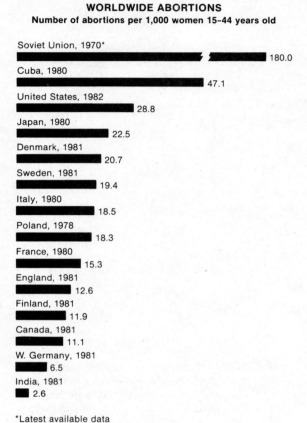

WORLDWIDE ABORTIONS
Number of abortions per 1,000 women 15–44 years old

Soviet Union, 1970* — 180.0
Cuba, 1980 — 47.1
United States, 1982 — 28.8
Japan, 1980 — 22.5
Denmark, 1981 — 20.7
Sweden, 1981 — 19.4
Italy, 1980 — 18.5
Poland, 1978 — 18.3
France, 1980 — 15.3
England, 1981 — 12.6
Finland, 1981 — 11.9
Canada, 1981 — 11.1
W. Germany, 1981 — 6.5
India, 1981 — 2.6

*Latest available data

29. Based on the information in the graph, we can conclude that

(1) the Soviet Union released information about its society more freely and frequently than other countries.
(2) women in the U.S. tend to have abortions at a higher rate than women in many European countries.
(3) the people in India don't practice birth control.
(4) the higher the education levels of the population, the higher the incidence of abortion among females.
(5) the higher the income level of the population, the higher the abortion rate among women.

30. According to the graph, communist nations—the former Soviet Union and China—had the highest rates of abortion. Which of the following most likely accounts for this fact?

(1) Communist countries are strong defenders of women's rights.
(2) The countries that have communist governments are overpopulated.
(3) Religion is not a part of the lives of women in communist countries.
(4) The government pays the medical costs for abortions, which are free in these communist countries.
(5) Birth control devices are not available under communist governments.

31. Anti-imperialists and isolationists have opposed American involvement in international affairs, but for very different reasons. For example, an anti-imperialist would say that American involvement in Vietnam was wrong because it was an attempt to dominate Vietnam. An isolationist, however, would say that American resources should be used at home.

Which of the following best explains the difference between anti-imperialists and isolationists?

(1) Anti-imperialists are against improper interference in other countries' affairs; isolationists are against making diplomatic and military commitments to other nations.
(2) Anti-imperialists are racially motivated; isolationists are not concerned with racial matters.
(3) Anti-imperialists are educated and concerned people; isolationists are selfish and lazy.
(4) Anti-imperialists are world travelers; isolationists have never left their own country.
(5) Anti-imperialists are powerful and influential people; isolationists are the common people.

Questions 32 and 33 are based on the following passage.

"The male form of a female liberationist is a male liberationist—a man who realizes the unfairness of having to work all his life to support a wife and children so that someday his widow may live in comfort; a man who points out that commuting to a job he doesn't like is just as oppressive as his wife's imprisonment in a suburb; a man who rejects his exclusion, by society and most women, from participation in childbirth and the engrossing, delightful care of young children—a man, in fact, who wants to relate himself to people and the world around him as a person."

Margaret Mead, "Some Personal Views"

32. The writer's opinion about role reversal in American society is that

   (1) males and females should remain in those roles that are best suited to their gender.
   (2) women should work outside the home and men should stay at home with the kids.
   (3) women should make fewer demands on men.
   (4) males can take on all of the roles of females.
   (5) men and women both should be able to perform roles not traditionally assigned to them by society.

33. What is the source of much frustration for modern men, according to the writer?

   (1) demands that they reverse roles with women
   (2) pressure to assume only traditional male roles and responsibilities
   (3) employers who do not pay them enough to allow their wives to stay at home
   (4) their own inability to relate to others as a person
   (5) the lack of excitement and thrill in their lives

Questions 34–36 are based on the following information.

Defense mechanisms are means by which people attempt to reduce frustration and anxiety. Five common mechanisms are described below.

compensation—offsetting a feeling of inferiority or failure in one area of life by achieving in another area

denial—refusing to accept some hurtful truth

fantasy—daydreaming; imagining a world of one's own

regression—retreating to early forms and patterns of behavior

sublimation—the use of a substitute activity to satisfy a motive

34. The mother and father of a child dying of cancer show no signs of stress, as they truly believe a cure will be found in time. The defense mechanism used is

   (1) compensation.
   (2) denial.
   (3) fantasy.
   (4) regression.
   (5) sublimation.

35. A husband who has lost an argument about buying a new sports car pouts and refuses to eat the dinner his wife has prepared. The defense mechanism used is

   (1) compensation.
   (2) denial.
   (3) fantasy.
   (4) regression.
   (5) sublimation.

36. Teddy Roosevelt was very small and sickly as a child; however, as an adult, he became an enthusiastic boxer, hunter, politician, and soldier, leading the Rough Riders during the Spanish-American War. The defense mechanism illustrated in Teddy Roosevelt's case is

   (1) compensation.
   (2) denial.
   (3) fantasy.
   (4) regression.
   (5) sublimation.

Questions 37 and 38 are based on the following cartoon.

America's Problem Child   —By Hungerford

37. This cartoonist attributes the cause of delinquency among children today to

(1) bad attitudes toward adults.
(2) poor education in the school.
(3) the increased number of divorces.
(4) low morals in society.
(5) the child's lack of purpose in life.

38. What belief of the cartoonist is shown in this cartoon?

(1) The need to keep our jails uncrowded is more important than teaching a child a lesson.
(2) Children who turn to crime should not be given the same concern as those who are victims of broken homes.
(3) Divorce is wrong when it starts victimizing the children and the society they belong to.
(4) Older people and children are the least deserving of, but most vulnerable to, harmful effects of crime.
(5) Children are our most valuable resource and do not belong in prison.

Questions 39 and 40 are based on the following passage.

The Noble and Holy Order of the Knights of Labor was organized in 1869 for all workers, regardless of race, nationality, craft, or skill level. They believed that organized labor could meet the force of big business.

The Knights were opposed to strikes and child labor and favored a federal bureau for labor statistics, equal pay for both sexes, and an eight-hour workday.

The organization peaked at over 700,000 members but quickly lost its strength after the Haymarket Square riot in Chicago. The riot started during a meeting to protest police brutality against striking Knights. Violence erupted when a bomb was thrown into a police-controlled crowd. Seven policemen and ten workers were killed, and 117 people were injured.

39. The most direct cause of the downfall of the Noble and Holy Order of the Knights of Labor was

(1) spontaneous revolts by its members.
(2) the Haymarket Square riot in 1886.
(3) the police brutality directed toward its strikers.
(4) the amount of work time lost by its members on strike.
(5) the ineffectiveness of its leaders in meeting the organization's goals.

40. Which of the following is supported by the information given in the passage?

(1) The Knights of Labor succeeded in at least one area—keeping peace among black and white workers.
(2) The events of 1886 proved that the leaders of the Knights of Labor were dishonest.
(3) The Knights of Labor kept the growth of monopolies and other big businesses to a minimum in the 1880s.
(4) The Knights of Labor's importance was in articulating the demands of laborers to big business.
(5) The federal government established child labor laws and the Bureau of Labor Statistics as a result of the Knights of Labor's influence.

Questions 41 and 42 are based on the graph below.

AMERICA'S DEBT
Owing more than it makes

*Federal and state governments, households, and nonfinancial business
**Third-quarter report

---

41. Which of the following statements is best supported by the information on the graph?

(1) The national debt is decreasing while the Gross National Product is increasing.

(2) The national debt is increasing while the Gross National Product is decreasing.

(3) The national debt is increasing at a rate as fast as the growth of the Gross National Product.

(4) The national debt is increasing at a rate slower than the growth of the Gross National Product.

(5) The national debt is increasing at a rate faster than the growth of the Gross National Product.

42. In which of the following years was the amount of the national debt more than 1-1/2 times that of the Gross National Product?

(1) 1965
(2) 1973
(3) 1978
(4) 1982
(5) 1985

Questions 43–45 apply to the following information.

Governmental systems are classified according to the way in which authority is held and exercised. Defined below are five types of governmental systems that operate in the world.

absolute monarchy—a system in which a royal family has the final authority in all governmental matters

constitutional monarchy—a system in which the authority of a member of royalty is limited by rules set forth by the government's constitution

parliamentary democracy—a system in which the people elect the governing legislature which in turn elects the prime minister

totalitarian state—a system in which a central authority runs a government that subordinates the rights of individuals

theocracy—a system in which the head of state is considered to be guided by God and in which religion plays a prominent role in the government

43. Under this system, a vote of "no confidence" can be given by the legislature to the leader of the government. After such a vote, the leader will resign immediately or will ask the people to select a new leader. The form of government described is

    (1) an absolute monarchy.
    (2) a constitutional monarchy.
    (3) a parliamentary democracy.
    (4) a totalitarian state.
    (5) a theocracy.

44. King John and his predecessors ruled England for many generations before the Magna Carta was instituted to make government more democratic. The form of government described is

    (1) an absolute monarchy.
    (2) a constitutional monarchy.
    (3) a parliamentary democracy.
    (4) a totalitarian state.
    (5) a theocracy.

45. Vatican City is an independent state located within Rome, Italy. The Pope holds supreme legislative, executive, and judicial power. However, the administration of the state is delegated to a governor and his lower officials. The form of government in Vatican City most closely resembles

    (1) an absolute monarchy.
    (2) a constitutional monarchy.
    (3) a parliamentary democracy.
    (4) a totalitarian state.
    (5) a theocracy.

Question 46 is based on the following quote.

"Please understand that we are not asking for a parade, a movement, or pity. But we do ask you to remember in your own way the 57,661 Americans who died in the war. Perhaps all of them died in vain."

These are the words of Al Santoli, a Vietnam veteran who recorded the verbal accounts of 33 veterans of the most unpopular war in U.S. history.

46. Which of the following statements would Santoli most likely support?

    (1) Vietnam veterans are heroes who should be honored as such.
    (2) Most Americans are unsympathetic to Vietnam veterans.
    (3) American soldiers sacrificed too much in the war.
    (4) The U.S. should have had welcoming parades and other signs of gratitude for returning Vietnam veterans.
    (5) Most Vietnam veterans were insulted by the monument built for them in Washington, D.C.

Questions 47–49 are based on the following chart.

RATING COMPARABLE JOBS
How state of Washington determines what a job demands

In number of points	Secretary I steno	Electrician	Clerk-typist I	Truck driver I	Registered nurse I
Knowledge and skills	122	122	106	61	280
Mental demands	30	30	26	10	122
Accountability	35	30	35	13	160
Working conditions	0	15	0	13	11
Total job points	187	197	167	97	573
Annual salary	$17,108	$25,404	$13,468	$20,856	$20,440

47. Which of the following did the state of Washington assume in establishing its job-rating system?

(1) Ratings of jobs would not be made public knowledge or be made mandatory.

(2) Annual salaries of its state employees are already comparable and fair.

(3) There is a fair and quantitative method of figuring what jobs are worth.

(4) Working conditions of office jobs would not be able to be rated.

(5) "Mental demands" could not be as easily rated as "knowledge and skills."

48. From the information in the chart, you can conclude that

(1) nurses and truck drivers earn about the same amount of money, so their jobs are comparable.

(2) a nurse's job is considered to have about the same worth as a truck driver's even though the nurse's job is more demanding.

(3) a truck driver earns slightly more than a nurse because his working conditions are slightly more difficult.

(4) although truck drivers' jobs are less demanding than nurses' jobs, the truck drivers are held in higher regard by society.

(5) a truck driver's knowledge and skills are more valuable than a nurses's.

49. What can you conclude about the rating the Washington team gave to the working conditions of secretaries and clerk-typists?

(1) The team was unable to determine what the working conditions of those two jobs would be.

(2) The raters considered the jobs to have the most difficult working conditions.

(3) The Washington point system is incomplete and inadequate at this time.

(4) The job raters felt that neither job is demanding in regard to working conditions.

(5) The team of raters thought the two jobs had very different working conditions.

Questions 50–52 are based on the following graph.

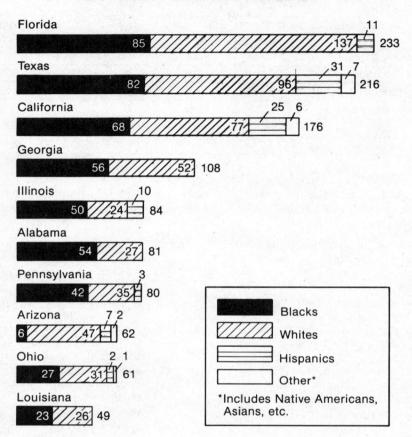

WHO IS ON DEATH ROW
Top 10 states; number of inmates by race

Florida
85 / 137 / 11 / 233

Texas
82 / 96 / 31 / 7 / 216

California
68 / 77 / 25 / 6 / 176

Georgia
56 / 52 / 108

Illinois
50 / 24 / 10 / 84

Alabama
54 / 27 / 81

Pennsylvania
42 / 35 / 3 / 80

Arizona
6 / 47 / 7 / 2 / 62

Ohio
27 / 31 / 2 / 1 / 61

Louisiana
23 / 26 / 49

█ Blacks
▨ Whites
☰ Hispanics
☐ Other*

*Includes Native Americans, Asians, etc.

50. Which of the following statements about capital punishment in populous states is best supported by the graph?

   (1) Florida judges have been consistently harsher in sentencing minorities than in sentencing whites.
   (2) A person convicted of a serious crime is more likely to be sentenced to capital punishment in Florida than in any other state.
   (3) Florida is the most dangerous state in the U.S. for victims of violent crimes.
   (4) There are no Asians on Death Row.
   (5) Violent crimes are much less common among Hispanics than among other minority groups.

51. Which of the following states has the most evenly balanced numbers of blacks and whites on Death Row?

   (1) Florida
   (2) Georgia
   (3) Illinois
   (4) Alabama
   (5) Arizona

52. Which of the following groups would most likely use this graph to support its position?

   (1) the U.S. Supreme Court
   (2) the Southern Governors' Conference
   (3) the National Prison Guards Union
   (4) the Florida State Legislature
   (5) the Coalition Against the Death Penalty

Questions 53 and 54 are based on the following passage.

Women have been a growing force in the political world since females first banded together to demand equality with men in late-eighteenth-century France. The late-nineteenth-century Industrial Revolution brought the working woman to the forefront as "female" skills came into demand in factories. The Women's Liberation Movement began making demands of its own in the early 1970s as equal pay, equal status, and "career" work for women became issues.

Despite many years of struggle, however, as of January 1983, working women had been at their present jobs an average of only 3.3 years. This median varied from a low of 0.6 years for teenagers to 11.9 years for women 65 and older. Hopefully, these figures will improve with each new generation as women become more insistent on the rights due them.

53. In the passage, the author has assumed that

   (1) women will want to remain on their jobs as long as men.
   (2) employers do not discriminate against women.
   (3) females should not join forces to demand equal rights for themselves.
   (4) working for one employer for an average of 3.3 years is the women's choice.
   (5) females in their teens make up the least desirable category of employees.

54. The author of the passage would agree with which of the following statements about the Women's Liberation Movement?

   (1) Its beginning in France helped women there make gains not seen in other countries.
   (2) Its achievements in the U.S. have far exceeded those in other countries.
   (3) It was helped by the Industrial Revolution when women gained higher status and pay in the workforce.
   (4) It has not made much progress in the two centuries since it began.
   (5) There are many issues concerning working women that still have to be addressed.

Questions 55 and 56 are based on the following passage.

In 1953, the U.S. Congress passed the Refugee Relief Act. This act increased the immigration quota for victims of war and disaster. In 1980, Congress raised the total number of persons permitted entry into the U.S. under the act from 290,000 to 320,000 yearly. This latter act also redefined a refugee as a person fleeing any part of the world, not just communist countries or the Middle East.

Despite the revamping of the law, however, some aliens still find it difficult to enter the U.S. with refugee status. Many resort to illegal means to enter the country, risking imprisonment and deportation if caught.

A number of these illegal aliens entering the U.S. are attempting to escape political persecution or war-torn conditions in their homelands. As the numbers of these people increase, so do the number of members in the Sanctuary Movement in the U.S. The Sanctuary Movement consists of American citizens and a network of churches who are banding together in ever-increasing numbers to assist illegal aliens in crossing the border, getting settled, and seeking official recognition as political refugees. Members of the movement have defied immigration laws for years, mostly for victims of Central American wars, by declaring the churches religious sanctuaries immune from the law.

55. What is the most likely reason that the members of the Sanctuary Movement think they should receive immunity from legal prosecution?

   (1) They are helping victims of Central American wars.
   (2) They are risking their lives to help the aliens.
   (3) They are a religious sanctuary network.
   (4) They are a large, growing group.
   (5) They are preventing the deportation of aliens.

56. The members of the Sanctuary Movement are most similar to which group in American history?

   (1) young men who resisted the draft
   (2) the Underground Railroad for runaway slaves
   (3) Vietnam war protestors
   (4) immigrants seeking religious freedom
   (5) civil rights activists

Questions 57 and 58 are based on the following passage.

Behaviorist psychologists have spoken highly of the benefits of positive reinforcement for much of the twentieth century. As a result, they have greatly influenced, for the better, education and parenting.

Teachers and parents are now more scientific and controlled in their approaches to teaching and child rearing and are therefore much better at these tasks than their counterparts were in past centuries.

57. The author's main point in this passage is that

(1) education and parenting are improved when positive reinforcement is made a part of each.
(2) positive reinforcement has no place in the field of teaching and parenting.
(3) behaviorists are basically educators and parents seeking better ways to do their jobs.
(4) all other forms of psychology have had negative effects on education and parenting.
(5) behaviorist psychology has a long historical tie to education and parenting.

58. The basic assumption underlying this passage is the author's belief that

(1) punishment is detrimental to the education and raising of children.
(2) parents and teachers in past centuries did not use methods of positive reinforcement.
(3) parents and teachers today are worse than those of the past.
(4) the problem with parents of the past is that they lacked control.
(5) behaviorist psychology has worked wonders with unruly children.

59. In the period following World War I, many Americans opposed American entry into the newly founded League of Nations and World War II. What belief were these Americans exhibiting?

(1) patriotism
(2) nationalism
(3) isolationism
(4) racism
(5) militarism

60. Between the years 1935 and 1957, America's birth rate had risen from 16.9 to 25 per thousand people. In 1967, 40 percent of the U.S. population was under 21 years of age, 46.5 percent under 25, and more than half under 30.

The most likely cause for this "baby boom" was

(1) the return of the young American soldiers from war in Europe and the Pacific
(2) the growth of the urban/suburban areas after World War II
(3) the increased mobility of the American family
(4) the continuing expansion of the middle class and its new, inflationary wealth
(5) the relaxing of moral sanctions against the use of artificial means of birth control

61. Mark Twain and Charles Dudley Warner's book, *The Gilded Age*, satirized the political corruption and hustle for the fast buck that characterized the post Civil War years in the North. These writers were probably most critical of which of the following developments during this period?

(1) a larger, more efficient railroad
(2) the increased use of technology in farming
(3) a growth surge in the steel industry
(4) the spreading of materialistic attitudes
(5) the spreading of anti-imperialism

Questions 62-64 are based on the map on page 281.

62. The Philippine Islands are considered to be in a key strategic location for U.S. defense overseas. Another country also considered to be a key strategic site for the U.S. would be

(1) Indonesia
(2) Australia
(3) Burma
(4) Taiwan
(5) Japan

THE PHILIPPINES' PRE-1991 STRATEGIC IMPORTANCE

☐ Major U.S. bases
■ Major Soviet bases
● Sea-lane choke points
▨ Soviet Naval forces

USSR

North Korea

South Korea

Japan

China

North Pacific Ocean

Vietnam

Burma

Okinawa

Taiwan

The Philippines

Guam

Indonesia

New Guinea

Indian Ocean

Australia

63. This map best supports the statement that

(1) both the U.S. and the former U.S.S.R. considered southeast Asia to be of strategic importance.

(2) the U.S. considered southeast Asia to be of strategic importance, but the U.S.S.R. did not.

(3) the U.S.S.R. considered southeast Asia to be of strategic importance, but the U.S. did not.

(4) neither the U.S. nor the U.S.S.R. considered southeast Asia to be of strategic importance.

(5) the Philippines was more important strategically to the U.S. than to the Soviet Union.

64. Which of the following statements is an opinion that cannot be supported by information on the map?

a. Countries allied with the U.S. were being outmaneuvered by Soviet naval forces.

b. There was a very strong American military presence in the Pacific Ocean.

c. Sea-lane choke points prevented American naval maneuvers in the Pacific.

(1) a only
(2) b only
(3) c only
(4) a and c
(5) b and c

Use the chart below to determine the reading skills areas in which you need to do the most review. Circle any items that you got wrong and pay particular attention to areas where you missed half or more of the questions.

Posttest Reading Skills Chart

Skill Area	Item Number	Review pages	Number Correct
Comprehension	**5**, **6**, **7**, 10, 13, **15**, **16**, 18, 24, 31, 32, 33, **51**, 57, 61, **62**	23–36	_____/16
Analysis	9, 11, 12, 17, 19, 20, 23, **28**, **29**, **30**, **37**, 39, **42**, **47**, **48**, **49**, 53, 55, 58, 60	37–67	_____/20
Application	1, 2, 3, 4, **8**, 21, **27**, 34, 35, 36, 43, 44, 45, **52**, 56	68–81	_____/15
Evaluation	14, 22, 25, 26, **38**, 40, **41**, 46, **50**, 54, 59, **63**, **64**	82–98	_____/13

Your score _____ out of 64 correct.
The numbers in boldface are questions based on graphics.

If you got fewer than 44 items correct, go back and find the areas in which you had the most difficulty. Then, review those pages that you need additional work in.

Now, circle the same numbers for the items that you circled in the chart above. This will give you additional information about the social studies content areas in which you need the most review.

Posttest Content Areas Chart

Skill Area	Item Number	Review Pages	Number Correct
History	9, 10, 13, 14, 15, 16, 23, 24, 25, 26, 31, 39, 40, 46, 59, 61	99–146	_____/16
Political Science	43, 44, 45, 50, 51, 52, 55, 56	147–175	_____/8
Behavioral Science	5, 6, 32, 33, 34, 35, 36, 37, 38, 53, 54, 57, 58	176–209	_____/13
Geography	1, 2, 3, 4, 7, 8, 29, 30, 60, 62, 63, 64	210–240	_____/12
Economics	11, 12, 17, 18, 19, 20, 21, 22, 27, 28, 41, 42, 47, 48, 49	241–263	_____/15

Posttest Answer Key

1. **(3)** Southern California is mild and dry most of the year, which best fits the Mediterranean description.

2. **(5)** The temperature changes and the cold winters indicate that the Corn Belt is located in the continental region.

3. **(2)** Hot, rainy weather all year is typical of rain forests.

4. **(4)** Dryness and extreme heat are typical of deserts.

5. **(2)** The robber's response and the look on his victim's face indicate that the victim is trying to explain the robber's own actions to him.

6. **(1)** The cartoonist is using this incident to show his opinion about psychiatrists. He shows that the psychiatrist is blaming the robbery on the robber's cry for psychiatric help.

7. **(3)** The top ten cities in predicted growth are all located in the South and West.

8. **(1)** New York is not in the South or the West. All the other choices are in those fast-growing areas.

9. **(4)** Reconstruction and industrialization after the Civil War required the nation's complete attention.

10. **(2)** The reform of the banks and the currency of the U.S. helped to maintain balance in the economy during World War I. The author's reference to "adjust to the financial strain" refers to "absorbing the shock of the expense."

11. **(2)** The farmworker's successful boycott had led to reduced profits and unfavorable publicity. As a result, the growers were forced to give in to the farmworkers' wage demands.

12. **(4)** With fairer wages, farm workers were less motivated to join the union.

13. **(4)** Because he was a reformer, we can infer that *trust* in this context refers to a combination of corporations that controls a single market.

14. **(4)** The passage says that Roosevelt was a trust-buster and champion of labor, yet he supported growth of industry as natural and beneficial. This suggests that he did not cater to either workers or big corporations.

15. **(3)** Germany, Austria-Hungary, Bulgaria, and Turkey comprised the Central Powers (represented by diagonal lines).

16. **(2)** The U.S., Great Britain, Italy, and Russia comprised the Allied Powers (represented in white).

17. **(3)** Conservative Republicans is the group listed that would be the most opposed to the kind of government spending that the British welfare system requires.

18. **(4)** The passage states that, "it is this latter provision [a guaranteed pension for retirees] that many feel is bankrupting the system."

19. **(1)** The welfare system must be supported by some revenue; taxes is the most likely source for this financial support.

20. **(5)** Many wealthy Britons have left the country, choosing to live in the U.S. where the tax burden is not as great as that in Great Britain.

21. **(3)** Sweden is the only industrialized nation represented that has a socialist form of government that provides generous welfare benefits to its citizens.

22. **(3)** By choosing a "cradle-to-grave" welfare policy, the British have shown that they place the welfare of their citizens over a concern about government spending.

23. **(3)** The passage states that the Ch'in Dynasty lost all its power when the people it had forced to work on the Great Wall finally rebelled against it.

24. **(5)** Choice (5) is the main idea of the passage. The other points are details and facts from the passage.

25. **(2)** The author is enthusiastic about the Great Wall, despite the suffering it caused. Therefore, he would probably feel the same about the pyramids of Egypt.

26. **(4)** Even though the author states that the people who built the Wall did not feel it was worth the effort, he states that the Great Wall holds great fascination for modern man.

27. **(5)** The widespread use of computers (5) is the only choice that relates to a similar sweeping change in industrial production.

28. **(4)** The line representing the products supplied per farm worker has risen steeply since the 1940s.

29. **(2)** The only choice that is supported by the facts in the graph is that women in the U.S. tend to have a higher rate of abortions than those in many European countries.

30. **(4)** One reasonable explanation for the high incidence of abortions in these two communist countries is that the government pays the medical costs for abortion.

31. **(1)** Choice (1) gives the correct definitions of an anti-imperialist and an isolationist; the others do not.

32. **(5)** Men staying home to care for young children is a reverse of their usual role, just as women working outside the home is a role reversal for them. The writer makes it obvious that both reversals are their rights.

33. **(2)** The writer implies that men are frustrated because of society's confining rules regarding appropriate behavior.

34. **(2)** The parents are denying the seriousness of their child's illness.

35. **(4)** Pouting and refusing to eat dinner is a form of childhood behavior.

36. **(1)** Teddy Roosevelt compensated for his feeling of physical inferiority by becoming physically active.

37. **(3)** The increased number of divorces (and the resulting broken homes) is seen by the cartoonist as the cause for delinquency among children.

38. **(3)** The cartoonist is blaming divorce for increased delinquency among children, victimizing them and society.

39. **(2)** The Haymarket Square Riot was the most direct cause of the downfall of the Knights of Labor.

40. **(4)** The Knights served an important purpose in stating clearly the goals of organized labor. The passage does not provide enough information for us to conclude anything else.

41. **(5)** The line representing the national debt rises more steeply than the line representing the gross national product.

42. **(5)** In 1985, the national debt was about 6-1/2 trillion dollars. This is more than 1-1/2 times the GNP of about 4 trillion dollars.

43. **(3)** Under a parliamentary democracy the legislature elects the leader of the government.

44. **(1)** Under an absolute monarchy a royal family rules and has final authority in all governmental matters.

45. **(5)** Under a theocracy the head of the government is considered to be guided by God and has supreme authority.

46. **(3)** The author states that perhaps all the American soldiers died in vain in Vietnam. That was a tremendous sacrifice for what he sees as little gain.

47. **(3)** The raters could not have completed the study without first believing that there is a fair and quantitative way to rate jobs.

48. **(2)** You arrive at the conclusion by comparing 573 job points for a nurse with 97 job points for a truck driver and then by looking at their similar salaries.

49. **(4)** A zero (0) rating indicates an opinion of no measurably bad working conditions.

50. **(2)** The graph shows that Florida has the most convicted criminals on Death Row.

51. **(2)** Georgia has 56 blacks and 52 whites on Death Row.

52. **(5)** The large number of inmates on Death Row could be cited by a group that opposes the death penalty.

53. **(1)** The writer assumes that women want to remain on their jobs longer than 3.3 years.

54. **(5)** The second paragraph indicates that the author believes that there are still many issues concerning women in the workplace that need to be addressed.

55. **(3)** The last sentence in the passage tells us that these people have declared their churches to be religious sanctuaries. Therefore, they believe they are immune from prosecution.

56. **(2)** The Sanctuary Movement members break the law to assist illegal aliens who are fleeing persecution and oppression. This activity is similar to that of members of the Underground Railroad who transported and hid slaves.

57. **(1)** The main idea expressed in the passage is that education and parenting are improved when positive reinforcement is made a part of each.

58. **(2)** In making the point, the writer assumes that parents and teachers in past centuries did not use methods of positive reinforcement.

59. **(3)** Only choice (3) isolationism refers to many Americans' desire to withdraw from international conflicts and concerns.

60. **(1)** Quick marriages after soldiers returned from war most likely caused the surge in births. The other choices given here are either not relevant or not significant.

61. **(4)** The statement in the passage, "The hustle for the fast buck," implies a criticism of spreading materialism.

62. **(5)** According to the map, the Philippines and Japan both have numerous U.S. bases. These indicate the area's strategic importance to the U.S.

63. **(1)** The presence of U.S. and Soviet naval forces suggests that both countries considered southeast Asia to be of strategic importance.

64. **(2)** There is not enough information on the map to indicate that the U.S. was being outmaneuvered by Soviet naval forces, choice (a), or that sea-lane choke points were preventing naval maneuvers in the Pacific, choice (c).

ANSWER KEY

CHAPTER 1: COMPREHENDING
Exercise 1
pages 24–25

1. **(4)** The main idea is that there was much abuse of power during the Nixon administration, a point stated at the end of the passage. Choices (1) and (3) are neither stated in nor supported by the passage. Choices (2) and (5) are ideas that support the main idea.

2. **(3)** The passage refers to John Dean's testimony, which led to formal charges against former president Nixon. The passage neither states nor implies that Nixon was found innocent (1), or was convicted (2). It is obvious that he was not executed (4). Because the former president resigned from office to escape impeachment proceedings, choice (5) is incorrect.

Exercise 2
page 27

(2) The point of the graph is to show the variety of methods this business uses to advertise. The title of the graph, "Advertising Spending for One Business," is a clue to the main idea. The other choices are either details, judgments, or facts not supported by the graph.

Exercise 3
pages 30–31

1. **(4)** The passage says, ". . . a primary target is the American citizen." Choices (1), (2), (3), and (5) are not stated in the passage.

2. **(2)** The passage says, ". . . sustain communication among hostages as much as possible." This means communicate as often as possible with other hostages. Choices (1), (3), (4), and (5) are not stated in the passage.

3. **(2)** The article says that you should not even appear to be capable of providing valuable information to the terrorists. This could put you in danger.

Exercise 4
page 33

Your answers may vary slightly; take Midlothian Road north to Peterson Road. Turn right on Peterson Road and drive east until you reach State Highway 45. Turn left on 45 and drive north to Gages Lake Road. Turn right on Gages Lake Road and follow it to Wildwood.

Exercise 5
pages 34–35

1. **(5)** If the middle income group spends 2 out of every 10 dollars on wants and the upper income group spends 6 out of every 10 dollars on wants; then the implication is that as one's income goes up, one has more money to spend on wants.

2. **(1)** When the author says, "At best, they have just enough food and shelter to stay alive," he is implying that the poor cannot even provide for their basic needs.

Exercise 6
page 36

(2) Since the cost of college has risen steadily, the implication is that this trend will continue. Choices (1) and (3) are judgments that cannot be supported by the graph. Choice (4) is a possible explanation for the rising cost of college but not an implication that may be drawn from the graph. Choice (5) is inaccurate.

CHAPTER 2: ANALYZING
Exercise 1
page 39

1. The *causes* are extended drought and extreme overpopulation, since they contributed to severe famine (the *effect*).
2. The *effect*, population growth in the Sunbelt states, has come from companies relocating (the *cause*).
3. The *effect*, emigration of the first pilgrims, was prompted by religious persecution (the *cause*).
4. The *cause*, unfair employer practices, brought about the establishment of labor unions (the *effect*).

Exercise 2
page 39

1. (d) The passage states that the tornado series of 1965 caused $300,000,000 in property damage.
2. (c) According to the passage, the combination of location, population density, and development leads to a greater potential for tornado damage in the Chicago area.
3. (b) Rotating air masses cause tornadoes. This is stated at the beginning of the passage.
4. (a) The tornado series of 1925 killed 740 people in five states. This is stated at the end of the first paragraph.

Exercise 3
pages 40–41

1. (5) The passage says in the third paragraph that U.S. auto makers were able to improve quality, increase automa-

tion, and reduce manufacturing costs; this means that the auto makers have become more competitive.
2. (2) The passage says that American car buyers have responded to the limit on Japanese exports by buying more European imports.
3. (2) California voters realized that to improve the quality of their schools they would have to pay higher taxes.
4. (5) According to the passage, California now leads states that have raised taxes to improve educational programs.

Exercise 4
page 43

(4) The sales went from about 5,000 cars (symbolized by half a car in the pictograph) in August '84 to about 10,000 cars (symbolized by a picture of a whole car) in August '85.

Exercise 5
pages 46–47

1. (2) According to the passage, the main source of stress for controllers is poor labor/management relations. Choice (2) is the only one that involves labor/management relations.
2. (1) This is the only choice given that can be proven with data. The other choices either are not true or are opinions.
3. (3) This answer is based on the quote "Controllers who were interviewed complained that their recommendations for providing safety backups and other measures were not being considered by their employers or the Federal Aviation Administration."

Exercise 6
page 49

(2) The house, located on the moon, with a "for sale" sign, is looked at longingly by the family. The father is holding a sign that says "new-house cost doubles in 10 years," indicating that home ownership is threatened by increasingly high costs.

Exercise 7
page 50

(1) The U.S. had a long history of making loans to the Allied Powers. The graph shows a very strong financial commitment. Choices (2), (4), and (5) cannot be derived from the graph, and choice (3) would not affect the decision to align with all the Allied Powers.

Exercise 8
pages 51–52

Exact words may vary.

1. The writer assumes that socialism is harmful for developing countries and that capitalism is better.
2. The writer assumes that Kennedy won the presidency in 1960 because he was more attractive on TV than Nixon was.
3. The writer assumes that, before westernization, China had a dreary past.
4. The writer assumes that there usually is trouble at a rock concert but not at a Christian rock festival.
5. The writer assumes that there are cheats in the welfare system and that doing volunteer work would stop their cheating. Also, the writer assumes that those on welfare do not already perform volunteer work in the community.

Exercise 9
page 52

Statements (c) and (e) are the assumptions that are made by the author. Statements (a) and (b) are stated directly in the passage. Statement (d) is the opposite of what the author implies.

Exercise 10
page 53

1. (4) The governor says that private corporations would be good at running prisons because they are running hospitals effectively. The assumption is that privately run prisons would require management skills similar to those needed by privately run hospitals.

2. (2) "Doing well" means making a profit. "Doing good" means doing good works for society.

Exercise 11
page 56

(3) By showing the bird full and proud in the beginning and featherless and weak at the end, the cartoonist assumes that, as government has grown larger over the years, it has eroded or taken away personal freedoms.

Exercise 12
page 58

1. (1) Since borrowers must choose between "high fixed interest rates" and rates "that can fluctuate" (go up or down), the conclusion is that borrowers must be prepared to choose between different mortgage options.

2. (2) Parents have the ultimate responsibility for the proper development of their children (since parental neglect is punishable by the state).

3. (1) Because many examples of the use of computers in the workplace are given, the conclusion that may be drawn is that computers will be present in almost all aspects of society's workplace.

Exercise 13
page 59

1. (3) By requiring businesses to give a year's notice before plant closings or layoffs, several community groups have given some employees a chance to plan their future.

2. (1) Because the 1920s, like the 1980s, saw a large rise in wealth concentration, they must have been boom years for the rich.

Exercise 14
page 62

1. Y   Snow and temperature patterns in the Northeast suggest that this is a forecast for a winter day in the U.S.
2. Y   The map indicates that only a small portion of the country has rain or snow.
3. Y   The temperatures increase in 10-degree increments as you travel south.
4. N   There is no snow in the Pacific Northwest on this map.
5. N   Rain is indicated for some parts of the East Coast, but not enough to warrant fear of flooding.
6. Y   Showers covering central Pennsylvania are shown on the map.
7. N   Florida is shown to be in both the 60- to 70-degree ranges.

Exercise 15
page 63

1. *I* That London may be one of the most pleasant cities on earth in which to live is an opinion and cannot be supported by the map.
2. *S* Since there appears to be little, if any, population in deserts, rain forests, tundras, and ice caps, it is possible to make this conclusion.
3. *I* This cannot be derived from this map; there is no information about economies of the regions represented.
4. *S* This can be concluded from the density of population above the equator and the number of deserts, semideserts, and tropical areas below the equator.

Exercise 16
pages 64-65
Exact wording may vary.

1. This speaker probably feels that social activism in Central America is the missionary's responsibility or obligation.
2. This speaker probably admires Japan's ability to produce cheaper cars.
3. This speaker probably resents or dislikes Six Flags Great America Amusement Park.

Exercise 17
page 65
1. (2) You can infer this from the last sentence, "Fortunately, Thurmond's filibuster did not prevent passage. . . ."
2. (5) A clue to the meaning of the word *filibuster* is that Thurmond "talked for more than twenty-four hours to purposely delay the vote. . . ."

Exercise 18
page 67
(4) If the men want to store nuclear waste in a citizen's garage, it can be inferred that nuclear waste disposal is "getting too close for comfort."

CHAPTER 3: APPLYING CONCEPTS
Exercise 1
page 70
1. **YES** Busing children would quickly desegregate schools.
2. **NO** Afro-American history courses do not address the problem of separate and unequal facilities.
3. **NO** The United Negro College Fund program provides funding for colleges where the vast majority of students are black.
4. **YES** Minority quotas would help desegregate colleges quickly.

Exercise 2
pages 70-71
nurture Verbal stimulation would be part of an environmental effect.
nature Cooing and crying are natural activities and do not involve the environment.
nurture Our attitudes toward people affect our actions toward them; this is an example of environmental influence.
nature Chemical makeup comes from nature.

Exercise 3
page 71
(4) This is the only choice that involves a violation of the Sherman Anti-Trust Act—price-fixing.

Exercise 4
pages 72-73
1. (2) The propaganda technique described is "glittering generalities" since the manufacturer speaks in general and vague terms. The statement does not tell us what the "leading product on the market" is.
2. (4) The propaganda technique used is bandwagoning. The announcer advises the residents to subscribe to the paper because practically everyone else does it.
3. (3) The propaganda technique used is transferring. The candidate expects the power or respect of the leader of the "Moral Majority" to "rub off" and favorably impress the voters.

Exercise 5
page 75

(2) This is the only choice given in which someone is punished for political activity.

Exercise 6
page 77

1. (3) The Electoral College system does not allow direct popular election of the president; a body of electors elects the president and vice president. Prior understanding of the electoral college system should have helped you make this choice.
2. (1) Conflicts between religious authority and governmental authority are described historically as issues of church vs. state.
3. (2) Prior knowledge of history would tell you that New Zealand is the only choice listed that is a British possession and that Maoris are natives of New Zealand.

Exercise 7
pages 78–79

(3) This is the only choice that is based on physical features as described in the passage.

Exercise 8
page 81

1. (3) This requires prior knowledge of Leif Ericson's place in history.
2. (2) To answer this you would have to know that the North Sea is located off the coast of Norway and that Leif Ericson was a Norwegian.

CHAPTER 4
Exercise 1
page 83

1. NO—5 In this case, there can be no legal contract because illegal activity has taken place.
2. YES In this case, there is a legal contract. The attorney is a representative of the seller and accepts the $5,000 check from the buyer. The buyer will receive the property after the deal is settled.
3. NO—2 The buyer seems to have made a clear offer, but the seller has not accepted; therefore, no settlement can be made.

4. YES The agreement is in writing and the valuables exchanged in the arrangement will be labor for room and board. The exchange of room and board for services performed is a perfectly legal exchange.

Exercise 2
page 84

1. (3) Montagu's race has no bearing on the believability of the hypothesis.
2. (3) How long Montagu has had the theory adds nothing to its believability.
3. (2) The fact that the term race is still widely used and accepted tends to dispute Montagu's theory.
4. (2) There appear to be valid reasons for classification by race based on physical features.
5. (1) Montagu has strong credentials in the anthropological field.
6. (1) Other noted professionals support Montagu's theory.

Exercise 3
page 84

1. (2) Hispanics are classified racially by their skin color, not by their common ancestry with others of European origin. This supports Montagu's belief that the concept of race based on skin color and physical features leads to errors.

Exercise 4
page 86

(5) The writer has done an organized and objective study based on extensive data.

Exercise 5
page 87

1. You should have written *patriotism* or *responsibility to his country*, since he chose to serve his country over getting married and settling down.
2. You should have written something like *principles* over his *career*, since he refused the project despite its prestige.

Exercise 6
pages 87–88

1. (5) The value of concern for lives and property after the sinking of the battleship *Maine* was the deciding factor in the United States' decision to enter the war.

2. **(3)** The passage states, "For good or for ill, the U.S. became less nationalistic." None of the other choices are stated directly or implied in the passage.

3. **(3)** The viewpoint that the U.S. is an imperialist nation would be held by someone who believed that the invasion of Grenada was an act of aggression.

Exercise 7
page 90

(2) From his portrayal of this situation, the cartoonist obviously values productivity over high wages.

Exercise 8
pages 91–92

1. **(3)** The statement "The ERA was not given enough time" is the conclusion made, but there are no facts to support that conclusion.

2. **(1)** The last sentence of the paragraph says that a majority of American citizens supported the ERA. Since feminist organizations supported the amendment heavily, and since the government failed to pass the ERA, we can infer that organizations working for the ERA have more popular than governmental support.

Exercise 9
page 93

1. adequate
2. inadequate: political map would show this better
3. adequate
4. inadequate: weather map would show this better
5. adequate
6. inadequate: population and world map would show this better
7. adequate
8. inadequate: population map would show this better

Exercise 10
page 94

1. **(1)** Russia, formerly a Soviet republic, is located in Asia. Choice (2) is untrue according to this map. None of the other choices are represented adequately on this map.

2. **(4)** There is no key to use to determine mountain height.

Exercise 11
pages 95–96

1. **(1)** There is no logical connection made by the writer between laws restricting the freedom of blacks and the bias shown against them by European immigrants.

2. **(3)** There is no logical reason to believe that if these laws did not exist there would not be racial bias.

Exercise 12
pages 97–98

1. **F** There is nothing in the graph to indicate what caused the gap.

2. **L** This is logical because the Japanese items could not have been sold in the U.S. in such great numbers had Americans not been receptive to buying them.

3. **F** It is not logical to say that only one factor led to a growing gap between American and Japanese exports.

4. **F** Other countries are not compared here.

Exercise 13
page 98

(3) It would be faulty reasoning to attribute the trade imbalance only to the low manufacturing costs of the Japanese. Additional factors, like the lack of an import tax, help to keep the prices of Japanese products low.

CHAPTER 5: HISTORY
Exercise 1: The New World
page 101
Understanding Ideas

1. **(2)** According to the passage and the map, France and England became rivals in the establishment of some settlements in the New World.

2. **(5)** The map shows that the French held little territory in the thirteen colonies. Choices (1), (2), and (3) cannot be supported by the map; and choice (4) is not true.

Exercise 2: Thirteen Colonies
page 102
Evaluating Ideas

(1) and (4) The chart says that New England has dense forests and rocky soil. These conditions are not desirable for farming. Also, the abundant rainfall, warm temperatures, and suitability for farming encouraged the emergence of the southern plantation system (4).

Exercise 3: The Revolutionary War
page 103
Understanding Ideas
1. (2) The passage states that the purpose of the first Continental Congress was to demand the colonists' rights as British citizens.
2. (2) The passage states, " . . . by the time of the second Continental Congress in May 1775, hostile encounters had already taken place between the English soldiers and the colonists."

Applying Ideas
3. (2) The struggle of India for its independence from Great Britain is the only event that can be compared to the American colonists' fight against Great Britain since both ultimately won freedom and established democracies. The other choices are not examples of anti-colonial wars.

Writing Activity 1
pages 104
Your answer might include the following points:
- the American Revolution proved that a small number of inspired people can overthrow a large and powerful nation.
- the American Revolution represented an experiment in government that symbolized the fundamental ideals of many people throughout the world.

Exercise 4: Federalists and Anti-Federalists
pages 105–106
Applying Ideas
1. A This represents an anti-Federalist viewpoint that states and territories should have sovereignty.
2. F The Federalists believed that the national government should have the power to coin money.
3. F The Federalists held that only the federal government should have authority to regulate trade.
4. A The anti-Federalists held that the states themselves should have the right to form their own local militias.

5. F Those who believed in a strong national government believed that only the federal government should have the right to make treaties with other nations.

Exercise 5: Disputes and Compromises
pages 106–107
Understanding Ideas
1. (1) Hamilton was a Federalist who believed in a centralized government for the thirteen separate states.
2. (4) As shown on the chart, the "Great Compromise" involved the creation of a two-house federal legislature to allow for fairness in representation.
3. (1) Counting slaves as only three-fifths of the population was detrimental to the southern states because it meant that they would have fewer representatives in the House of Representatives.
4. (3) The Bill of Rights was an important addition to the Constitution because it guaranteed rights to the colonists.

Analyzing Ideas
5. (5) From the quote we can infer that Washington believed that ratification of the Constitution by the United States was surprising given the many differences among the states. None of the other choices are stated or implied in Washington's quote.

Writing Activity 2
page 107
Your answer should include the fact that had slaves been counted as part of the population, the South would have had greater representation in the House of Representatives. Thus, the legislators would have been sympathetic to the needs of the South and would have voted accordingly.

Exercise 6: The Western Frontier
pages 108–109
Analyzing Ideas
1. (3) Based on the passage, you can tell that Jefferson believed that the Constitution did not specifically allow for the president to expand the territory of the U.S. Choices (1), (2), (4), and (5) are facts that are stated in the passage, not opinions.

Understanding Ideas

2. **(4)** This is stated directly in the passage. The passage states that Lewis and Clark established friendly relations with the Indians, not that relationships improved greatly, choice (1). Choices (2) and (5) are not true, and although choice (3) is true, the fact had little to do with the American belief in Manifest Destiny.

Evaluating Ideas

3. **(4)** Only choice (4) is supported by the passage which says that Jefferson was reluctant to go beyond powers stated directly in the Constitution. However, when he did go along with the Louisiana Purchase, he laid the basis for future presidents to use implied powers.

Exercise 7: The War of 1812
page 110

Understanding Ideas

1. **(2)** According to the passage, the forcing of American seamen to join the British Navy was proven and contributed to the War of 1812.

Analyzing Ideas

2. **(3)** The death of the British ally, Tecumseh, marked the end of the united Indian resistance in the Midwest and South, thus directly affecting the outcome of the War of 1812.

Understanding Ideas

3. **(1)** The passage states that one result of the war was that "U.S. dependence on Europe was broken" since the war had forced the U.S. to learn to do without Europe's economic and political help.

Exercise 8: The Monroe Doctrine
page 111

Applying Ideas

1. **(2)** and **(4)** The only situations listed that represent attempts to enforce the principles of the Monroe Doctrine are the American opposition to the Spanish control of Cuba and the American blockade of Cuba. In both cases, the United States was trying to prevent European involvement in the Western Hemisphere.

Exercise 9: The Vote on Secession
page 113

Understanding Ideas

1. **(c)** Virginia split in two over the issue of secession, with the western part loyal to the Union. This was the origin of the state of West Virginia.

2. **(d)** Texas seceded from the Union despite the fact that only the eastern part of the state voted to do so.

3. **(a)** Kentucky was a border state that remained in the Union despite being a slave state.

4. **(b)** Mississippi is a solidly southern state that voted overwhelmingly to secede from the Union.

Exercise 10: Secession and States' Rights
page 114

Analyzing Ideas

(2) Lincoln did not issue an order for emancipation for the entire country out of loyalty to the four border states that remained with the Union despite the fact that they were slave states.

Exercise 11: North vs. South
page 115

Applying Ideas

1. N   3. S   5. S   7. N   9. N
2. S   4. N   6. N   8. B   10. S

Exercise 12: Brother Against Brother
pages 116–117

Analyzing Ideas

1. **(5)** The passage says, "As a result of this [Emancipation] proclamation, the Union Army's ranks were swelled by 180,000 former slaves who fought against the Confederacy."

Applying Ideas

2. **(2)** Catton said, ". . . we move to make a living reality out of the great ideal of equality of all Americans. . . ." Based on that, you could assume that Bruce Catton would most likely support the actions of the Civil Rights workers of the sixties.

Evaluating Ideas

3. (2) Bruce Catton repeatedly points out that the Civil War obligates Americans to promote freedom at home and abroad.

Applying Ideas

4. (2) The other main event in U.S. history that forced women to become equal partners in the work force was World War II. As was the case for the Civil War, women were forced to take the place in the work force for many men who had to go to war.

Exercise 13: Reconstruction and Healing
page 118

Applying Ideas

1. (4) The Freedmen's Bureau Act, whose function was to provide food, education, and work in the Reconstruction South, is sometimes regarded as the nation's first federal welfare system.

2. (3) The Fifteenth Amendment guaranteed voting rights to all citizens and is a logical basis for opposition to discriminatory voting requirements.

Exercise 14: Industrial Revolution
pages 119–120

Understanding Ideas

1. (5) One of the most important aspects of the industrial revolution was the ability to mass-produce goods. Factories that adopted the method of using interchangeable parts were able to produce more goods than before.

2. (5) The U.S. had more miles of railroad than all of Europe and Russia and was recognized as the industrial leader of the world. Based on that, you can see that dependable transportation is a key to mass production and sale of goods.

Analyzing Ideas

3. (2) The maps show more dots in the North than in the South. Moreover, the larger population centers are shown to be in the North. Since industry was related directly to population growth, you can infer that there was more industry in the northern states than in the southern states during the period 1870-1900.

Understanding Ideas

4. (4) From the maps it appears that industries and the cities that grew up around them were usually established near bodies of water such as the Atlantic Ocean, the Great Lakes, and the Mississippi River.

Exercise 15: Laissez-faire Business Policies
page 121

Applying Ideas

The actions that represent economic activity without government intervention are:

(1) Major airlines engage in a price war, setting competitive prices for air fares.

(2) The absence of a usury law, a law that sets the maximum interest rate that can be legally charged for a loan.

(5) Banks charge whatever rate of interest the market will bear on passbook savings accounts.

Exercise 16: Growth of Big Business
page 122

Analyzing Ideas

(2) The passage says "This attitude contributed to the social problems that emerged at the end of the nineteenth century." Based on this, you can infer that big business grew in the U.S. at the expense of public welfare.

Exercise 17: The New Immigrants
page 123

Understanding Ideas

1. (3) The only statement that is true and may be proven by reading the graph is that the trend at the turn of the century was for immigrants to come to the U.S. from eastern, central and southern Europe in greater numbers than twenty years earlier.

2. (3) Of the regions listed, northwest Europe experienced a reduction in the numbers of immigrants coming to the U.S. It is the only region shown in which the bar for the period 1891-1910 is substantially shorter than the bar for the period 1871–1890.

Writing Activity 3
page 123

Your answer might include the following points:

- Naturalized Americans today do not always accept today's "new Americans" as readily as our ancestors did; overt discrimination may not be as widespread today as it was during the nineteenth century, but it still exists.
- "New Americans" are competing with native Americans for America's dwindling number of jobs.
- Many of today's "new Americans" are coming from Mexico, India, the Middle East, and southeast Asian countries.
- Many of today's "new Americans" are not as motivated to learn English and therefore persist in speaking their native language, thus creating a need for bilingual programs in schools.

Exercise 18: Political Machines
pages 124–125

Evaluating Ideas

1. **(5)** Based on Plunkitt's definition of "honest graft" and "dishonest graft," you should have arrived at the judgment that political bosses appeared to have no sense of right and wrong.

Understanding Ideas

2. **(4)** According to the information in the passage, another name for "honest graft" as described by Plunkitt might be profiting from inside information on government purchases. Choices (1), (3), and (5) are described as "dishonest graft." Choice (2) is not mentioned by Plunkitt.

Exercise 19: Progressive Reform
pages 126–127

Evaluating Ideas

1. **(5)** In his statement, Riis points out, " the greed of capital that wrought the evil must undo it . . ." By capital, he means private industry. Riis would likely agree with the position that private industry is morally responsible for helping to correct social problems.
2. **(3)** Riis believed that justice should come from the public conscience, as represented by private citizens who established settlement houses. Choice (1) is incorrect because the "Four Hundred" do not represent the public

conscience. Choices (2) and (5) are incorrect because machine politicians and businessmen who believed in Social Darwinism are the very ones Riis attacked for creating the conditions. Choice (4) is incorrect because Riis says legislation cannot undo the evil.

Exercise 20: Imperialism vs. Isolationism
page 128

Applying Ideas

1. **(4)** An example of American imperialist policy is the U.S. control of most of the Panama Canal Zone, because it is a case of the U.S. controlling a foreign territory.
2. **(1)** In making his decision, President Grover Cleveland was abiding by the principles of rule by "consent of the governed" put forth by the Declaration of Independence.

Exercise 21: World War I
page 129

Analyzing Ideas

The events that most directly contributed to the U.S. entering the war on the Allied side were:
- **(4)** Germany's attack on the passenger ship, the *Lusitania*
- **(5)** threats to U.S. neutrality

Writing Activity 4
page 130

Your answer might include the following points:
- Both the twenties and eighties were dominated by conservative politics, with the Republicans in power.
- As in the twenties, the Reagan Administration cut taxes for the rich with the belief that economic benefits would "trickle down" to the poor.
- Also, as in the twenties, social programs have been cut, hurting the poor and middle classes.

Exercise 22: The Jazz Age and the Lost Generation
page 131

Analyzing Ideas

(1), (2), The statements that reflect assump-
and (5) tions by this writer are: (1), (2), and (5). Choice (3) is incorrect because the writer felt that American society was hurt by its young artists and writers flocking to Paris. Choice (4)

is incorrect because the writer believed that young people's striving for individuality and self-expression represented a breakdown in America's moral fabric.

Exercise 23: The Crash and Depression
page 132
Analyzing Ideas

(4)   The rise in unemployment from 4 million in 1930 to 11 million by 1932 is a result of the Depression, not a cause. The other choices are causes that are stated in the passage.

Exercise 24: The New Deal vs. the Reagan Revolution
pages 133–134
Understanding Ideas

1. (3)   The entire passage compares and contrasts the two men's policies and personal styles.

Analyzing Ideas

2. (5)   When, in the last paragraph, the author says, "Opinions are sharply divided," she is expressing the opinion that the verdict is still out on Reagan's stature as president.

3. (2)   While it is obvious that the author has respect for both men's personal styles, her positive references to the New Deal reveal an admiration for Roosevelt's policies.

Writing Activity 5
page 134

Your answer might include the ideas expressed below.
Franklin Roosevelt and Ronald Reagan appealed to the American people because both:
- were reassuring in their style, manner, and way of speaking.
- were very experienced politicians.
- knew how to use the media—radio and television—to their best advantage.
- had immediate popular support for the programs needed to correct America's problems.

Exercise 25: The World at War
page 135
Understanding Ideas

1. T   4. F
2. F   5. F
3. T

Exercise 26: World War II
page 136
Applying Ideas

1. (4)   Choice (4) is correct because an internationalist believes in maintaining good relations with other nations. Choice (1) is incorrect because Roosevelt says "we can't isolate ourselves from the rest of humanity." Choices (2) and (5) are incorrect because the quote makes no mention of one country controlling or not controlling another. Choice (3) is incorrect because Roosevelt's language is not warlike.

2. (5)   The passage says, "Six million others were slaughtered by the Nazis for no other reason than that they were Jewish and thus considered to be racially inferior to Germans."

3. (2)   The writer shows concern for the concentration camp inmates and is upset by "man's inhumanity to man."

Writing Activity 6
page 137

You might argue one of the following points:
- President Truman was justified in dropping the bomb because the action ended a long, bloody war and saved American lives.
- President Truman was not justified in dropping the bomb because there can never be any justification for taking another human life.
- President Truman was not justified because the action opened the door for nuclear war and the everpresent threat of the destruction of mankind.

Exercise 27: The Truman Era
page 138
Applying Ideas

(1), (2), and (4)   The situations that represent modern-day attempts to enforce the principles of the Truman Doctrine are: (1), (2), and (4). Choices (3) and (5) do not represent the U.S. support of free peoples who resist attempted control by armed minorities or outside pressures. The Soviet Union, friendly to Cuba, sought to establish missile bases there, (3). Duvalier was forced out of Haiti because of his abuse of political power, choice (5).

Exercise 28: The Eisenhower Years
pages 139–140
Applying Ideas
1. **(4)** The undeclared war in Vietnam most closely resembled the situation in the Korean War. Both were undeclared wars that resulted from the U.S. policy of containing communism.

Understanding Ideas
2. **(3)** The *Brown* v. *Board of Education* decision is significant today because it said that there could not be "separate but equal" educational facilities. This serves as the legal basis for school busing to achieve desegregation.

Analyzing Ideas
3. **(1)** The passage stresses that Dwight Eisenhower was a war hero. The other choices either are not true or do not account for such great popularity.

Exercise 29: The New Frontier
page 141
Understanding Ideas
1. **(2)** This choice summarizes the Kennedy administration's participation in the Peace Corps and Vietnam abroad as well as in civil rights issues at home

Analyzing Ideas
2. **(4)** From reading the passage, it may be assumed that Cuba, a communist nation, was an ally of the Soviet Union.

Writing Activity 7
page 141
You might argue either of the following points:
- President Kennedy was justified in trying to overthrow Castro because Castro's friendliness toward the Soviet Union threatened, indirectly, our national security.
- President Kennedy was not justified in trying to overthrow Castro because no country has the right to meddle in the political affairs of another country.

Exercise 30: The Great Society
pages 142–143
Understanding Ideas
1. **(2)** The passage outlines the contributions that former president Johnson made in the areas of civil rights and economic opportunity.

2. **(5)** The passage shows how the Vietnam War and the protests against it disrupted American society.

Evaluating Ideas
3. **(4)** The thrust of the passage is that the war in faraway Vietnam had a big impact on American society.

Exercise 31: Nixon and Watergate
page 144
Evaluating Ideas
1. **(3)** Of former president Nixon's foreign policy initiatives, history will likely credit him most for reestablishing relations with the People's Republic of China.

2. **(5)** The opinion best supported by the evidence presented in the passage is that "the president of the United States is not above the law." It was President Nixon's involvement in the cover-up of the break-in and the subsequent impeachment action that led to the first presidential resignation in U.S. history.

Exercise 32: Closing the Twentieth Century
page 146
Evaluating Ideas
1. **(3)** This choice illustrates Carter's commitment to peace. Choice (1) is incorrect because it is not very historically significant. Choices (2) and (4) are incorrect because many Americans did not agree with Carter's policies toward the shah of Iran and Somoza. Carter likely will be remembered unfavorably for his failure to gain the hostages' release, choice (5).

Understanding Ideas
2. **(1)** Reagan's foreign policy is characterized generally as one of anticommunism. None of the other choices reflect this foreign policy emphasis.

Evaluating Ideas
3. **(3)** The passage shows that, despite his high approval ratings during the Persian Gulf War, President Bush lost favor because of economic troubles in the U.S.

CHAPTER 6: POLITICAL SCIENCE

Exercise 1: Types of Government
page 149

Applying Ideas

1. **O** A system of government in which decisions are made by a "few top men" in the People's Republic of China is an example of an oligarchy.

2. **M** Authority to rule that is inherited and that was justified by a God-given right is an example of an absolute monarchy.

3. **M** A system of government headed by a king and in which power is passed down is an example of a monarchy.

4. **DE** A system of government in which a prime minister heads the legislature and cabinet is an example of a parliamentary democracy.

5. **DI** A system of government in which one person has total control and who usually comes to power after a revolution is an example of a dictatorship.

Exercise 2: Making Laws
pages 150–151

Applying Ideas

1. **C** The power to declare war is stated in the Constitution.

2. **C** The power to approve presidential appointments is stated in the Constitution.

3. **E** The Constitution states that Congress has the power to provide and maintain an army and navy. At the time the Constitution was written, there could not be an air force. Therefore, the establishment of an air force is an application of the elastic clause.

4. **C** As the passage states, the power to impeach a president is stated in the Constitution.

5. **E** The authority to advance Daylight Savings Time is not significant enough to be stated in the Constitution and, therefore, represents an application of the elastic clause.

6. **E** This goes beyond the powers stated above.

7. **C** The power to admit states is granted in the Constitution.

8. **C** This is an example of the power of Congress to maintain the army.

Exercise 3: The Legislative Branch
page 151

Analyzing Ideas

(1) and (3) Choices (1) and (3) are logical conclusions that can be drawn from the information on the map. According to the reading, the Supreme Court decided that redrawn legislative districts must be proportional to the population. The fact that the Ninth Congressional District is so much smaller than the others implies that its population is the densest. Also, you could conclude that, if the districts had been drawn to equalize land area, the population apportionment would not have been fair.

Exercise 4: The Executive Branch
page 153

Understanding Ideas

1. **(3)** Presidents until FDR followed Washington's precedent. As defined by this section, a precedent is an earlier action that serves as a justification for a later action.

2. **(3)** The history section of this book states that President Roosevelt created a number of agencies to deal with the state of the economy. Washington's presidency was too far removed, in years, from the Kennedy and Johnson administrations, and President Truman did not create as many agencies as had Roosevelt.

Exercise 5: Setting Precedents
page 154

Understanding Ideas

1. **(b)** Just as Polk had done in Mexico, Johnson escalated the buildup in Vietnam without Congress's declaration of war.

2. **(c)** The national emergency that prompted Roosevelt's extensive use of executive power was the Great Depression; the national emergency that forced Lincoln to expand his authority was the Civil War.

298 SOCIAL STUDIES TEST

3. (a) Carter's assumption of the role of mediator in the Middle East can be linked to the precedent set by Teddy Roosevelt in his mediating between disputing Russia and Japan.

Exercise 6: Enforcer of Laws
page 154
Applying Ideas
(5) In the passage, the term "strong president" is used to describe one who dominates the legislative branch. The decription of Andrew Jackson best fits that definition.

Writing Activity 1
page 155
Your answer might include the following points:
Direct Election
- The president and vice president of the United States should be elected by direct vote because the principle on which the electoral college operates is unfair; a candidate who loses a state by a narrow margin also loses the state's electoral votes.
- Electors may cast their ballots as they choose because they are not legally bound to vote for the winner of the popular vote.

Electoral College
- The system should not be changed because the Founding Fathers intended for the president and vice president to be elected by the electoral college.

Exercise 7: Interpreting Laws
page 156
Understanding Ideas
1. (4) The only issue common to all five decisions is the defending of an institution's or individual's civil liberties. Choices (1), (2), and (3) are not illustrated by the cases, and choice (5) is the opposite of the Supreme Court's intent.

Analyzing Ideas
2. (3) The Miranda case affected police procedures during an arrest. None of the other cases have anything to do with the mechanics of local law enforcement.

Writing Activity 2
page 157
Your argument might include either of the following points:
YES
- The president's appointing Supreme Court justices who agree with his political philosophy is an abuse of power because the Supreme Court should be as independent as the Constitution intended it to be. A lack of independence hurts its ability to serve as a "check" on the executive branch.

NO
- The president has the right to appoint whomever he desires to the Supreme Court in order to have the court support his administration's policies.

Exercise 8: Separation of Powers
pages 157–158
Applying Ideas
1. (1) Of the choices, only choice (1) was the result of actions of the judicial branch. The other choices were the result of actions of either the legislative branch or the executive branch.
2. (5) According to the passage, the Voting Rights Acts outlawed restrictions on voting. Choices (1), (2), (3), and (4) did not involve the issue of literacy tests for voters.

Exercise 9: The Enactment of a Law
page 159
Understanding Ideas
(2) Choice (2) is supported by the part of the chart that shows that a bill must go to a conference committee for compromise. The chart does not indicate that a bill may be introduced directly by the president (1). A filibuster (as you read in the "Reading Skills" section) is an acceptable means by which a vote on a bill may be delayed (3). Bills introduced by *either* house may be amended as shown in the illustration (4). Bills may become law without the president's signature (5).

Exercise 10: System of Checks and Balances
page 159

Understanding Ideas

2. (a) legislative   (b) executive
3. (a) legislative   (b) executive
4. (a) legislative   (b) executive
5. (a) judicial   (b) legislative
6. (a) executive   (b) legislative

Exercise 11: The Bill of Rights
page 161

Applying Ideas

1. (4) According to the passage, the Fifth Amendment includes the "right to remain silent," one of the rights read to an accused. The Sixth Amendment gives the accused the right to call a lawyer.

2. (3) The quote refers to the First Amendment, the guarantee of freedom of speech. An American citizen is guaranteed freedom of speech as long as this freedom does not infringe upon the rights of others.

Writing Activity 3
page 161

Your argument might include either of the following points:

YES

- Schools that censor their student newspapers deny students freedom of the press. Freedom does not exist when students are told what to write—and what *not* to write.

NO

- Schools have the right to make sure that student newspapers live up to the school's standards. The newspaper is owned by the school, and students often get academic credit for working on the newspaper staff.

Exercise 12: Political Parties
page 163

Understanding Ideas

(1) Democratic Party; controlled the presidency from 1933 to 1953
(2) Republican Party; controlled the presidency for twelve terms
(3) Answers will vary.

Writing Activity 4
page 163

Your answer might include the following points:

YES

- The Republican Party was once a third political party. Such a political shift could happen again. If the third party represents enough people, it could succeed.

NO

- Third parties historically have not succeeded in gaining control of the presidency, so it is unlikely that they will do so in the future.
- The two-party system in the U.S. is rooted in tradition; therefore, a successful third party cannot be established.

Exercise 13: Political Labels
pages 164–165

Applying Ideas

1. (5) Because the speaker advocates a return to an earlier policy (arming oneself as in the Old West), the speaker is classified as a reactionary.
2. (2) Because the speaker advocates social improvement through governmental action, the speaker may be considered a liberal.
3. (4) Because the speaker advocates maintaining the existing order (the law should remain the way it is), the speaker may be considered to be a conservative.

Exercise 14: Public Opinion
page 166

Analyzing Ideas

(1), (2), and (4) The fact that Truman won the election even though Dewey was predicted to win suggests that voters might have changed their minds between the time of the surveys and the time of the election, choice (1). The fact that the voters were not as committed to Dewey as the pollsters were led to believe [choice (2)] is a second hypothesis that may be drawn since Truman defeated Dewey. A third hypothesis that can be drawn based on the poll results is that the sampling of voters might have been too small or that the pollsters didn't ask the right people, choice (4). Neither choice (3) nor choice (5) can be supported by the information in the chart.

Exercise 15: Public Opinion Polls
page 167
Evaluating Ideas
(1) The best choice is (1), which is based on the hypothesis that the early announcements of Reagan's victory discouraged Carter's supporters from voting.

Writing Activity 5
page 167
Your answer might include some of the following points:

YES
- The job of the television news departments is to report the facts as they see them; if this means predicting election outcomes, then the television networks have that right.

NO
- It is unfair for television news stations to predict the outcome of an election before all votes are cast because the practice discourages potential voters from voting for the losing candidate.
- Television, in predicting the outcome of an election, influences the outcome; this practice hurts the electoral process in a democracy.

Exercise 16: Powers of State Governments
page 170
Understanding Ideas
1. (3) Choice (3) is an infringement of the freedom of the press, a right guaranteed by the Constitution.

Evaluating Ideas
2. (3) The most likely reason for forbidding states to grant titles of nobility is that doing so would violate one of the key principles on which the American Revolution was based, that "all men are created equal."

Exercise 17: State vs. Federal Powers
page 170
Understanding Ideas
1. B	3. F	5. S
2. B	4. F	6. S

Exercise 18: The Judicial Branch
page 171
Understanding Ideas
1. (3) According to the passage, circuit courts, county courts, district courts, and superior courts handle civil cases that involve greater monetary rewards; personal injury suits usually involve large monetary rewards.

Applying Ideas
2. (4) Because the murder case has already gone to trial, and the accused has been sentenced, the decision must be appealed and referred to the state appellate court.

Exercise 19: County Expenditures
pages 172-173
Analyzing Ideas
1. (4) County B has a greater concentration of children because of the larger proportion spent on schools (75% vs. 10%).
2. (4) Because the proportion of money spent for law enforcement in County A is higher than that spent for law enforcement in County B, there must be a greater need for law enforcement services in County A. Also, the proportion of money spent for law enforcement in County A is the second highest expenditure after general and public assistance.

Writing Activity 6
page 173
Your answer should include one of these four types: weak mayor-council plan, strong mayor-council plan, commission form, and council-manager form.

Exercise 20: The Plight of the Cities
page 174
Understanding Ideas
Answers for three through nine may be in any order.
(1) cities
(2) sharks
(3) upper income flight to the suburbs
(4) school troubles
(5) racism
(6) crime
(7) ghettos
(8) continued decay
(9) tax squeeze

Exercise 21: Problems of the Cities
page 175
Understanding Ideas
(2) The title, "Vicious Circle," means that the problems of America's big cities are so interconnected that it is hard to know where to start to correct them. Choice (1) is not the main point of the cartoon. Choice (3) might be true but is not the focus of the cartoon. Choice (4) is the opposite of what the cartoonist is saying, and choice (5) is not an implication that may be drawn from the cartoon.

CHAPTER 7: BEHAVIORAL SCIENCE
Exercise 1: Types of Scientists
page 177
Applying Ideas
1. **biologist**—A biologist studies humans and their physical functions.
2. **sociologist**—A sociologist studies societies of today like modern-day Israel.
3. **anthropologist**—An anthropologist traces a culture from its earliest origins.
4. **psychologist**—A psychologist studies a person's personality and mental capabilities.

Exercise 2: The Scientific Method
page 177
Analyzing Ideas
The order of the steps is :
4. carrying out an experiment or research
2. hypothesizing about the problem
5. drawing a conclusion and doing further research
1. observing a situation
3. designing an experiment or developing a method of research

Exercise 3: Physical and Cultural Anthropology
page 179
Applying Ideas
1. **cultural anthropologist**—The sentence says that Turnbull studies every aspect of their unique life; a cultural anthropologist studies a people's culture.
2. **physical anthropologists**—The sentence states that the Leakeys analyzed skeletal remains dug up in Africa; a physical anthropologist studies the development of human physical characteristics.

Exercise 4: Evolution of Culture
page 180
Analyzing Ideas
2, 5, 1, 3, 7, 6, 4

Exercise 5: Emerging Civilizations
pages 180–181
Analyzing Ideas
1. (4) According to the passage, art was created because people had more time for leisure since they did not need to focus as much on basic survival. Choices (1), (2), (3), and (5) are not stated in the passage.

Understanding Ideas
2. (4) According to the passage, the development of goods and the trade between villages and towns created the need for written records of transaction. This led to the development of written language.

Evaluating Ideas
3. (5) According to the passage, goods created a demand that contributed to the development of villages and towns around trading centers. The other choices are either not referred to or are contrary to what the passage says.

Exercise 6: Race and Culture
page 182

Evaluating Ideas

(2), (4), The practice of casting one's eyes
and (5) down when talking to an older person is rooted in Mexican cultural tradition, choice (2). The African custom of wearing loin cloths is dictated by both geography and history, choice (4). The closeness of the Japanese family comes from Japanese history or tradition, choice (5).

Choice (1) does not indicate a cultural difference, but a biological difference. Differences in learning styles cannot be linked to either history or geography, choice (3).

Writing Activity 1
page 182

Your description might include one of many ethnic subcultures within the U.S.—Mexican, Polish, East Indian, etc. You might write about distinctive foods introduced by these cultures as well as family relationships—nuclear or extended.

Exercise 7: Religion and Culture
page 184

Understanding Ideas

(1) folklore   **(4)** ritual
(2) supernatural   **(5)** tabu
(3) shaman

Exercise 8: Understanding Ethnocentrism
page 185

Applying Ideas

1. **(5)** When an American woman describes European women's refusal to shave their legs as "masculine," she is being ethnocentric. Clean-shaven legs is an American standard of beauty, and European women are being judged by an American cultural standard. None of the other choices show the act of judging one culture by the standards of another.

Evaluating Ideas

2. **(3)** Choice (3) is the only objective assessment of the Hindu rite of cremation shown. Choices (1), (2), and (4) are value judgments and therefore are not objective. Choice (5) reflects an argument in favor of the practical benefits of cremation, not the cultural aspect.

Exercise 9: Cultural Diffusion
pages 186–187

Understanding Ideas

1. **(2)** The only example of cultural diffusion shown is the Pygmies' use of prefabricated materials to build their houses. Choice (1) led to cultural diffusion, choices (3) and (5) have no relationship to the process of cultural diffusion, and choice (4) is a result of cultural diffusion expressed in the passage.

Evaluating Ideas

2. **(3)** The passage states that "the group is weakened when the rules begin to bend or are ignored" and that "once primitives come into contact with the outside world, an innocence and unquestioning contentment is lost." These words suggest that the author thinks that the effect of cultural diffusion on the Pygmies has been negative.

3. **(5)** The author's emphasis on the words, *civilized, advanced,* and *primitive* indicate an effort to avoid being ethnocentric; this attitude suggests that cultures described as *civilized, advanced,* and *primitive,* may not be what we think they are.

Exercise 10: The Pygmies
page 187

Analyzing Ideas

(1), (2), That Pygmy camps are smaller than
and (4) plantations, choice (1), is obvious. Since all of the Pygmy camps represented begin with the word *Apa,* it must refer to "camp" or "tribe," choice (2). No villages are shown outside of plantations, choice (4).

Exercise 11: Primary and Secondary Groups
pages 188–189

Applying Ideas

1. S   3. S   5. S   7. S   9. S
2. S   4. P   6. S   8. P   10. P

Writing Activity 2
page 189

Your description should include your family, friends, work group or members of a club or team. You should explain how the degree of intimacy between you and other group members determines whether the group is a primary or secondary one.

Exercise 12: Nuclear and Extended Families
page 190
Applying Ideas

1. **N** Because the couple moves away from their inlaws, the situation describes a nuclear family.
2. **E** Because the law requires the husband and wife to live in the same compound as other relatives, the situation describes an extended family.
3. **E** Because family members other than the immediate family are involved in the rearing and care of the children, an extended family is described.
4. **E** Because the elderly live with their children who are required to support them, the situation described is that of an extended family.
5. **N** A single-parent family is an example of a nuclear family.

Exercise 13: The Family
pages 190–191
Analyzing Ideas

1. **(2)** Because the mother is the head of the Seminole household, the mother's brother is more important to the family structure than the father, who is not a blood relative. Choices (1), (3), (4), and (5) are not supported by the facts in the passage.
2. **(2)** Because the passage states that inheritance and lines of descent are through the mother's side of the family and that women are the heads of their households, we can infer that women are central figures in both the nuclear and extended families.

Writing Activity 3
page 191
Your description should indicate whether or not your family is nuclear or extended, whether or not it is headed by one or both parents, and should describe the degree of interaction between the members.

Exercise 14: Changing Families
pages 192–193
Evaluating Ideas

1. **(2)** Both black and white boys who lived with their stepfathers reported a higher percent of delinquent acts than boys who lived with their real fathers or no father at all.

Analyzing Information

2. **(4)** Because the percentage of two or more delinquent acts is highest among boys who live with their stepfathers, it might be hypothesized that the poor relationship between stepfathers and stepsons causes the boys to act out their anger by committing delinquent acts.

Understanding Ideas

3. **(1)** Fifty-four percent of those black males who had a real father present reported no delinquent acts.

Exercise 15: Role Reversal
page 194
Applying Ideas

1. Claude—The mother traditionally stays at home with the kids, so Claude is reversing roles.
2. Dr. Scott (woman); Nurse Davis (man)—Men are predominantly the doctors and women the nurses; qualities of warmth and caring are usually attributed to female, rather than male, nurses.
3. Jimmy (home economics); Betty Sue (auto mechanics)—Traditionally, a girl is expected to take home economics classes and a boy is expected to take auto mechanics.

Exercise 16: Roles and Status
page 194
Applying Ideas

1. ascribed—One is born into a racial category; therefore, being a member of the mongoloid race is ascribed status.
2. achieved—One must undergo training to become a policeman, so the status is achieved.
3. ascribed—Because age confers a special status on members in certain cultures, becoming a senior citizen is an example of an ascribed status.
4. achieved—Obtaining a GED certificate is an achievement.
5. ascribed—One is born into royalty; it may not be earned.

Exercise 17: Social Status
pages 195–196
Evaluating Ideas

1. **(3)** The passage states, "money is not the only criterion that determines status in our society. . . . the degree of formal education also contributes to social status in America." The other choices are neither stated in nor supported by the passage.

Applying Ideas

2. **(3)** The occupation of brain surgeon is the only one shown that indicates high earnings along with a high level of formal education; therefore, it would be considered to have the highest status in American society today.

Exercise 18: Social Classes
page 196
Analyzing Ideas

(1), (3), (4), and (5) In the quote, the "replacements" the writer describes are members of the working class and include more Hispanics and blacks than did his previous middle-class students, choice (1).

Working-class people moving into a formerly middle-class neighborhood represents social mobility, choice (3).

The quote states that the "replacements were more often working class . . . took achievement tests less well," choice (4).

According to the quote, the "replacements . . . collected more welfare," choice (5).

Writing Activity 4
page 196

Your answer might include the following points:

YES
- People are still able to improve their lot with education and hard work
- The middle class is constantly growing

NO
- Illegal immigrants are competing with native Americans for fewer jobs
- The poorer class is growing larger every day
- Big business, by taking over smaller firms, is making it hard for the small businessman to succeed

Exercise 19: Social Deviation
page 197
Evaluating Information

(1), (2), (4), and (5) Each of these laws is violated because a significant number of people do not believe they are vital to the welfare of society. As a result, most of them are unenforceable. Laws against shoplifting (3) and kidnapping (6) *are* enforceable.

Exercise 20: Psychoanalysis
page 199
Applying Ideas

1. The **hunger drive** represents the id in the case described because the passage states that id consists of all the basic drives and instincts we are born with.
2. Lenny's **limiting himself to five cookies** represents the functioning ego. The passage states, the ego "keeps us from having 'too much of a good thing.' "
3. The **guilt** Lenny experiences represents the superego because, according to the passage, the superego acts as the conscience.

Exercise 21: Behaviorism
page 200
Applying Ideas

1. **(3)** Conditioning involves the use of positive or negative reinforcement to encourage a certain behavior (work). Human nature is not a psychological explanation for human behavior, choice (1). Conditioning is explained by behavioral theory, not psychoanalytic theory, choice (2). Choices (4) and (5) are incorrect because conditioning involves both negative and positive reinforcement, not just one type of reinforcement.
2. **(4)** This is the only choice that represents the use of a positive reinforcement (a reward) to encourage good behavior. Choices (1) and (2) are punishments. While choices (3) and (5) are intended to help the child with his grades, they do not reward good behavior.

Exercise 22: Behaviorism and Psychoanalysis
page 201
Applying Ideas

1. **P** Psychoanalytic theory attributes adult behavior (Kevin's stubbornness) to childhood influences (Kevin's difficulty in toilet training).
2. **B** Behavioral theory involves conditioning (David's waking up on his own in response to the negative reinforcement of the alarm clock).
3. **B** The reward for Lillie's losing weight is the applause of fellow members of Weight Watchers; therefore, she is conditioned to remain on her diet. Conditioning is an element of behavioral theory.

4. **P** The linking of adult behavior (Al's smoking) with a childhood occurrence (lack of oral stimulation) is a feature of psychoanalytic theory.
5. **B** The reward of a "smiley face" appearing on the computer screen conditions Johnny to strive for the correct response. Johnny is being conditioned, an element of behavioral theory.

Writing Activity 5
page 201
Answers will vary according to individual experience.

Exercise 23: Frustration and Conflict
pages 202–203
Analyzing Ideas
1. **avoidance-avoidance**—Jose has a sore tooth, the pain of which he wants to avoid, but he also wants to avoid the dentist who can take care of the problem.
2. **approach-approach**—Keisha wants to go out with Lionel, to whom she is attracted, but she also wants to be with her best friend on her birthday.
3. **approach-avoidance**—Hal needs a new car, a goal that attracts him, but is repelled by the idea of getting deeper into debt.

Writing Activity 6
page 203
Answers will vary according to individual experience.

Exercise 24: Recognizing Conflicts
page 203
Understanding Ideas
1. **(b)** One is caught between two undesirable choices—the devil and the deep blue sea.
2. **(c)** One is attracted to honey but at the same time is repelled by the bee's sting.
3. **(b)** One is caught between two undesirable choices—a rock and a hard place.
4. **(c)** One is attracted to the rose because of its beauty but repelled by the thorn it carries.
5. **(a)** One wants two things but cannot have both—having the cake and enjoying the pleasure of eating it.

Exercise 25: Defense Mechanisms
pages 204–205
Applying Ideas
1. **(3)** The dishonest politician is assigning a bad trait of her own to another person, her opponent.
2. **(5)** The man's reaction (joining a campaign to have X-rated films banned) is the opposite of his true feelings (he enjoys watching them).
3. **(4)** The man, in his mind, is transferring his aggression toward his coworkers to the bowling pins.

Writing Activity 7
page 205
Answers will vary.

Exercise 26: Theory and Neuroses
page 207
Understanding Ideas
1. Because Phobic Phil and Immaculate Isabel's neuroses are linked to childhood experiences, the **psychoanalytic theory** of psychology would best explain their actions.
2. If Claude receives attention only when he complains about being ill, his behavior is conditioned. The **behavioral theory** of psychology would best explain his actions.

Exercise 27: Neuroses
pages 207–208
Applying Ideas
1. **(3)** **obsessive-compulsive:** George is obsessed with order. Keeping his record albums in special groupings is a compulsion.
2. **(5)** **fugue state:** Sylvia left her home and responsibilities without making a conscious decision to do so.
3. **(2)** **conversion-reaction:** Lavonna's sickness is a reaction to the guilt of having an affair with her husband's friend.
4. **(1)** **phobia:** Bill has an irrational fear that may be traced to a childhood experience.

Writing Activity 8
page 208

Your description should be based on one of the following disorders:
- phobia
- conversion-reaction
- obsession-compulsion
- depressive reaction
- fugue state

Exercise 28: Psychoses
page 209

Evaluating Ideas

(3) This is the only choice that suggests a biological basis for the development of schizophrenia. Because identical twins develop from a single egg, it would follow that both members of a set of identical twins would be much more likely to be schizophrenic than two non-twin siblings.

CHAPTER 8: GEOGRAPHY

Exercise 1: The World According to Herodotus
page 212

Analyzing Ideas

1. (2) Sardes is located exactly in the center of Herodotus's world.

Understanding Ideas

2. (3) Ethnocentrism is the judging of another culture based on one's own cultural values. Since Herodotus and others like him believed their country was at the center of the world and that other countries were located around them, this belief is similar to the concept of ethnocentrism.

Exercise 2: Latitude and Longitude
page 217

Understanding Ideas

1. (3) North Africa
2. (1) The North Atlantic Ocean
3. (2) the United States

Exercise 3: Time Zones
page 219

Applying Ideas

1. (2) Since San Francisco lies in the Pacific time zone, which is two hours behind Chicago, which lies in the Central time zone, it would be 10:00 P.M.

2. (3) Since Salt Lake City, Utah, lies in the Mountain time zone, which is two hours behind New York, which lies in the Eastern time zone, it would be 2:00 A.M.

Exercise 4: Climate and Its Effect
page 222

Analyzing Ideas

1. (3) The passage discusses how the sun's rays strike the equator to form a right angle. The result of this is that the Northern and Southern Hemispheres experience the "opposite" seasons.

Understanding Ideas

2. (4) According to the passage, when one climate zone experiences a particular season, the other zone experiences its opposite (the mirror image effect). The opposite of the North Temperate Zone, in which lies the U.S, is the South Temperate Zone, in which lies the southern area of South America.

Exercise 5: The Topography of the Earth
pages 223–224

Understanding Ideas

1. (3) Because most of the elevations shown in the map are 500 feet or above, and less than 1,000 feet, they represent mostly hills.

2. (1) According to the passage, hills and plateaus that rise from the plains share the same climate characteristics of the plains near which they are located.

Evaluating Ideas

3. (3) The existence of a road and a school would suggest that the area is populated.

Writing Activity 1
page 224

Applying Ideas

Answers will vary, but they should explain how the topography of one's location affects the climate there during the different seasons of the year.

Exercise 6: Water's Effect on Climate
pages 224–225
Analyzing Ideas
1. **(2)** Because the drop in temperatures from July to December in Verkhoyansk, Siberia, is steeper than in the Lofoten Islands, it can be concluded that Verkhoyansk experiences more extremes in temperature.

Applying Ideas
2. **(2)** The passage states that "the Pacific Ocean's many warm currents moderate the climate from the western edge of Alaska, down the Canadian and American coasts . . ." Since Washington is located along the Pacific Coast, and South Dakota is not located near a large body of water, you can conclude that it is likely to be colder in South Dakota than in Washington.

Writing Activity 2
page 226
Answers will vary, but you should explain how your location near a large body of water (if it applies) affects the climate during summer and winter.

Exercise 7: The Distribution of Moisture in the Air
page 227
Analyzing Ideas
1. **(1)** According to the passage, precipitation results when warm air is cooled and becomes less able to hold moisture. Since temperatures generally are warmer near large bodies of water than inland, precipitation is likely to be more frequent and heavy along the coasts of the Arctic than inland.
2. **(5)** Florida is a peninsula—surrounded by water on three sides. The frequent precipitation that results from its location does not evaporate as easily as in states that are not surrounded by water; therefore, Florida is likely to be most humid during the summer.

Writing Activity 3
page 227
Answers will vary.

Exercise 8: Air Pressure and Winds
page 228
Analyzing Ideas
(2) and **(4)** According to the diagram, westerlies are restricted to the 30- and 60-degree latitudes, north and south. In the diagram, westerlies are shown blowing west to east.

Exercise 9: Prevailing Wind Patterns
page 229
Evaluating Ideas
1. **(2)** A mirror image is the reverse effect of a condition. According to the diagram, the wind conditions are reversed for the northern and southern hemispheres.

Writing Activity 4
page 229
Answers will vary according to location.

Exercise 10: Population Distribution and Migration
page 231
Analyzing Ideas
1. **(2)** Since there is an even distribution of population in Iowa as shown on the map, it can be inferred that lowlands allow for an even distribution of population. None of the other conclusions are supported by the map.

Applying Ideas
2. **(3)** West Virginia is the only state represented that is not primarily flat; therefore, the distribution of its population would be most unlike Iowa's.

Writing Activity 5
page 231
Answers will vary based on students' locations.

Exercise 11: World Population
page 233
Evaluating Ideas
1. **NO** The opposite is true; based on the information in the graph, the population of undeveloped countries exceeds that of developed countries.
2. **YES** The graph shows more dramatic increases for undeveloped nations than for developed nations from 1750 to 2000.
3. **YES** In 1750, the world population for both developed and undeveloped countries was nearly 1 billion; by the year 2000 it will be about 6½ billion. This figure represents more than a five-fold increase.
4. **YES** According to the graph, the population of developed countries has lagged behind that of undeveloped countries since 1750.

Exercise 12: Standards of Living Around the World
page 234
Evaluating Ideas
1. **(3)** China is an underdeveloped nation with a population larger than India's. Canada, Brazil, Australia, and France are all developed nations. None have a problem with large growth rates, as do China and India.
2. **(2)** Of the five choices, England has the most in common with Japan—it is an island, it is heavily industrialized, and it is densely populated.

Exercise 13: Regional Water Shortages
pages 236–237
Evaluating Ideas
1. **(4)** The prediction based on the graph does not take into account the possibility that new technologies for finding, processing, or transporting fresh water supplies will be found by the year 2020.
2. **(4)** Since the predicted water shortage is less severe with a two-child average family size than with three-children families, it stands to reason that the water shortage would be further reduced with an even smaller average family size.

3. **(5)** The Southwest, which includes the desert areas of Arizona, New Mexico, parts of southern California, and Nevada would have the most limited supply of water.

Exercise 14: Nuclear and Solar Energy
page 238
Understanding Ideas
1. **(1)** Illinois, with eight, has the greatest number of nuclear power plants.
2. **(3)** For the most part, the states that have the largest numbers of nuclear plants are also the states that have the largest populations and greatest amount of industrial production. Therefore, they are higher users of energy than states with smaller populations.

Evaluating Ideas
3. **(1)** Montana is the only state listed that is not highly industrialized and has no nuclear plants. Nebraska is also not highly industrialized, but it does have one or two plants.
4. **(2)** Because the map shows a large number of nuclear power plants in the most populous states, this supports the contention that nuclear power plants are dangerously close to densely populated areas.

Writing Activity 6
page 238
Your answer might include the following points:
YES
- Few alternatives exist for those states that need electrical energy; therefore, dependence on nuclear power plants is worth the risk they pose to small numbers of people.
- Technological progress brings some risks with it; to abandon using nuclear power plants is to stand in the way of progress.
- The threat of nuclear power plants to human life is being blown out of proportion; most nuclear power plants are operated safely.

NO
- Events like the Three Mile Island and Chernobyl disasters prove that nuclear power plants threaten human life and health.
- America has an abundance of coal reserves that has been relied on in the past to produce the electrical energy needed to run our industries and homes.

- Safe forms of power, such as solar energy, should be explored fully before risking the potential dangers of nuclear energy.

Exercise 15: World Trade
page 240
Understanding Ideas

1. **Japan**—Great Britain and Japan, being island nations, have few natural resources. Both import the raw material needed to manufacture goods they sell in the world market.
2. **Saudi Arabia**—Saudi Arabia and South Africa both have abundant supplies of natural resources—petroleum and gold, respectively—which they export in exchange for the basic goods required by their populations.
3. **the U.S.**—The U.S. has, and the former Soviet Union had, an abundance of mineral resources that helped establish their positions as world powers.

CHAPTER 9: ECONOMICS
Exercise 1: The Basics of Economics
page 242
Applying Ideas

1. e
2. c
3. a
4. b
5. d

Exercise 2: Economic Systems
page 244
Understanding Ideas

1. **communist** Under the communist system of government, the state controls the economy.
2. **capitalist** A capitalist economy is based on the system of free enterprise with very little government interference.
3. **socialist** Under socialism, the government regulates many economic activities with the goal of equalizing the distribution of wealth.

Writing Activity 1
pages 244–245
Answers will vary based on the topic selected.

Exercise 3: Supply, Demand, and Equilibrium
page 248
Understanding Ideas

1. (4) The supply and demand curves intersect at .60; therefore this would be the market rate for painting houses.

Analyzing Ideas

2. (3) According to the information in the passage, in general, when prices fall, demand increases. Therefore, demand for painting houses would increase. Choice (1) is the opposite of what the passage states. Choice (2) is unlikely, since some house-painting companies would have to exist to satisfy demand. Choices (4) and (5) are incorrect because there is no basis for them in the passage.

Exercise 4: Diminishing Return
page 249
Understanding Ideas

1. (4) The company became less efficient when it took eight workers to do the same job that it previously took only six workers to do.

Analyzing Ideas

2. (3) The situation describes a case in which increased labor costs (hiring of more workers) did not result in increased profit (return on investment).

Writing Activity 2
page 250
Your answer might include the following points:
OIL PRODUCERS

- Raising of oil prices will bring more money into developing economies of Third World nations.
- If industrialized nations can get good prices for the goods they export to oil-producing nations, oil-producing nations should be able to get good prices for their product.

CONSUMERS

- With a reduced supply of imported petroleum, the price of oil and oil-derived products such as gasoline would increase.
- With increased petroleum prices, demand, or consumption of gas and other oil-based products, probably would fall.
- With increased imported petroleum prices and lowered demand, gas stations might become unprofitable.
- With increased imported petroleum prices, domestic (U.S.-based) oil companies might recover from financial difficulty and supply more oil than they had in recent years.

Exercise 5: The Federal Reserve System
page 253

Understanding Ideas

1. **F** The chief role of the Fed is to regulate the nation's supply of money and credit.
2. **T**
3. **F** The discount rate, not the prime rate, is the interest rate that the Fed charges member banks to borrow from it.
4. **F** The Fed neither coins money nor sets the prime rate to influence the money supply. It sets the reserve ratio and the discount rate.
5. **T**

Exercise 6: Money and Monetary Policy
pages 253–254

Applying Ideas

1. **(5)** When too much money circulates, the Fed follows a tight money policy by increasing the reserve ratio and the discount rate. Both measures take money out of the hands of consumers.
2. **(4)** When too little money is in circulation, the Fed follows a loose money policy by lowering the reserve ratio and discount rate. Both measures put more money in the hands of consumers.

Analyzing Ideas

3. **(3)** According to the quote, Will Rogers admires a central banking system (the Federal Reserve System). The Fed keeps the economy on a steady course during unstable economic times. Choice (1) is incorrect because the system is not regarded to be foolproof. Choices (2) and (4) are incorrect because the system did not exist since colonial times or since the beginning of human civilization. Choice (5) is critical of a central banking system.

Exercise 7: Government and Fiscal Policy
pages 255–256

Understanding Ideas

1. **(4)** The tale of Pinocchio involves a boy whose nose grows longer each time he tells a lie. In the cartoon, Congress is shown to be lying about the pledges it has made to cut government spending.

Analyzing Ideas

2. **(1)** This is the only statement that justifies and supports the idea that a federal deficit may be acceptable. Choice (2) contradicts the quote. Choice (3) is not supported in the passage. Choices (4) and (5) are unrelated to the facts presented in the passage.

Writing Activity 3
page 256

Your answer might include the following points:
YES

- National expenditures for the poor are being cut while expenditures for defense are on the rise.
- The poor have no lobbyists who have been effectively pleading their case for the saving of social programs.
- There has been a perceptible shift away from concern about social services for the nation's poor.

NO
- The money spent for social programs during the 1960s has contributed greatly to the nation's budget deficit.
- Many of the programs established in the 1960s have failed so it is a continued waste of the taxpayers' money to continue to support them.
- It is the states' responsibility to provide for their poor, not the federal government's.

Exercise 8: Measures of Economic Activity
pages 258–259
Analyzing Ideas
1. **(1)** According to the table, in the year 1974, prices increased 10.9 percent—a marked increase over previous yearly increases. Choice (2) refers to a period of several years, not the year 1974. Choices (3), (4), and (5) cannot be inferred from the information in the table.
2. **(3)** Based on the information in the right-hand column of the table, prices have generally risen since 1960.

Evaluating Ideas
3. **(3)** In the cartoon, the "flying carpet" is a credit card. This suggests that Americans' spending habits have not been curtailed by inflation but have been supported more and more by credit.

Exercise 9: Unemployment
pages 261–262
Applying Ideas
1. **(4)** The situation of construction workers being unemployed for part of the year is an example of seasonal unemployment.
2. **(2)** The situation of computers gaining importance in the workplace is an example of structural unemployment— unemployment caused by a rapid change in technology that changes employment needs.

3. **(1)** The situation of construction workers being laid off because of a slow economy and rehired when the economy improves is an example of cyclical unemployment.

Exercise 10: Displacement of Workers
pages 262–263
Understanding Ideas
1. **(4)** According to the graph, the bar measuring displacement in the area of durable good manufacturing is highest—35 percent.
2. **(3)** According to the graph, the lighter bar, which shows the percent of total employees, is higher for wholesale and retail workers (nearly 22 percent) than for any other category shown.

Evaluating Ideas
3. **(2)** The longest bars for displaced workers are for the durable and nondurable goods manufacturing industry. This fact suggests that they were hardest hit by the recessions of the 1970s and early 1980s.

Writing Activity 4
page 263
Your answers might include the following points:
ACCEPT
- The poor and unemployed will always be with us; we can never employ all the people in this country.
- Some people don't want to work in spite of any effort to make them employable. These are the people who make up the "below 4 percent" statistic.

REJECT
- Full employment is a worthy goal to strive for; to accept any level of unemployment is to weaken the resolve to reach the goal.
- It is government's responsibility to see that every person contributes to society by engaging in meaningful work.